TUSCANY & UMBRIA

European Regional Guide

PASSPORT BOOKS
a division of *NTC Publishing Group*
Lincolnwood, Illinois USA

Published by Passport Books, a division of NTC Publishing Group, 4255 W. Touhy Avenue, Lincolnwood (Chicago), Illinois 60646-1975 U.S.A.

Written by Christopher Catling

Copy editor: Dilys Jones

Edited, designed, and produced by AA Publishing. Maps © The Automobile Association 1993.

The contents of this publication are believed correct at the time of printing. Nevertheless, the publishers cannot accept responsibility for errors or omissions, or for changes in details given. We have tried to ensure accuracy in this guide, but things do change and we would be grateful if readers would advise us of any inaccuracies they may encounter.

Library of Congress Catalog Card Number: 93-83186

ISBN 0-8442-9971-5

Published by Passport Books in conjunction with The Automobile Association.

Color separation: Daylight Colour Art Pte, Singapore

Printed by Printers Trento S.R.L., Italy

Cover picture: **Siena rooftops**
Title page: **Majolica plate**
Opposite: **Nórcia shop front**
Pages 4–5: **Chianti vineyards**

·CONTENTS·

Introduction 5
The Region 6
The City and The Countryside 8
People and Customs 10
The Lower Arno and Apuan Alps 12
Florence and The Upper Arno 30
Umbria 50
Central Tuscany 76
The Etruscan Coast 98
Regional Map and Map Symbols 109
Practical Guide 112
Glossary 118
Index 119

FEATURES

Villas and Gardens *20*
The Florentine Renaissance *38*
Florence and the Medici *42*
Land of Saints *54*
Festivals *72*
Food and Wine *82*
Writers in Tuscany *90*
The Ancient Etruscans *104*

MAPS

Tuscany and Umbria (region) *7*
The Lower Arno and Apuan Alps *13*
Garfagnana Motor Tour *17*
Lucca Town Walk *18*
Pisa Town Walk *25*
Pistóia Town Walk *27*
Florence and the Upper Arno *31*
Arezzo Town Walk *32*
Casentino Motor Tour *34*
Cortona Town Walk *35*
Firenze (Florence) Art Tour *37*
City of the Medici Tour *37*
Oltrarno Town Walk *37*
Arcetri Walk *46*
Fièsole Town Walk *47*
Umbria *51*
Assisi Town Walk *53*
Lake Trasimeno Motor Tour *59*
Gúbbio Town Walk *61*
Valnerina Motor Tour *63*
Castelluccio to San Lorenzo Country Walk *65*
Orvieto Town Walk *67*
Perugia Town Walk *69*
Spoleto Town Walk *71*
Spoleto Motor Tour *75*
Central Tuscany *77*
Chianti Motor Tour *80*
Pienza Motor Tour *87*
San Gimignano Town Walk *89*
Siena Town Walk *94*
Volterra Town Walk *97*
Volterra Motor Tour *97*
The Etruscan Coast *98/99*
Maremma Motor Tour *106*
Sovana Walk *108*
Tuscany and Umbria *110–111*

The main entries in this book are cross-referenced to the regional map on pages 110–111. All heights on maps are in metres.

·INTRODUCTION·

This guide reveals the true character and flavour of Tuscany and Umbria, its people, legends and traditions, with detailed information and special features, illustrated throughout in full colour.

Specially drawn, easy-to-follow maps accompany over 25 walks and tours which take you out and about into the countryside as well as round the most popular towns and cities.

With practical information and a glossary of useful words and phrases, this is an invaluable guide to visiting this fascinating region of Italy.

·THE REGION·

'Over such trivialities as these many a valuable hour may slip away, and the traveller who has gone to Italy to study the tactile values of Giotto, or the corruption of the Papacy, may return remembering nothing but the blue sky and the men and women who live under it.'

E M Forster's often quoted observation is worth repeating – nobody else has summed up quite so concisely the attractions of Tuscany and Umbria. To put it in slightly different terms, the region appeals equally to fresco freaks who cannot get enough of medieval and Renaissance art, and to those who just want to rent a rural villa and relax with no fixed purpose to their days, soaking up the local atmosphere.

A little local colour for the season's visitors

Nowhere else in the world is there so much outstanding art in churches, museums and art galleries. Napoleon looted some of the choicer and more portable pieces, now in the Louvre in Paris, and English collectors made discreet purchases that have ended up in London's National Gallery, but the vast majority of the region's paintings, frescos and sculpture remains in situ. Even the most remote village church is likely to contain some treasure and travelling in Tuscany and Umbria can still throw up unexpected surprises; for art lovers the region offers the familiarity of great and famous works as well as the pleasures of treading uncharted paths.

But art is only one part of E M Forster's formula. Many people come to the region for nothing more demanding than shopping in local markets, sampling local wines, dining in rustic restaurants, savouring equally the romance of Tuscan landscapes and the balmy climate. Such visitors may find their sentiments echoed in the words of the poet Laurie Lee, who wrote: 'I'd had my fill of Florence, lovely but indigestible city. My eyes were choked with pictures and frescos, all stamped one on top of the other, blurred, their colours running. I began to long for those cool uplands, that country air, for the dateless wild olive and the uncatalogued cuckoo'.

To escape from Florence, Laurie Lee set off to walk to Siena and he made a sensible choice. The countryside between these two great cities corresponds most closely to the popular image of Tuscany, as depicted in travel brochures and tourist authority posters, a landscape of vineyards and castle-topped hills, of basking villas surrounded by sculptured cypress trees. First-time visitors are sometimes surprised to discover that not all of this vast region is similarly pastoral. Anyone arriving at Pisa will encounter the most developed part of Tuscany first, the heavily populated Arno Valley which, from Pisa up to Florence, is one continuous conurbation. Many of the plains and valleys in Tuscany and Umbria are similarly developed.

The rest consists of hilly to mountainous terrain, a varied and often dramatic landscape of olive groves, chestnut woods and sheep pasture. Spontaneous exploration is infinitely rewarding, but it pays to choose a small area and get to know it well. Memorable holidays depend upon using minor roads where almost any journey involves negotiating steep gradients and innumerable hairpin bends. It is only possible to travel slowly, and only right to do so, taking every opportunity to stop and admire a view, listening to the constant buzz of summer's insect life and the clang of a distant sheep bell.

Summer sees the biggest influx of visitors to the region but each season has its merits. September, October and even November are perfect months for avoiding crowds, enjoying warm but tolerable temperatures, seasonal dishes combining game and wild *funghi* and the general sense of well-being that surrounds the *vendemmia*, the grape harvest. This is a particularly festive time of year when, on any Sunday, visitors are likely to find village churches decorated and trestle tables set up in the main square for a *sagra* (feast) in honour of chestnuts, wine, olive oil, mushrooms, truffles, wild boar, salami, suckling pig – whatever happens to be the local speciality, including the humble cabbage and haricot bean.

Despite shorter days, winter brings clear skies and views that are not obscured by summer's haze. Hilltop cities are crisply outlined against blue skies and the low sun throws the sculptures on church façades into deep relief. Fewer tourists are about and museums can be delightfully empty. Shopkeepers have more time to stop and chat and visitors will see more of the ordinary life of the region.

Spring and early summer is the best time for wildflowers and there is a sense of freshness and renewal in the air as the snows melt in the mountains, rivers are in full spate and the hillsides are bright green with new foliage. In summer the noon heat dictates an early start to the day; churches, which are generally open by 7am, can be explored in the relative cool of the morning, followed by a reviving *espresso* before the museums open. By noon it is time to shop for picnic food or rest before a restaurant lunch; then a sleepy torpor descends as everything shuts for the long siesta. Life returns when shop shutters open again from 4pm and there is a magical time in the early evening when everyone, or so it seems, takes to the streets for the *passeggiata*, parading with friends in stylish clothes. To end the day it is best to dine *al fresco,* lingering under the stars, even if it does jeopardise your well-intentioned plans for an early start the next day.

In the Piazza della Signoria, nearly 500 years ago, the Florentines burnt Savonarola; today people meet here for more peaceable reasons

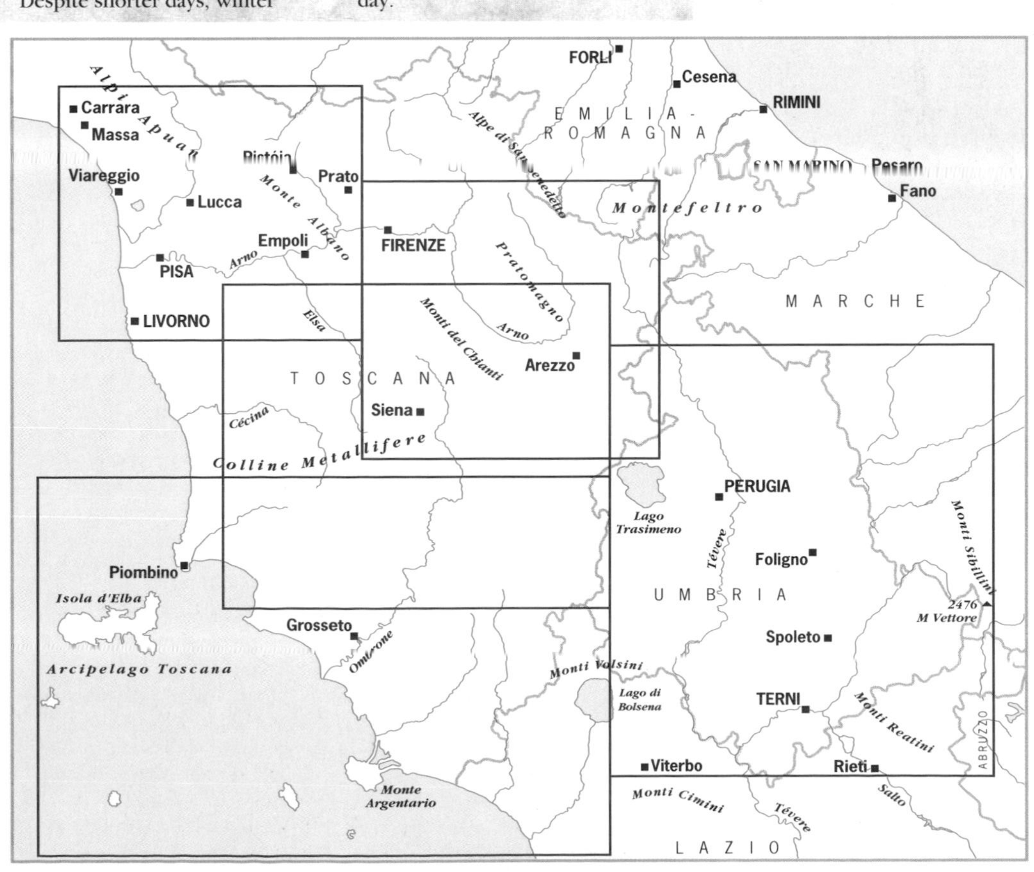

THE CITY AND THE COUNTRYSIDE

Those who have visited several cities in Tuscany and Umbria will begin to notice that, despite the strongly marked individuality of each place, there are certain underlying similarities. Nearly every city is surrounded by walls, often dating to the Etruscan or Umbrian foundation of the city between the 5th and 3rd centuries BC, later patched up, heightened or extended by Roman and medieval builders. Once inside these sheltering walls, there is a very real sense of stepping back several centuries and leaving the modern world behind, especially now that many towns prohibit traffic from entering the narrow medieval streets.

Siena's famed Campo is dominated by the 750-year-old Palazzo Pubblico

On entering a strange town, it is a fairly safe assumption that the main square can be reached by taking any road that leads uphill. Almost universally called the Piazza del Duomo, del Comune or del Popolo, this was deliberately sited on the crown of the hill so that its public buildings, the symbol of civic pride, could be seen from afar. Visitors arriving in the early evening will find the square and the main street full of people and the sound of their voices, echoing off the surrounding buildings, can rise to a considerable volume in the absence of traffic. The *passeggiata*, or evening stroll, is an aspect of town life that has changed little over the centuries, except for the dress of the participants, and it takes place against a backdrop of equally ancient buildings. These are the monuments that form the main focus of interest for the traveller: the cathedral and the town hall. Sometimes, too, there will be a fountain, as in Perugia, Bevagna, Siena and Panicale, its central position and fine sculpture an indication of the importance of water to a community often under the threat of seige.

The cathedral, or *duomo* – from *domus Dei*, house of God – may well be built over the crypt of a much earlier church or even on the foundations of an Etruscan or Roman temple. A surprising number have unfinished façades, a craggy cliff of broken stone and brick – usually because the money ran out or, as in the case of San Lorenzo in Florence, because the patrons could not agree on which of the competing designs should be built. These stand in contrast to the refreshing beauty of façades built in the Pisan Romanesque style, a delightful filigree of arcading and inlaid marble, or the sculpture covered façades of cathedrals in Siena, Assisi and Orvieto.

Interiors tend to be dark, lit only by small windows of alabaster or muddy yellow glass. Exceptions are Pope Pius II's cathedral in Pienza, flooded with light from tall, clear glass windows, reminiscent of a Protestant church in the Low Countries or Germany, or Siena and Orvieto, with their fine stained glass. Most cathedrals are built on the basilican plan, with a central nave flanked by lower side aisles. This plan, based on the Roman basilica, the hall of the magistrate, developed not long after Constantine the Great issued the Edict of Milan in AD313 granting official status to the Christian religion. Some churches differ from the Roman prototype only in that the high altar occupies the place of the magisterial chair, raised on a dais high above the nave, with a crypt below sheltering the relics of the local saint. Notable examples are at Barga, San Miniato in Florence and San Gregorio Maggiori in Spoleto, all enjoyable for their classical purity.

The town hall, with its accompanying tower, can usually be found close to the cathedral. Many of these Palazzi Comunali date from the 15th century, although begun as early as the 12th or 13th centuries; their construction was often interrupted by civil strife, lack of funds or the Black Death that ravaged the region from 1340. They represent an ideal rarely achieved in practice, of independent and relatively democratic local governments consisting of representatives of the guilds, the aristocracy and the people.

Representatives, or *priori*, were elected in theory to serve for a finite time (sometimes as little as two months) so that no one individual could dominate local government. In practice, instead of broadly based government, wealthy *signori* often imposed their own personal authority and, as in the case of the Medici family, were able to establish hereditary dynasties.

Even so, the town hall, built at public expense via a system of taxes and rates, provided the focus for local decision-making and the administration of justice.

Councillors, officials and leading citizens met to debate in the Great Hall. Official pronouncements and political speeches were made to the public from a balcony or raised platform, called the *ringhiera*, in front of the building, a word that gave rise to the verb 'to harangue'.

Many town halls are austere from the outside but, as in Siena, Florence and Perugia, contain richly frescoed rooms. They continue to serve as centres of local government but many also house the *pinacoteca* or *museo civico* (art galley and municipal museum), so that there is every chance to admire their Renaissance interiors.

Other place-names regularly encountered include the *bargello*, the town prison and palace of the judge, and the *rocca*, castle, or *fortezza*, fortress. Many of these castles, built by occupying imperial or papal garrisons to subdue the town, are now in ruins, though their cliffside or hilltop positions make them worth visiting for the views alone. Rural buildings also required defending from bandits and constant warfare, and the countryside is dotted with fortified manors (*castelli*) and villages (*borgi*). Undefended farmhouses began to be built from the 16th century in the relative peace that followed Tuscan subjugation by the Medici Dukes and in Umbria by the Papal States.

The plains of Tuscany and Umbria often have the colourless monotony associated with mechanised agro-industry, but the higher slopes are less easy to cultivate and pasture and woodland predominate. Here, depending on the season, there is an astonishing profusion of brilliantly coloured wildflowers. Even in winter, roadside verges support hellebores and spurges with their vivid lime-green flowers. The woodlands in spring are carpeted with snowdrops, bluebells, anemones and violets. May is the month of irises, which are particularly beautiful and profuse around Assisi.

In summer, any scrap of uncultivated land will be a patchwork of scarlet poppies, sky-blue chicory, small pink convolvulus, wild perennial sweet peas, white campion and ox-eye daisy, geraniums and pink and red-flowered mallows – while shady walls and damp rock faces will be covered in small ferns and yellow and white-flowered saxifrages. In autumn, countless cyclamen raise their fragile heads and the hillsides are a blaze of gold from the turning leaves.

The Romans were the first to extract marble from the Carrara quarries

PEOPLE AND CUSTOMS

In *A Traveller in Italy*, H V Morton described emerging from a museum full of ancient Etruscan sculptures and recognising the same faces on the street as he had been studying on the urns and tombs – the same full dark eyes, long inquisitive nose and 'Mona Lisa smile' echoing each other in flesh and carved stone over the distance of more than two millenia. Others, such as John Ruskin and D H Lawrence, have come to a similar conclusion: that the vibrant soul of the ancient Etruscans lived on to inspire the art of the Renaissance and continues to be evident in the people of modern Tuscany and Umbria.

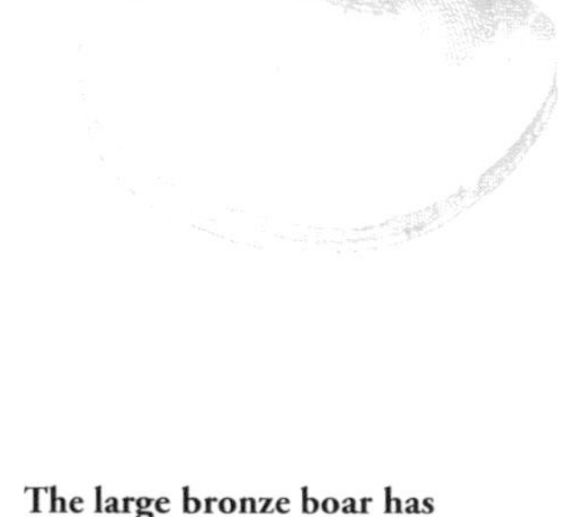

Ask a Tuscan whether this is true and the answer will be, 'Of course!' A scholar of ancient history might be more reserved, pointing to the fact that the language, art and religion of the ancient Etruscans were absorbed into Roman culture so that it is impossible to trace any distinctive Etruscan identity after the first century BC. Medical researchers have, however, isolated certain gene segments that are unique to the people who live in the region bounded by the Arno and the Tévere (Tiber), lending scientific weight to what was previously a romantic notion.

When educated Tuscans and Umbrians assert that they are Etruscan they mean numerous different things. That bald statement, for example, is used to justify the all-too-prevalent practice of tomb robbing. Among trusted friends at intimate dinner parties, a bronze figurine or painted vase might be brought out for admiration. An ordinance of 1934 allows Italians to keep antiquities they owned prior to that date; in theory everything discovered since then belongs to the state but it is difficult to prove precisely when an object was acquired. If challenged, the proud owner of an ancient brooch will argue that art is meant to be enjoyed, not left forgotten in the ground, and that, anyway, 'it is our heritage; we are Etruscan'.

That same phrase, 'we are Etruscan', is also used when Rome is being discussed, usually in contemptuous terms. The capital is seen as symbolising centralised bureaucracy, insensitivity to local views, inactivity and ineffective government. Some Tuscans and Umbrians speak as if they regret ever having joined a united Italy, even though both regions voted enthusiastically to do so in referenda in 1860. Their enthusiasm for a federal Europe within the European Community stems from disillusionment with Rome and the desire for greater regional autonomy, especially over the allocation of funds and subsidies.

Umbrians, in particular, still feel rueful that they did not receive more economic aid from Rome when they needed it most, when Marshall Plan funds were available for reconstruction after World War II. That explains why the

The large bronze boar has dominated Florence's Straw Market for centuries; rubbing its snout is supposed to bring good luck

communists continue to enjoy electoral success in today's relatively affluent Tuscany and Umbria. Initially communism was the cause espoused by anyone opposed to the fascism of the 1930s and 1940s and many courageous deeds of resistance were carried out under its banner. After the war the party encouraged the self-help ethic that enabled local farmers to set up co-operatives and food-processing plants and to improve the local infrastructure, building new roads linking remote rural areas to populous city markets. Local communism is not rampantly ideological or Marxist; it is pragmatic and would be called social democracy elsewhere in Europe.

Umbrians and Tuscans love to draw telling distinctions to prove that their souls are superior to those of the Romans – ancient or modern. For example, Rome was the builder of straight roads and planned towns with a regular street grid, oriented on the four cardinal points of the compass. The Etruscans and Umbrians, by contrast, built hilltop towns threaded by a maze of winding streets. Roman art is cold; Etruscan art, reborn in the Renaissance, vibrantly sensual. Romans are seen as hotheaded imperialists always in a hurry to get somewhere else – look at the way they drive. Etruscan and Umbrian roads zigzag and meander as if built for a people with no great desire to go far from home or depart from familiar surroundings – indeed, unlike other Italian provinces, Tuscany and Umbria have never seen the mass migration of their rural poor to the Americas or northern Europe.

Tuscans and Umbrians, in summary, see themselves as gracious, cultivated people in love with their land and its traditions. Yet no account of their character would be complete if it omitted one fact; that Tuscans and Umbrians sometimes seem to dislike each other even more than they do the Romans. This is seen in the passionate support given to local festivals which, for all their colour and pageantry, are thinly disguised re-enactments of ancient hostilities.

Campanalismo, which some translate as 'parochialism', is particularly strong in the region: that same bond of loyalty that unites a community of people all born within the sound of the ancient parish bells often excludes friendships with the people of a neighbouring community. Cities a few miles apart are 'foreign'; different accents can be detected in Perugia and Assisi, Florence and Siena, separated by no great distances, and of course the citizens of each town argue that their dialect is the purer form of Italian. Sienese with long memories pretend never to have heard of Florence, still smarting from a defeat inflicted 400 years ago.

Anthropologists, who have found a rich field for their studies in Tuscany and Umbria, explain all this through conflict theory; competition for scarce resources in highly populated regions leads to communities emphasising and exaggerating their differences. Tuscans and Umbrians would never accept such a bald reduction. They say that tradition and the past matters to them because it is a constant source of succour and inspiration. This finds expression in the region's rich tradition of craftsmanship and artistic endeavour – and art is defined in very broad terms. Equal respect is accorded to the producers of fine wines and olive oils, to the quarrymen of Carrara, to the seamstresses who make gorgeous festival costumes as to the painter or bronze caster. The region has also produced some world-renowned fashion designers. One of them, Emilio Pucci (who designed the smart and practical uniforms worn by Florentine traffic police) speaks for many Tuscans and Umbrians when he acknowledges his deep debt to the past and describes himself as the direct heir of an artistic tradition stretching back to the Renaissance and beyond to the dawn of Etruscan time.

The Palio, Siena's ancient annual horse race, is an integral part of the city's culture

THE LOWER ARNO & APUAN ALPS

Anyone with a window seat on the flight into Pisa will see the whole of the lower Arno plain laid out below as the aeroplane makes its final descent. Pisa itself, once a thriving port, now stands 8km from the sea. The Arno threads through the city glinting silver in the sunlight but, on dull days, more closely resembles Virginia Woolf's description: 'swirling past with its usual coffee-coloured foam'. Immediately around the Arno estuary the normally blue Tyrrhenian sea is cloudy and muddy with the silt that the river has been depositing for centuries. As a result Pisa is now landlocked, separated from the coast by mudflats, marshes and woodland. Along the coast itself is the Marina di Pisa, which, like many Italian resorts, has become a grid of neatly divided beach plots bedecked with sun loungers and colourful beach umbrellas lined in precisely measured rows.

To the north you may catch a glimpse of the port of Massa, the point from which Carrara marble is shipped to all corners of the globe. Nearer to Pisa is the unmissable escarpment of the Apuan Alps (Alpi Apuane), rising sheer from the flat Lucchese plain, named after the city of Lucca. The lower slopes of these mountains are covered in a green mantle of chestnut, oak and birch woodland; this gives way to what looks like snow but is, in fact, exposed limestone, forming an extensive chain of peaks and plateaus stretching for miles to Tuscany's northern border.

On arrival in Pisa it is difficult to escape the fact that this is one of the most industrially developed parts of Tuscany. Whichever road is taken from the city, there is little open countryside between one town and the next. The Arno Valley road, leading to Florence, passes through the furniture-making town of Cáscina, through Pontedera, where motorcycles are made and Empoli, a major centre for the manufacture of industrial glass. The Lucchese plain, running parallel to the Arno to the north, leads to Florence by way of the great textile towns of Pistóia and Prato, the centre of Italy's rag trade.

This is not the Tuscany of the popular imagination and most visitors have only one concern; to escape as quickly as possible to the greener countryside of central Tuscany or Umbria. To do so, however, is to miss some remarkable art and architecture and although it takes a certain dogged determination to drive through dreary industrial suburbs and find parking space, Pisa, Lucca, Prato and Pistóia are all rewarding cities.

Pisa provides an introduction to some of the best, and most idiosyncratic, Romanesque architecture in Europe. Quite apart from the tipsy charm of the Leaning Tower, the cathedral and baptistry form a bizarre ensemble of extraordinary shapes influenced by the Moorish architecture of Andalucia and North Africa. The cathedral was consecrated in 1138 when Pisa was approaching the peak of its prosperity as a great maritime power. Pisa's navy inflicted a decisive defeat on the Saracens in 1062 to conquer Sicily. In 1135 it captured the port city of Amalfi, its main rival, and for the next 150 years Pisa reigned supreme as the main trading city in the western Mediterranean. Twelfth-century chroniclers describe Pisa as a cosmopolitan city of 30,000 inhabitants, comparable to Venice in the exotic splendour of its buildings and the riches stored in its warehouses.

Though frequently at war with the Muslims, Pisa was influenced by Arabic thought. Nicolo Fibonacci, the Pisan mathematician, is credited with introducing Arabic numerals to Europe along with the concept of the Golden Section, which in turn influenced Pisan architects and engineers. This is evident in the precise geometry of the panels decorating the cathedral, forming complex patterns of squares, diamonds and triangles in light and dark marble. These alternate with exuberant arabesque reliefs depicting real and mythical beasts fancifully intertwined with foliage to create a carpet-like effect.

The strongest defining feature of the Pisan Romanesque style, however, is the distinctive four-storey colonnade of the cathedral façade, echoed by the blank arcading of the Leaning Tower and baptistry, with its rhythmic interplay of columns and arches. This style greatly influenced other churches in the region, notably in Lucca and Pistóia.

Visitors to Pisa can also admire the work of two remarkable artists, the father and son team of Nicola and Giovanni Pisano. They were responsible for completing the baptistry and adding the enormous dome with its spiky Gothic crown, but their best work consists of the pulpit by Nicola inside the baptistry (1260) and that of Giovanni in the cathedral (1300).

It is not an exaggeration to say that the Pisanos created modern figure sculpture. The critic Vasari says they learned their technique from copying Roman sarcophagi brought back to Pisa as spoils of war, though that does not account for the unprecedented realism and expressiveness of their pulpit reliefs. It took another 100 years

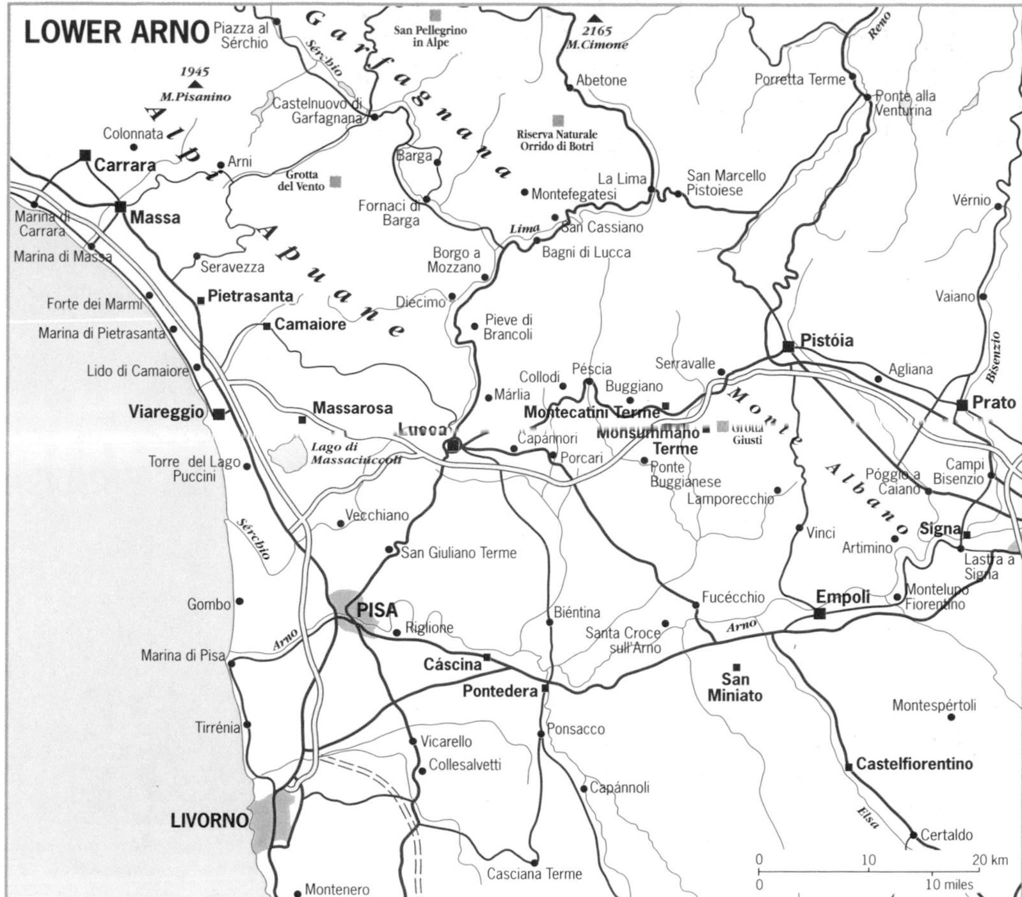

for Tuscan artists to catch up; not until the early Renaissance did other artists create work of such compelling vigour. If seeing this work whets the appetite, there are other fine Pisano pulpits in Pistóia and Siena cathedrals, but their great masterpiece is the Fontana Maggiore in the Umbrian capital, Perugia.

Pisa's decline began in 1284 when the city's navy was all but destroyed by the Genoese at the Battle of Meloria, fought off the coast near Livorno. Pisa's harbour, which had only been kept clear by continual dredging, finally silted up and the city fell prey to Florence in 1406. Lorenzo de'Medici attempted to reconcile Pisa to Florentine rule by funding the revival of its ancient, but decayed, university, where the city's native Galileo (1564–1642) studied and taught. Even so, Pisa's fate was sealed and, in Shelley's words, the city became 'the grave of an extinguished people' until, after heavy bombing in World War II, it revived as an industrial centre and thanks to the international airport became the gateway to Tuscany.

Those who find the region's industrial sprawl depressing should, after visiting Pisa, drive north to the atmospheric town of Lucca, sparing time to see at least one of the palatial villas built by the Lucchese nobility in the foothills of the Apuan Alps, and then up the Sérchio Valley. Quarries and 19th-century paper mills around Borgo a Mozzano soon give way to a landscape of rugged beauty, known as the Garfagnana. In this undiscovered region mountain villages cling to the sides of wooded ravines and the urban splendours of Pisa seem very far away. Either side of the Sérchio Valley rise the dazzling white peaks of the Apuan Alps, composed of deeply folded and striated limestone streaked with harder layers of marble. Hang-gliding enthusiasts practice their death-defying sport here, watched by nomadic wild sheep and even the occasional soaring eagle. This is a misanthropist's paradise; visitors will not encounter many fellow travellers, but will find plenty of scope for walking, admiring the magnificent views and observing nature in the wild, rocky valleys of the huge Parco Naturale delle Alpi Apuane and the Parco dell'Orecchiella.

North from Pisa, the Apuan Alps are streaked with white marble quarries

BAGNI DI LUCCA

MAP REF: 110 B5

In the 19th century, Bagni di Lucca was one of the foremost spa towns in Europe. Under the patronage of Napoleon's sister, Elisa Baciocchi, it was frequented by the crowned heads of Europe and distinguished foreign visitors, such as Byron, Shelley, the Brownings and Montaigne. Though ostensibly visiting Bagni for the curative properties of the local waters, the 19th-century elite found time for romance, boating, reckless gambling and, according to Elizabeth Barrett Browning, waspish gossip and scandal.

Today the grand spa hotels are in need of their own rejuvenation and the casino – built in 1837 and one of the first licensed gaming establishments in Europe – is locked and shuttered; long-standing plans to restore the building to its full imperial glory have yet to be implemented. Despite this decay the town retains a certain charm; the River Lima flows through the centre and steep wooded hills rise above the town making it feel enclosed and apart from the busy world. The main square is dominated by the neo-classical Circolo dei Forestieri, once an exclusive club, now a restaurant. Literary pilgrims can cross the bridge behind this building and seek out the forlorn Protestant cemetery where Marie Louise de la Ramée (1839–1908), better known as the best-selling romantic novelist, Ouida, is buried.

Nineteenth-century Europe's favourite spa resort, Bagni di Lucca

Nearby The mountain road north from Bagni leads through magnificent chestnut woods to Montefegatesi, a high-lying hamlet perched on its own miniature peak below the impressive bare limestone heights of the Alpi Apuane (Apuan Alps). From the car park at the entrance to the village a track leads for 5km to the Orrido di Botri gorge, a dramatic ravine. To vary the journey, return through San Cassiano, a small village with a fine Romanesque church covered in sculptural reliefs.

The hump-backed Ponte del Diavola (Devil's Bridge) in Borgo a Mazzano

BARGA

MAP REF: 110 B5

Barga is the most appealing town in the Sérchio Valley. The town's narrow alleys are beautifully paved with stone hewn from the surrounding hills and the complete absence of traffic makes Barga a perfect place for leisurely exploration. All lanes eventually lead up to the Romanesque

The countryside around Lucca

cathedral, standing on a grass-covered terrace with mountain views on every side.

The stone corbels running round the eaves of the cathedral are carved with intricate interlaced knots as well as beasts and armoured knights. An intriguing freize above the north portal depicts a banquet; some interpret this as the Wedding Feast at Canaa, others as a scene from some lost medieval folk tale. Inside, the pulpit carved by Bigarelli di Como in the early 13th century is a *tour de force*; it stands 5m high on pillars rising from the backs of man-eating lions. The pulpit reliefs depict the Evangelists, the Three Magi, and the Annunciation, Nativity and Baptism of Christ. The huge wooden figure of St Christopher in the apse dates from the early 12th century and, to the right of the high altar, charming terracottas by Luca della Robbia depict angels drawing curtains aside to reveal a gilded tabernacle. Alongside the church is a small museum of local archaeology.

In summer Barga hosts a renowned music festival; the main venue is the 18th-century Teatro dell'Accademia dei Differenti in Piazza Angelico.

BORGO A MAZZANO

MAP REF: 110 B5

Borgo a Mazzano is the main industrial centre of the Sérchio Valley, a town of factories and early 19th-century paper mills. Its main attraction is the striking Ponte del Diavolo (Devil's Bridge – also known as the Ponte della Maddelena) just to the north of the town. The local legend says that the bridge was built with the aid of the Devil who demanded the first soul to cross the bridge as payment. The wily villagers ensured that the first to cross the bridge was not a human but a dog. In reality, the arched bridge, with its pronounced hump, was built in the 11th century under the patronage of the Countess Matilda. This remarkable woman, born in 1046, inherited the title of imperial margrave from her distant ancestors, the Germanic Lombards who invaded northern Italy in the 6th century. Matilda endowed the region with a number of fine Romanesque churches; the best are Pieve Santa Maria, near Diecimo, and San Donato, both to the south of Borgo a Mazzano, and Pieve di Brancoli, located in a characterful hilltop town on the opposite bank of the Sérchio.

CARRARA

MAP REF: 110 A5

Carrara is famous throughout the world for its snow-white, fine-grained marble, the favoured material of sculptors since Roman times and worked to such good effect by artists as different in their styles as Michelangelo and Henry Moore. In the steep-sided valleys located to the north and east of Carrara, over 300 quarries produce 500,000 tons of marble a year, extracting huge blocks of dazzling white stone with pneumatic drills and diamond edged 'wire' for export through the nearby port of Massa.

To find out about the local industry it is best to start at the Mostra Nazionale Marmi e Macchine, on Viale XX Settembre, a museum that explains the history and techniques of marble extraction. From there it is possible to visit some of the quarries which offer guided tours by heading for Colonnata, east of Carrara. Finally, return to the town centre where marble workshops, such as the Atelier Niccoli in Piazza XXVII Aprile, admit visitors. To see the local marble used to good effect visit Carrara's fine cathedral, with its Pisan-style façade.

It is impossible to escape the presence of Pinocchio in Collodi

COLLODI

MAP REF: 110 B5

Large signs featuring Pinocchio and his remarkable nose line the roads leading to Collodi. Carlo Lorenzini (1826–90), the author of *The Adventures of Pinocchio,* was born in Florence but frequently visited Collodi where his uncle lived at the Villa Garzoni. Fond childhood memories led Lorenzini to adopt Collodi as his pen name. The tiny village seized this opportunity to create a Pinocchio theme park in the late 1950s and the local economy thrives on the sale of puppets and other souvenirs. The Parco di Pinocchio consists of a museum, playground, maze and garden where there is a bronze statue of Pinocchio by Emilio Greco (1956) along with tableaux and mosaics based on Venturino Venuri's illustrations for the book.

The other great attraction of Collodi is the Villa Garzoni, which has one of the grandest hillside gardens in Italy. The villa was built for the Garzoni family between 1633 and 1662 in baroque style. The frescoed interior contains original furnishings and the homely kitchen where, it is claimed, Collodi dreamed up his famous children's story. The breathtaking gardens fall steeply away from the villa down a series of terraces decorated with waterfalls, grottoes and fountains. The underlying formality of the garden is relieved by the sheer bravado of the scheme, devised by Ottaviano Diodati in 1786. Off the main staircase, alleys and thickets conceal terracotta nymphs, a maze and a bathhouse, complete with a concealed stage where musicians could play without being able to spy on the amorous games of the villa's aristocratic guests.

EMPOLI

MAP REF: 110 B4

Empoli is a far from attractive town, specialising in glass manufacture, but it is worth pushing through the dreary suburbs for the delicate Romanesque Collegiata Sant'Andrea in Piazza Farinata. The lower part of the attractive green and white marble façade dates from 1093, while the upper part was successfully completed in the same spirit in the 18th century. The picture gallery in the adjacent baptistry houses choice works by Florentine masters, including a celebrated *Pietà* fresco by Masolino, a *Virgin and Child* attributed to the young Filippo Lippi and a *gonfalone*, or processional banner, by Bicci di Lorenzo, showing St Nicholas of Tolentino shielding Empoli from a hail of arrows representing the Black Death.

Sant'Andrea's marble façade, in the style of San Miniato in Florence

Nearby Two outstanding Medici villas lie to the east of Empoli. The gloriously sited Villa La Fernandina, at Artimino, fulfils everyone's idea of the perfect rural retreat. The villa was built as a hunting lodge for Ferdinand I by Buontalenti in 1594 and it stands high above unspoiled Tuscan countryside. Numerous chimneys punctuate the villa's roofline, earning it the nickname 'Villa of a Hundred Chimneys'. These are matched inside by numerous fine fireplaces carved from dove-grey *pietra serena*. The villa houses a small museum of Etruscan bronzes and ceramics, and an excellent restaurant serves its own estate-bottled wines.

A scenic road links this villa, by way of Comeana, to the Villa di Póggio a Caiano, sheltered behind high walls from the scruffy town of the same name that surrounds it. This was Lorenzo de'Medici's favourite retreat, the place where he wrote his sonnets celebrating nature and the Tuscan landscape which inspired Botticelli's *Primavera*. The villa was built between 1480 and 1485 by Giuliano da Sangallo who, inspired by the 1st-century treatise *De Architectura* written by Vitruvius, sought to build a villa in the style of ancient Rome. The graceful curving staircase, which lends grace and femininity to the classical design, was added in 1807. Within, the central atrium is covered in frescos glorifying the deeds of the Medici, painted in the 16th century by various artists including Andrea del Sarto and Pontormo. The villa is surrounded by extensive parkland, laid out in the English landscape style in the 19th century.

MOTOR TOUR

The remote and mountainous Garfagnana region remained isolated from mainstream events between 1115, when the Countess Matilda died, bequeathing her feudal domain to the pope, and the 19th century when it became part of Tuscany. The region has no great buildings or works of art, but the valleys leading off either side of the upper Sérchio Valley are renowned for their wild and unadulterated natural beauty.

From Barga follow the signs north to Castelnuovo di Garfagnana.

Castelnuovo di Garfagnana
The main town of the upper Sérchio Valley is dominated by the 12th-century *rocca* which

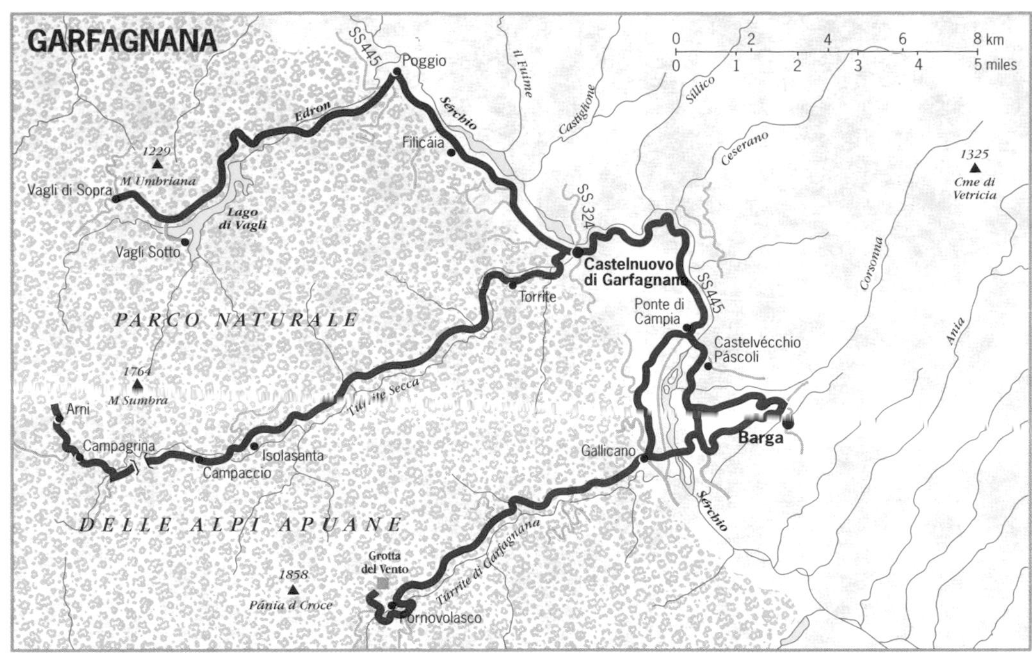

controlled the mountain road connecting Genoa and Lucca. Ludovico Ariosto, the author of the epic *Orlando Furioso*, was governor here between 1522 and 1525, responsible for stamping out banditry and collecting tolls. He needed the job to pay for the publication of his work but found the 'rough, wild, horrid crags' depressing and eventually resigned, confessing that 'I am not a man to govern other men'. It is worth making the long and tortuous 32km drive northeast from Castelnuovo to the monastery of San Pellegrino in Alpe for the outstanding scenery and an informative museum of peasant life in the Garfagnana.

Follow the SS445 north, signposted Aulla, and turn left after 8km, following the signs for Vagli di Sopra.

Vagli di Sopra

This ancient mountain hamlet stands close to the man-made Lago di Vagli. The village of Fabbriche was drowned when the lake was dammed and can sometimes be seen in the water's depths. The landscape has a rugged beauty; the views stretch north to Monte Pisanino, the highest peak in the Apuan Alps (1,945m) and the whole surrounding landscape is protected as a Parco Naturale.

Return to Castelnuovo and take the first right at the entrance to the town, signposted to Massa. After 17km, turn right for Arni.

Arni

Arni is noted for the curious geological formations called the Marmitte dei Giganti, the Giants' Cooking Pots, great hollows scoured by the swirling waters of the Túrrite Secca. Some of the craters are 20m across and it is possible to climb to the bottom, but with care! Nearby, the road to Carrara continues through the Galleria del Cipollaio, a tunnel carved through the marble heart of the mountain.

Return to Castelnuovo and head south on the western bank of the Sérchio, following signs for Borgo a Mazzano. After 12km, leave the main road following signs for Gallicano, passing through the village on the Grotta del Vento road, which climbs alongside the Túrrite di Garfagnana mountain stream for 8km.

Grotta del Vento

The Cave of the Wind is just one of the great network of caverns that riddle the heart of the Apuan Alps. Guided tours of 1, 2 or 3 hours' duration take the visitor to the icy depths of the cave system with its eerie subterranean landscape of pools, streams and stalactites.

Retrace the route to Gallicano and cross the river. Turn right then left to return to Barga.

The lively town of Castelnuovo di Garfagnana has wild surroundings

LIVORNO

MAP REF: 110 A4

After Pisa's harbour silted up, Cosimo I initiated a scheme to transform the small fishing village of Livorno into Tuscany's main port. Work began in 1577 when a new city of wide avenues and canals was laid out by Buontalenti. In 1608 Livorno was declared a free port, open to traders, regardless of religion or race, and it soon attracted a large population of Dutch, Spanish, English and African merchants as well as Jewish refugees from religious persecution. English involvement began with Sir Robert Dudley, the illegitimate son of Elizabeth I's favourite, the Earl of Leicester, who was appointed marine engineer to the Medici Dukes and designed the impressive mole, the sea wall protecting the harbour, completed in 1621. The British architect Inigo Jones, who was one of Buontalenti's students, designed the city's new cathedral in 1605. By the 18th century Livorno was a favourite resort of British travellers, who called the city Leghorn, anglicising its medieval name, Legorno. The poet Shelley (1792–1822) was the city's most famous resident; he celebrated the Livornese landscape in *Ode to the West Wind* and *To a Skylark* and it was from the port that he set out on his last fateful voyage to Viareggio in July 1822.

Today, rebuilt after heavy Allied bombing in World War II, Livorno is Italy's second busiest port after

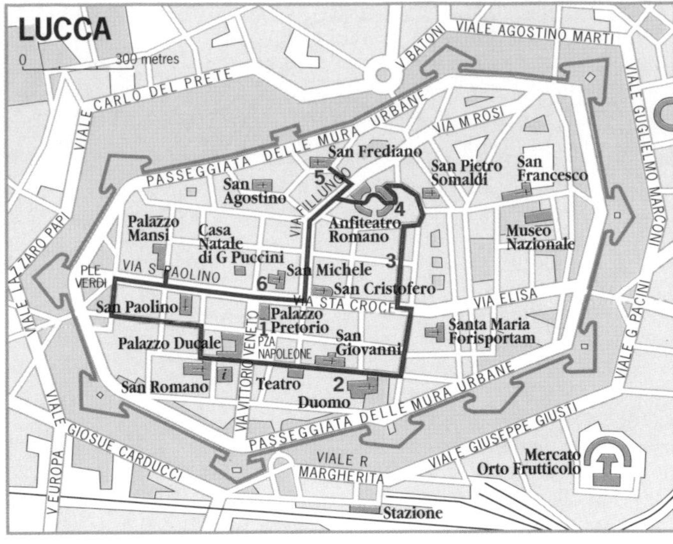

Génova (Genoa). The main sights lie along the Via Grande. On Piazza Michele, fronting the port, is a monument to Ferdinand I (1595). The four chained Moors, added in 1623, serve as a reminder that, despite its reputation as a progressive city, Livorno had a notorious slave market and launched piratical attacks on North African traders. Beyond, in Piazza Grande, is Inigo Jones' cathedral, almost entirely rebuilt after the war. Jones' design for London's Covent Garden was modelled on this square. Further up is the ugly Piazza Repubblica with the brick Fortezza Nuova (1590) to the left. More characterful, if somewhat run down, is the Piccola Venezia (Little Venice) quarter south of the Fortezza, an area of canalside *palazzi*, warehouses and workshops.

On the eastern side of the city is the English cemetery (Via Verdi 63) where Tobias Smollett is buried along with other members of Livorno's British and American community. Further out, the Museo Civico, in the Villa Fabbricoti, has a good collection of works by the late 19th-century Italian impressionists, the *Macchiaioli* (literally, 'spot makers').

LUCCA

MAP REF: 110 B5

Lucca is a most appealing city. Remarkably, it remained independent of the Tuscan Grand Duchy, carved out by Cosimo I, until 1847. The town's red-brick walls are a reminder of the city's commitment to autonomy; they were begun in 1500 when the threat of Florentine aggression was very real and remain the best-preserved example of Renaissance city defences in Italy. The upper ramparts were planted with plane

Lucca's Church of San Michele, where Puccini was a choirboy

trees in 1817 to create a continuous shady avenue, 4km in length, from which there are fine views over the city. Within the walls, Lucca preserves its Roman street plan and numerous churches with Pisan Romanesque façades (greatly admired by the critic John Ruskin, who recorded that his interest in medieval architecture literally began in this city). The Lucchese have adopted the bicycle as their favoured mode of transport and the absence of cars makes the city feel all the more intimate and human in scale.

TOWN WALK

Start from the car park in Piazzale Verdi and walk down Via Vittorio Emanuele, taking the second right, Via Vurlamacchi, to San Romano Church. Inside is Matteo Civitali's Renaissance tomb of San Romano (1490) but the church is rarely open. Turn left by the church, right under the ochre-coloured aerial corridor, and left, through a gate, to enter the Palazzo Ducale and admire Ammannati's Mannerist colonnade (1578) on the left. Exit through the opposite arch into Piazza Napoleone.

1 The name commemorates Napoleon's sister, Elisa Baciocchi, who briefly ruled Lucca as her private principality in 1805. Her successor, the Duchess Maria Louisa, who ruled from 1817, is commemorated by Lorenzo Bartolini's statue in the square. To the right is the neo-classical Teatro del Giglio (1817), with its ornate lampstands, where the operas of Puccini, who was born in Lucca, are performed in summer.

Walk past the theatre, and bear left through Piazza San Giovanni to the Duomo (Cathedral) di San Martino.

2 The cathedral façade, begun in 1204, is an outstanding example of Pisan Romanesque architecture and is covered in intricate panels of green and white marble depicting a host of symbolic birds and beasts. The rich carvings around the portal illustrate the Labours of the Months. Inside, on the left, is the much praised, though rather ponderous, marble tabernacle of Matteo Civitali (1484). It shelters one of medieval Europe's most greatly revered relics, the *Volto Santo*. According to legend this crucifix was carved by Nicodemus, a witness to the Crucifixion, and thus it was believed to be an exact portrait of the dead Christ. The fame of the image led to some interesting corruptions: the mythical St Vaudeluc, worshipped in medieval France, probably derives from 'Saint Vault de Lucques', the holy face of Lucca, and in Germany the bearded Virgin, Santa Kummernis, may be the result of untutored village carpenters making imprecise copies of the original. In reality, the figure probably dates from the 11th century.

The transept contains the remarkable tomb of Ilaria del Carretto (1408), an early Renaissance masterpiece by Jacopo della Quercia.

Walk down the left-hand side of the church, first left, then right, into Via della Rosa. Head left past Santa Maria Forisportam (13th century) then left and first right to enter Via Guinigi.

3 This street has some of Lucca's oldest surviving *palazzi*, untouched since they were 'modernised' in the 15th century by the insertion of Renaissance door and window surrounds. The striking Torre Guinigi, with trees growing from its upper storey, was the stronghold of Paolo Guinigi, political leader of the city from 1400 to 1430.

At the end of the street turn right, then left past San Pietro Somaldi (13th century) following Via Busdraghi and through a tunnel into the Anfiteatro Romano.

4 This striking elliptical *piazza* preserves the exact outline of the Roman amphitheatre and is the atmospheric centre of local community life.

Exit through the opposite side of the square, turn right, right again and left for San Frediano Church.

5 San Frediano has an outstanding mid-12th-century font, big as a fountain and carved with scenes showing Moses (in medieval armour) with an entourage of camels passing through the divided Red Sea.

Cross the piazza in front of the church and turn right in Via Fillungo, Lucca's main shopping street, noting the art nouveau *ironwork that graces several shop façades. The Church of San Cristofero, halfway down on the left, has a fine 13th-century wheel window and is used as an art gallery. At the bottom turn right for Piazza San Michele.*

The rooftops of Lucca from the Torre Guinigi

6 Lucca's most beautiful square is surrounded by Renaissance palaces and occupies the site of the Roman forum. San Michele church has a 13th-century façade to rival that of the cathedral, covered in panels of huntsmen in pursuit of barbaric beasts.

With your back to the cathedral, take the left-hand exit from the square, Via San Paolina, which leads back to Piazzale Verdi. The fourth turning right leads to the city art gallery, housed in the Palazzo Mansi; this retains some of its original 17th-century furniture and has a delightful rococo fresco of The Judgement of Paris.

Bargain-price mercandise at a Lucca street market

VILLAS AND GARDENS

'A villa in Tuscany'; this simple phrase conjures up all sorts of associations – rural tranquillity, a refuge, an oasis, a Garden of Eden. Tuscan villas and their gardens carry a whole weight of symbolism that sets them apart from any mere farmhouse or country abode. Originally, of course, the villa was just that: a functional building at the centre of an agricultural estate. One such villa, at Settefenestre near Orbetello in the Maremma region, was excavated in the mid-1970s. Dating from the 1st century BC, it was found to be subdivided into two main parts: the living quarters of the landowners, decorated with frescos, stucco work and mosaic floors, and the working part with the granary, oil press, wine cellars, stables, byres and slave quarters.

By the mid-2nd century AD, however, an entirely new type of villa was being built that had nothing to do with agriculture. The Villa Adriana, near Rome, was built for the Emperor Hadrian between AD125 and 134. It is a vast complex, a city in miniature but without the noise, the stench and the crowds. Within its high encircling walls the Villa Adriana contained baths, libraries, theatres and temples, gardens full of statues and an artificial grotto representing Hades, guarded by a statue of the three-headed Cerberus. Hadrian built his villa as a place where the intellectual elite of his day could meet, read, take exercise and contemplate the fundamental mysteries of life; already the villa had come to represent a vital ingredient in the balance between public and private life, and a man was regarded as incomplete who did not find time for reading, thinking and recharging his batteries in the company of like-minded friends.

In the 15th century Cosimo de'Medici revived the idea of the villa as a kind of club, a meeting place for men of refined sensibilities. Cosimo would retreat to the Villa di Careggi (today a nursing home in the northern suburbs of Florence), 'not so much for the purpose of improving my fields as myself'. Here he would read his 'favourite Plato' and devote himself to pursuing 'the true road to happiness'.

Lorenzo de'Medici, Cosimo's grandson, spent much of his youth at the same villa. Lorenzo threw himself into gardening, raising

The magnificent hillside gardens of the Castello Garzoni in Collodi

cows, pigs, Sicilian pheasants and racehorses, and experimenting with new methods for manufacturing cheese.

The philosophy of humanism was also a direct product of villa society. The Villa di Careggi was the principal meeting place of the Platonic Academy, founded by Cosimo. Members of the Academy included Lorenzo de'Medici, Aeneas Silvius Piccolomini (later Pope Pius II), Politian, Masilio Ficino (the translator of Plato's works), the Greek scholar John Argyropoulos and other leading thinkers of the day. It functioned as a philosophical debating society whose members met to gain nourishment and instruction from discussing classical texts and talking long into the night, convinced of the power of words, knowledge and persuasion to make the world a better place. One member of the Academy, Leon Battista Alberti, undertook a typically humanistic enterprise: the description of architecture in terms of mathematical principles to do with ratio and proportion. His treatise, *De Re Aedificatoria* (1452), laid down the essential rules for the archetypal villa: it had to be built on top of a hill to take advantage of the views, its rooms would all radiate off a central hall or atrium, its windows should be large and numerous to admit light and air, and 'the harmony and concord of all the parts [should be] achieved in such a manner that nothing could be added or taken away or altered except for the worse'.

In 1480 Lorenzo de'Medici employed Giuliano da Sangallo to build such a villa at Póggio a Caiano, east of Florence. Sangallo, like Alberti, went back to Roman prototypes, as described by the 1st-century AD author Vitruvius in his treatise *De Architectura*. The result, scarcely changed to this day, is a simple but dignified building that anticipates the designs of Palladio by several decades. The villa at Póggio a Caiano served as the prototype for scores of villas that now dot the slope of Fiésole to the north of Florence and of Bellosguardo to the south. They include the splendid Villa della Petraia (1575) and the Villa di Castello (1537), which are open to the public, and others, such as La Pietra, the home of the distinguished art historian Sir Harold Acton, and the Villa dell'Ombrellino, former home of Edward VII's mistress, Alice Keppel, and her daughter Violet Trefusis, which can not.

The villas of Lucca, standing in the foothills of the Apuan Alps, north of the Lucchese plain, are far more ornate; several were remodelled in the 17th and 18th centuries, when the villa was no longer conceived of as a refuge for gentlemen scholars but rather as the setting for elaborate parties, theatrical entertainments and romantic frivolities. The Villa Reale in Márlia (also known as the Villa Imperiale and the Villa Orsetti Pecci-Blunt) was transformed into a magnificent imperial residence by Napoleon's sister, Elisa Baciocchi. Niccolò Paganini was her court musician and the magnificent *teatro verde*, an outdoor theatre of clipped yew trees, is the setting for an excellent summer music festival. The Villa Mansi, 3km east of Márlia near Segromigno Monte, and the Villa Torrigiani, a short way south near Camigliano, both have lively façades embellished with statues and baroque flourishes. At all three of these villas, however, and most notably at the Villa Garzoni further east in Collodi, the building itself is not the main attraction: rather it is the gardens, with their formal terraces, fountains, statuary and staircases.

Italian gardens, in the formal style, may disappoint those who consider flowers to be an essential ingredient. The predominant colours are the shadowy dark greens of cypress, box, yew and ilex (holm oak), offset by lichened stonework and terracotta. The trees and shrubs are rarely allowed to follow their own inclinations, but are clipped into crisp geometric shapes that mirror the architecture of the villa itself; even the cypress avenues are planted to imitate stone colonnades. The essence of these gardens is their theatricality: the virtuoso waterworks, the carvings of amorous nymphs, lecherous satyrs and statuesque deities, create a world of mythical allusion and a counterpoint between human artifice and, in the words of Pliny, the 'negligent beauties of rural nature'.

The gardens of these four villas, together with the Boboli Gardens in Florence, represent some of the best surviving examples of the Italian formal garden style. They now have another quality which Vita Sackville West found especially enchanting, the precious patina of age. 'The abrasion of hard edges and the falling out of mortar are a gain', she wrote, 'for the lichen laps over the bruised moulding and the mortar is replaced by a cushion of moss'.

Of all the Medici villas, Poggio a Caiano was the favourite of Lorenzo the Magnificent

PÉSCIA

MAP REF: 110 B4

Although the region around Péscia is one of the most densely populated and heavily built-up areas of Tuscany, it also serves as a major centre for horticulture. The flat alluvial plain of the Valdinievole (Vale of Mists) is reminiscent of Holland; every inch of free space is used for growing asparagus, carnations, gladioli, lilies and chrysanthemums and for mile after mile the SS435 road linking Lucca and Péscia is lined with nursery gardens. Anyone with an interest in gardening should visit one of the nurseries that sell direct to the public (*vendita direta*) to see what is in fashion among Italian gardeners. For a price, visitors can take home young cypress trees, box clipped into all imaginable shapes, beautiful terracotta urns and marble statues in more questionable taste.

In Péscia itself, the utilitarian hangar-like building at the entrance to the town is the site of Italy's largest flower market. Over 3 million cut flowers are auctioned and despatched daily, all before 8am. Péscia, a rather scruffy town, has few other attractions. San Francesco church contains scenes from the life of St Francis painted in 1235 by Bonaventura Berlinghieri, only seven years after the saint's death; the portrait of the saint is said to be an exact likeness.

Nearby Buggiano is an attractive village of stucco-fronted houses painted in pastel colours. At Ponte Buggianese, San Michele church contains the stark frescos of the modern Italian artist, Pietro Annigoni.

MONTECATINI TERME

MAP REF: 110 B5

Montecatini Terme is the most enjoyable of Tuscany's spa towns because of its extensive public gardens and the palatial grandeur of its *belle epoque* bathhouses.

Most of the nine major thermal establishments are located within the Parco delle Terme, a large and immaculately maintained park of shaded avenues, green lawns and fountains. The Stabilimento Tettuccio, built under the patronage of the Grand Dukes of Tuscany at the beginning of this century, is the most splendid; visitors can sip the spa's warm saline liver-restoring waters in its elegant café. The marbled interior, with its pools and fountains, was designed by Ugo Giovanozzi in the 1920s and is embellished with *art nouveau* tiles and paintings of aristocratic water nymphs by Galileo Chini. Other nearby buildings include the neo-baroque Leopoldina pavilion, the neo-Palladian Regina arcade and the Torreta, with its pseudo-medieval tower and *loggia*, the venue for afternoon concerts.

From the lower town visitors can take the funicular railway (from Viale A Diaz) or drive to Montecatini Alto. This ancient upper town, surrounded by olive groves, offers fine views over the Valdinievole. The traffic-free main square is ringed by a circuit of antique shops and restful pavement restaurants. The effects of a good meal can be walked off by climbing to the *rocca* and exploring the narrow stone-paved alleys.

Nearby Serravalle, as its name suggests (literally 'Shut the Valley'), has two fortresses commanding the Montecatini to Pistóia road, the old (11th century) and new (14th century). To the south, at Monsummano Terme, the Grotta Giusti cave was discovered in 1849 and the green lakes in its depths are fed by hot springs. These, too, are used for thermal treatment; white-robed patients come to breathe the vapours that wreathe eerily around the cave's stalagmites and stalactites.

The Stabilimento Tettuccio spa in Montecatini Terme

TAKING THE WATERS

Montecatini Terme is the most splendid of Tuscany's several spa towns. Along with Bagni di Lucca, Chianciano Terme, Bagno Vignoni and Satúrnia, Montecatini throngs with visitors during the main season, which lasts from April to September. A typical cure lasts for a week and often twice as long; the benefit of taking the waters is cumulative and it takes time for the body to be flushed clean of impurities. The waters are drunk to relieve liver complaints and urinary, digestive and gynaecological disorders. Bathing and hydro-massage are prescribed for rheumatism and mud packs for skin conditions – everything from simple ageing to allergies, acne and dermatitis. Breathing the sulphur laden fumes from naturally hot thermal springs is also said to relieve respiratory problems.

It is easy to be cynical about the real medical value of such apparently simple cures for such complex and chronic conditions. The Italians, though, are firm believers, as are the many German, Austrian, Belgian, French and Dutch visitors who flock to these spas. The British are conspicuously absent from this Euro-*mélange*. This is curious when you consider that Britain once had its own thriving spas – at Bath, Buxton, Cheltenham, Brighton, Leamington and Tunbridge Wells. British gamblers and con men, bride hunters, young aristocrats fleeing disgrace and debt as well as poets and literati once filled Europe's spa towns, as Thackeray recounts in *Vanity Fair* and Trollope in *The Way We Live Now*. Bagni di Lucca used to be enlivened by the antics of the British, who organised boating parties along the River Lima and, when the river dried up in summer, horse races on which large sums of money were staked.

Today's spa towns are far more sedate, and if the British have gone it is perhaps more to do with the fact that spa treatment is not available on the National Health, whereas it is in less sceptical European countries, including Italy itself; otherwise the British would no doubt also be queuing for a form of treatment that involves no pain and encourages self-indulgence.

After all, as water-cure specialists continually stress, taking the waters is only a part of the cure; equally important is total relaxation. When visitors check into a spa hotel, uniformed porters immediately seize their bags; guests are pampered from the moment of arrival and encouraged to do nothing more stressful than take a stroll or snooze in the sun. Even the strain of deciding what to eat is removed; the dining rooms of most spa hotels serve a fixed, no-choice menu of 'healthy' food in minute portions accompanied by more of the obligatory water – to the benefit of local cafés where visitors sit sipping forbidden coffee and eating calorie-laden pastries.

The splendid architecture of Montecatini Terme, its marble palaces, its splashing fountains, its grand cafés with their tea-time concerts and well-tended lawns, are all designed to be easy on the senses and induce a feeling of well-being.

In such a beguiling atmosphere, romance thrives, and therein lies another part of the appeal. Chianciano Terme is an unofficial matchmaking agency for affluent widows and widowers of all European nations. Friendships are made and blossom rapidly among couples rejuvenated by the water cure. Not for nothing does the town have numerous luxury shops selling rings, jewellery, furs and expensive clothes, everything for the newly engaged couple determined to make the most of their remaining years. That is why Tuscany's spa towns are such serious business; without them the regional economy, along with hundreds of hoteliers and shopkeepers, would be considerably poorer than they are.

There are some fine buildings in Montecatini Terme

•PISA•

Like the Pyramids and the Taj Mahal, the Leaning Tower of Pisa is one of a handful of sights that enjoy worldwide renown. Consequently Pisa attracts a phenomenal number of tourists and the Campo dei Miracoli, the green lawn from which the Leaning Tower protrudes, can feel like the most crowded place on the globe at the height of summer. Jealous detractors from rival cities even claim that the Pisans deliberately built the tower to lean so as to attract tourist revenue!

The more conventional account of the tower's history says that subsidence caused it to slip sideways during construction, when it was still only 10.5m tall. Although begun in 1173, the Tower was not completed until 1350 and it has continued to move inexorably sideways ever since. Experts recently predicted that the tower would collapse within 200 years if corrective steps were not taken. As a consequence, it will be closed for an uncertain number of years while the Italian authorities spend 300 billion lire curbing the tilt once and for all. At 54.5m high, the tower leans 4.5m from the perpendicular, thus enabling Galileo to perform a famous experiment; dropping stones from the top, he proved that the velocity of falling bodies is the same, regardless of their weight. Even disregarding the tilt, the Leaning Tower is an enthralling building and it is partnered by three other buildings of great interest: the cathedral, begun in 1063, the baptistry of 1152 and the Camposanto (cemetery) of 1278.

The Leaning Tower of Pisa

The façade of the cathedral is, like the tower, covered in a rising series of delicate colonnades, the characteristic feature of Pisan Romanesque style. The biblical scenes on the bronze doors date from 1602 and were designed by Giovanni di Bologna. Today the main entrance is through the south transept, which also has fine bronze doors illustrating the Life of Christ, designed by Bonnano da Pisa in 1180.

The interior was devastated by fire in 1595 and most of the undistinguished frescos date from the 17th century. Pride of place is given to Giovanni Pisano's outstanding pulpit carved with New Testament scenes in a style that anticipates the best Renaissance sculpture. The mosaic in the vault, of Christ in Majesty, was completed by Cimabue in 1302 and the bronze lamp hanging from the nave was not the one that inspired Galileo's discovery of pendulum motion, despite what local guides say; the lamp was cast in 1587, six years after Galileo's discovery.

The baptistry, resembling a papal crown, is a monumental building whose dome was one of the largest in Christendom when it was completed by Nicola and Giovanni Pisano in 1284. The dome shelters a graceful baptismal font of inlaid marble dating from 1246. The pulpit, with its animated scenes from the Life of Christ, was an early work of Nicola Pisano and it set the style for similar pulpits found all over Tuscany.

Pisa's medieval cemetery, the Camposanto (Holy Field), lies to the north of the cathedral, enclosed by marble walls. According to Pisan legend, shiploads of earth were brought back from the Holy Land by 13th-century crusader ships to add extra sanctity to the burial ground, but this did not prevent many frescos being destroyed by an Allied bomb in 1944. Among the surviving frescos is a gruesomely realistic *Last Judgement* by an unknown 14th-century artist, and the cloister contains many fine examples of funerary sculpture, including reused Roman sarcophagi.

TOWN WALK

Away from the Leaning Tower and the crowds, Pisa (map ref: 110 B4) is a bustling and characterful city with numerous sights of interest on both banks of the River Arno.

From the cathedral, walk up Piazza del Duomo to the Piazza Manin city gate, then turn back for one of the best views of the whole Campo dei Miracoli ensemble. Return up the right-hand side of Piazza del Duomo and enter the Museo delle Sinopie.

1 This museum contains the remains of frescos removed from the Camposanto cemetery. The exhibits consist largely of *sinopie*, preliminary drawings scratched into the surface of the plaster undercoat. In true fresco, the artists painted on to wet plaster so that the pigment was absorbed into the surface; the artists had to work fast, hence these sketches were made to map out the main

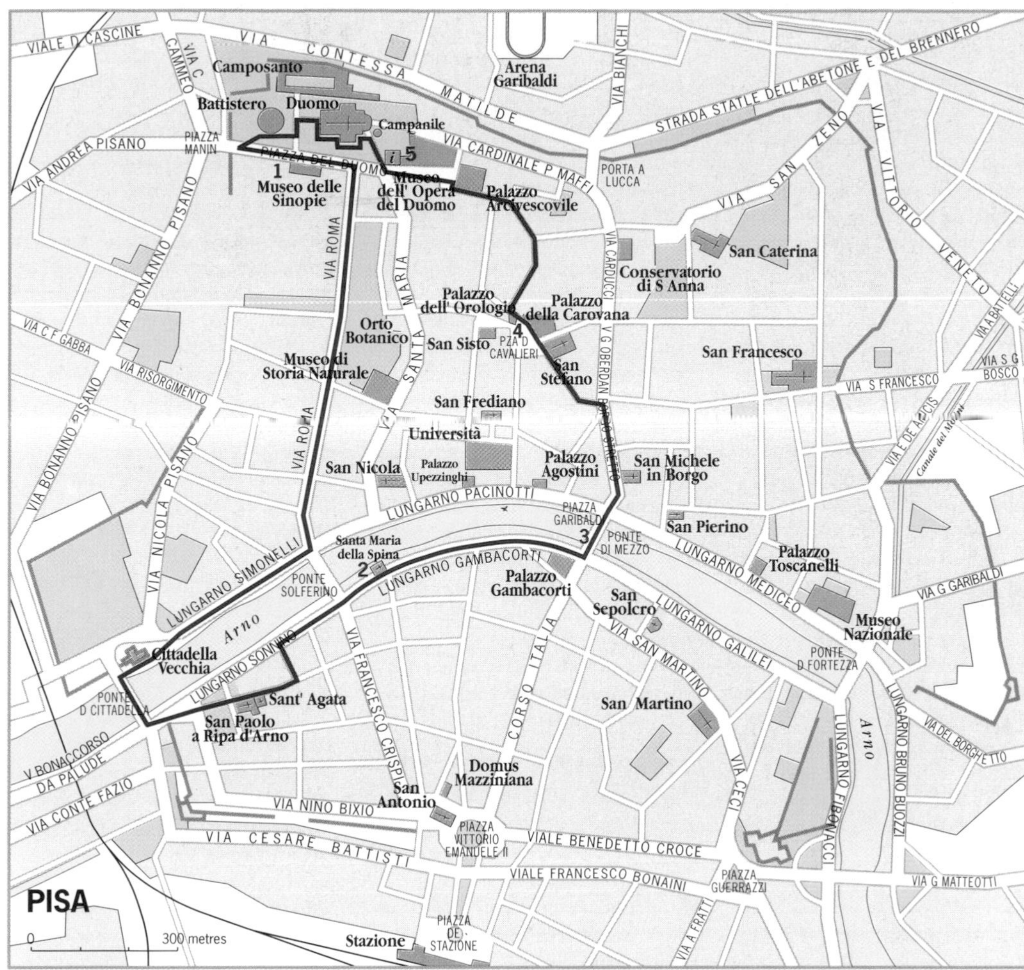

components of the composition before the final plaster coat was laid.

Turn right out of the museum and first right down Via Roma, past the entrance to the somewhat neglected Botanical Gardens, the Orto Botanico, and down to the Arno embankment. Turn right along the Lungarno Simonelli, past the Cittadella Vecchia, the medieval fortress and shipyard. Cross the Arno at the next bridge and turn left to reach San Paolo a Ripa d'Arno, a 12th-century church with a splendid façade. Walk to the left of the church, down Via San Paolo, to see the Romanesque chapel of Sant'Agata, built in brick with a prismatic roof. Take the first left to return to the Arno and turn right to reach Santa Maria della Spina.

2 This pretty Gothic church, sadly isolated in a dull and traffic-torn part of Pisa, is as prickly as its name suggests. The church was built to house a thorn from Christ's crown and the 14th-century builders used the thorn theme to great architectural effect; the roofline bristles with pinnacles and miniature spires, while the south façade is covered in gabled niches sheltering statues of Christ and the Apostles.

Continue along the embankment to the next bridge, the Ponte di Mezzo.

3 This is a good spot to watch the sun go down behind the palace-lined embankments of the Arno. It is also the venue for the Gioco del Ponte, a ritual battle held on the last Sunday in June, when rival teams from the north and south sides of the river fight to push a cart across the bridge into the other's territory.

Cross the bridge to Piazza Garibaldi and walk up the arcaded Borgo Stretto, Pisa's main shopping street. Take the first left, Via Dini, to reach the Piazza dei Cavalieri.

4 This square is dominated by Vasari's Palazzo della Carovana (1562), covered in black and white *sgraffito* decoration. An imposing statue of Duke Cosimo I stands in front of the palace as if to emphasise the humiliation of Pisa, which fell under Florentine domination in 1509.

The town hall of the once independent city was demolished to make way for this new palace, which served as the headquarters of the Cavalieri di Santo Stefano, the Knights of St Stephen, who launched several piratical attacks against the Turks. Spoils from their campaigns are displayed in the Church of San Stefano to the right of the palace. To the left is the Palazzo dell'Orologio incorporating the Torre Gualandi; in 1208 Count Ugolino, with his two sons and grandsons, was walled up in the tower and starved to death, accused by political rivals of betraying Pisa to the Genoese. The grim story is told in Dante's *Inferno* (Canto XXXIII) and Shelley's poem, *The Tower of Famine*.

Pass under the arch beneath the clocktower of the Palazzo dell'Orologio and take the right-hand street, Via Martiri, which bends left to join Via San Giuseppe. On the right, just before you emerge back in the Campo dei Miracoli, is the Museo dell'Opera del Duomo.

5 This museum contains numerous works of art taken from the cathedral and Baptistry, including Giovanni Pisano's exquisite *Virgin and Child* carved in ivory. There is an unusual view of the Leaning Tower from the courtyard.

PISTÓIA

MAP REF: 110 B5

Pistóia was once a byword for viciousness and intrigue. The pistol, invented in the 16th century, was named after the town because it was as inconspicuous and deadly as the little daggers used by the Pistóiese to murder their enemies in the city's dark alleys. Dante had no good word to say for the citizens, indeed, he had cause to hate them, as the long-running feud between the Bianchi and the Neri, the Blacks and Whites, began in Pistóia. What started as a family quarrel grew into a political conflict that enmeshed all of Italy, and resulted in Dante's exile from Florence. Despite this dark reputation, Pistóia has one of the most characterful main squares in the region, and it is worth negotiating the traffic-torn suburbs to explore the historic centre.

The buildings of the Piazza del Duomo are so different in style that they ought not to harmonise; yet they do, forming an ensemble that delights the eye by their sheer variety. The looming watchtower was heightened in the 14th century by three upper storeys of green and white marble that match the arcaded façade of the cathedral alongside. Inside the cathderal is the tomb of Dante's friend and fellow poet, Cino di Pistoia (died 1337) who is depicted in relief lecturing to a class of young boys, one of whom allegedly represents Boccaccio.

The chapel of St James contains an extraordinary silver altar begun in 1287; scores of silversmiths laboured for 200 years to make the 628 figures of saints. Behind the cathedral, the Gothic Palazzo del Comune, completed in 1355, bears the Medici crest, a reminder that Pistóia finally surrendered to Florence in 1329. The courtyard and ground floor rooms are used to display rugged bronze sculptures by the Pistóia-born abstract artist, Marino Marini (1901–80). The Museo Civico above contains a good range of works spanning the 12th to 19th centuries.

Pistóia's busy vegetable market containing the old well

TOWN WALK

This walk takes in the network of narrow medieval alleys surrounding the Piazza del Duomo and three outstanding church pulpits that illustrate the rebirth of Tuscan figure-carving in the 13th century.

Start from the graceful baptistry opposite the cathedral, designed by Andrea Pisano and completed in 1359. Walk down Via Roma and turn right in Via Cavour to reach the striped church of San Giovanni Fuorcivitas on the left.

1 Fuorcivitas – from *fuori città*, outside the city – refers to the fact that the original 8th-century building stood beyond the city walls. It was rebuilt in the 12th century in Pisan Romanesque style. The dark interior contains Luca della Robbia's glazed terracotta *Visitation* and a masterful pulpit carved with New Testament scenes by Gugliemo da Pisa in 1270.

Opposite the church the Vicola del Cacio leads into Piazza della Sala where you can browse among the fish, meat, vegetable and herb stalls of the town's market. Leave the square by the upper right-hand corner, the Via del Lastrone, a typically narrow Pistóian alley where it is easy to imagine conspirational figures lurking in dark doorways. Turn right in Via D. Orafi, the main shopping street, and immediately left in Via del Duca. Continue on through Piazza del Spirito Santo and Via Rossi to the Church of Sant'Andrea.

2 Sant'Andrea, partnered by an ancient Cedar of Lebanon, has a good Romanesque relief above the portal illustrating the Journey of the Magi and dated 1166. Inside is the best of the city's three pulpits, completed in 1301 by Giovanni Pisano and hailed as his masterpiece, surpassing even the pulpit he made for Pisa's cathedral the following year. The scenes in relief illustrate the Nativity, the Massacre of the Innocents, the Adoration of the Magi, the Crucifixion and the Last Judgement.

Backtrack down Via Sant'Andrea and take the first left, Via delle Belle, down to the tree-filled square fronting the baroque church of San Carmine. Turn right, cross Via del Carmine and follow Via delle Pappe to the Ospedale del Ceppo on the left.

3 *Ceppo* refers to the hollowed-out tree used to collect charitable donations to fund the work of this hospital cum orphanage. The façade features garishly coloured 16th-century terracottas depicting the Seven Works of Corporeal Mercy, from the workshops of Giovanni della Robbia.

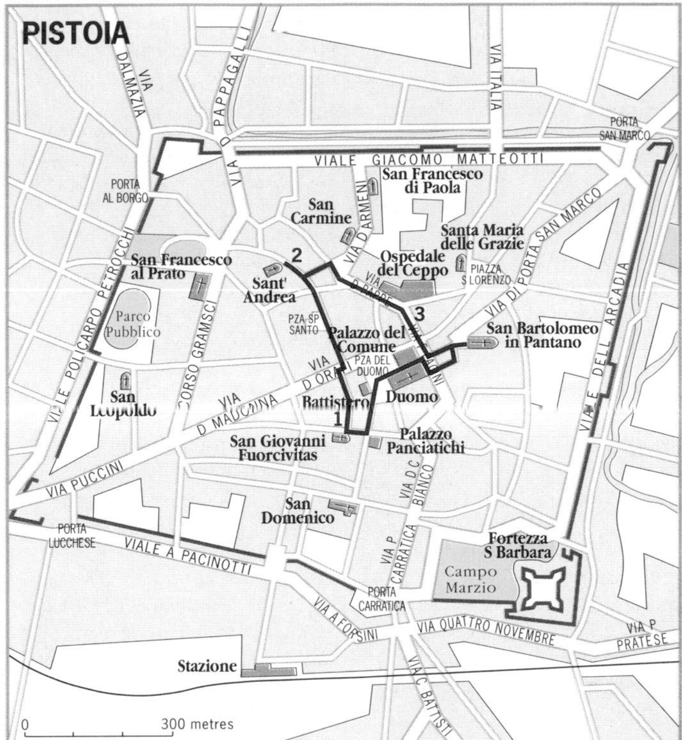

Continue down Via F Pacini and take the fifth turning on the left for San Bartolomeo, which houses a damaged pulpit carved by Guido da Como in 1250. Return to Via F Pacini and take the alley opposite to climb back to the Piazza del Duomo.

PRATO

MAP REF: 110 C5

Prato, meaning meadow, is now surrounded by miles of depressing industrial hinterland; it is one of the few cities in Tuscany that still makes its living from the textile trade, just as it did in the Middle Ages. In the 19th century Prato was proud to be called the Manchester of Tuscany and today three out of every four woollen garments exported from Italy are made here.

The city's most famous citizen, Francesco di Marco Datini (1330-1410) was the subject of Iris Origo's fascinating biography, *The Merchant of Prato*. Datini, whose motto was 'For God and Profit', virtually invented the science of accountancy. Though he spent most of his life in Florence, he endeared himself to his fellow citizens by leaving his very considerable wealth to local charities.

At the heart of Prato is the spacious Piazza del Duomo where the faithful gather five times a year (Easter Sunday, May 1, August 15, September 8 and Christmas Day) to pay reverence to the Virgin's Holy Girdle. According to legend the girdle was given to Thomas, the doubting apostle, by the Virgin Mary just before her assumption into heaven. When another merchant of Prato, Michele Dagomari, married a Palestinian woman descended from Thomas, the girdle formed part of her dowry and Dagomari brought it to Prato in 1141. The girdle is shown from the delicate external pulpit on the right-hand side of the cathedral façade. Modern casts have replaced Donatello's dancing cherubs from the pulpit base; the originals (1438) are now in the Museo dell'Opera del Duomo, to the left of the cathedral.

Agnolo Gaddi's frescos (1392–95) inside the cathedral depict the Legend of the Girdle but they are hidden behind the huge reliquary in which the girdle is locked for most of the year.

Pistóia's Palazzo Communale: Medici crest

Easier to enjoy are Filippo Lippi's scenes from the Martyrdom of John the Baptist (1452–66) behind the high altar. These lyrical frescos convey none of the gruesome horror of the Baptist's story; Salome, a portrait of Lippi's mistress, Lucrezia Buti, dances demurely at the banquet of Herod and the head of St John is presented as if it were a delicacy at a Tuscan dinner party.

The narrow streets north of the square lead to the Piazza Comune with its 19th-century statue of the Merchant of Prato and a pretty fountain known as *Il Bacchino*, the little Bacchus. The original fountain, of which this is a copy, is one of the exhibits in the excellent Galleria Comunale, housed in the Palazzo Pretorio alongside, a 14th-century building of skyscraper proportions. Other works in the collection include Bernardo Daddi's *Story of the Holy Girdle* and Filippo Lippi's *Madonna del Ceppo*, which includes another portrait of the celebrated merchant.

Green and white stripes and rich sculpture in Prato Cathedral

Northwest of Empoli, the town of Vinci lies among olive hills

SAN MINIATO

MAP REF: 110 B4

San Miniato is an airy town of sweeping views and open green spaces. It stands only 140m above sea level and yet visitors can feel on top of the world by climbing to the *rocca* that commands the highest point in the town; the views stretch down the Arno Valley all the way to the sea. The *rocca*, destroyed in World War II but faithfully reconstructed, was built by Frederick II around 1240.

The town's old name, San Miniato dei Tedesco – of the German – indicates that this was an important stronghold first of the Lombards and then of the Hohenstaufen Holy Roman Emperors. The Countess Matilda, who ruled the region as the last of the Lombardic imperial margraves, was born here in 1046; the town's other defensive tower, now the cathedral campanile, is called the Torre di Matilda in her honour. Frederick II, like his grandfather, Frederick Barbarossa, used San Miniato as a base for his ultimately fruitless attempts to reassert his territorial claims to Italy. San Miniato remained an enclave of unwavering support for the emperor's cause during the conflicts of the 12th and 13th centuries, and was the seat of the Imperial Vicarate in Tuscany.

One of Frederick II's chief counsellors, Pietro della Vigna, leapt to his death from the tower of the *rocca*, falsely accused of plotting against his master, as Dante records (*Inferno*, Canto XIII). The 12th-century Palazzo dei Vicare dell'Imperatore still survives from this era in the tree-shaded Prato al Duomo, alongside the much restored cathedral. The cathedral's Romanesque brick façade is unusually decorated with 13th-century majolica roundels. The Museo Diocesano in the cathedral sanctuary contains good paintings and carvings gathered from churches in the vicinity. Further down the hill is the characterful Piazza della Repubblica where the long façade of the Seminario is decorated with incised (*sgraffito*) figures of saints, dating from the 17th century, and shelters some well-restored 14th-century shopfronts.

The Museo Vinciano is packed with models of the great man's inventions

This model of Leonardo's famous tank is based, like the others in the Museo Vinciano, on the sketches in his *Codex Atlanticus*

VIAREGGIO

MAP REF: 110 A5

Viareggio is the largest resort on the Versilia, Tuscany's Riviera, which stretches northwards to the port of Massa. A visit to any of the beaches here involves an encounter with Italy's regimented beach culture. Much of the wide sandy strip is divided into privately owned bathing establishments where visitors pay a high price for access and use of the tightly packed sun-loungers; at least the sexes are no longer segregated as they once were. Wilder undeveloped beaches, shaded by groves of parasol pine, can be found further south towards Torre del Lago.

Viareggio itself has a strict grid of streets running at right angles to the seafront promenade. This was laid out in the 1860s with a boardwalk, but the original timber buildings were destroyed when the town went up in flames in 1917. The new buildings that rose from the ashes in the 1920s reflect the popular Liberty style of the time, Italy's version of *art nouveau*. The seafront boulevard is lined with stately hotel buildings and fish restaurants in this 1920s style, notably the magnificent Gran Caffé Margherita, designed by Galileo Chini and Alfredo Belluomini.

Nearby Giacomo Puccini (1858–1924), born in Lucca, wrote all of his stirringly dramatic operas (with the exception of *Turandot*) in his villa at Torre del Lago, south of Viareggio. The approach to Puccini's home passes through extensive pine forests and the villa itself stands on the western shore of the Lago di Massaciúccoli, a shallow lake where the gun-mad Puccini would take pot shots at passing wildfowl.

The villa is preserved as a shrine to the composer, every piece of furniture exactly as it was when he died. Puccini and his wife are buried in a mausoleum appropriately located between the piano room, where he composed his work, and the gun room where his rifle ('my second favourite instrument') is displayed.

A popular festival featuring Puccini's operas is held every August in the outdoor theatre in Torre del Lago. Visitors can also hire boats in the village to explore the lake and its many marshy inlets.

THE DEATH OF SHELLEY

Viareggio's Piazza Shelley, with its bust carved by Urbano Lucchese (1894) commemorates the tragic end of the poet's short and tempestuous life. Shelley became a permanent exile in 1818, at the age of 26, exchanging debts and harassment in England for the freedom of Tuscany. He and his second wife Mary (author of *Frankenstein* and daughter of the feminist Mary Wollstonecraft) befriended Byron and became the stars at the centre of an artistic circle whose number included Edward Trelawney and Leigh Hunt.

In 1822 dark premonitions cast a shadow over their freedom, when Mary suffered a near-fatal miscarriage and Shelley saw the ghost of a dead child beckoning from the sea. In August that year he sailed to Livorno to visit Byron, who was living in Montenero, south of the port. On the return journey his schooner, *Ariel*, was hit by a sudden and violent squall. Shelley was drowned, as was his friend, Edward Williams, and the boat boy. The poet's body was found two weeks later, washed up on the shore at Gombo, just north of the Arno estuary. Trelawney, Byron and Leigh Hunt cremated the body on the spot where it was found, pouring libations of wine, salt and frankincense on to the red-hot ashes. Even then the bizarre business took a romantic turn; Shelley's body was consumed but his heart remained entire, as if unwilling to remain on a foreign shore – it was returned to England and finally laid to rest in Bournemouth.

VINCI

MAP REF: 110 B4

Leonardo da Vinci's birthplace lies to the north of Empoli in the foothills of Monte Albano. The 13th-century *rocca* in Vinci has been well restored to create the Museo Vinciano, a highly enjoyable museum that displays over 100 machines invented by Leonardo; the models, based on his notebook sketches, include a bicycle, prototype helicopter (and parachute), submarine, tank and machine gun. The models are beautifully made and leave the visitor in awe at the extraordinary fertility of Leonardo's imagination. This is also one of the very few museums in Tuscany and Umbria that children will be reluctant to leave.

The actual house in which Leonardo was born is not in Vinci itself but in the village of Anchiano, 3km further up into the Monte Albano foothills along the delightfully scenic road to Pistóia. The birthplace, a simple [illegible] groves, contains another museum dedicated to the Renaissance genius.

***Art nouveau* in the town of Viareggio**

FLORENCE AND THE UPPER ARNO

Speeding between Florence and Arezzo on the A1 *autostrada*, most travellers are unaware of the unique landscape that lies between the two cities. The A1 follows the Arno upstream to Arezzo, but here motorway and river part company. The Arno turns north and from here up to its source, 56km away on the slopes of Monte Falterona, the countryside becomes more and more wild, the woodland more dense, the roads narrower and more tortuously winding and the villages smaller and fewer. This is the Casentino, the remote upper valley of the Arno, a land of ancient hermitages and monasteries – La Verna, where St Francis received the stigmata, Vallombrosa, founded by the Florentine San Giovanni Gualberto in protest against church corruption, and Camáldoli, founded by San Romauldo as a place of solitary meditation.

Time has literally stood still here, for the monks of Camáldoli have been tending the 1,200 hectares of beech, chestnut and pine forest since it was presented to them in the 11th century, planting 5,000 new trees a year and creating, in the process, a rich ecological enclave. The monks of Vallombrosa have followed a similar regime to create their own glorious woodland, celebrated by Milton as the 'Etrurian shades'.

Those in the know come to this area to feast on wild strawberries, gather wild mushrooms and picnic in the cool shade beside the numerous waterfalls and rushing mountain streams. Nature seems at its most benign here. The meadows around Stia are grazed by white cattle with faces more like deer than cows and an ancient pedigree; their ancestors were revered by the ancient Etruscans and Romans and offered in sacrifice to their gods. In spring these meadows are carpeted with the same dancing wildflowers that Flora scatters in Botticelli's *Primavera*. Yet every so often here in the Casentino nature gathers its forces to wreak havoc downriver upon the urbane Florentines. Once in every century or so the Arno, swelled by torrential autumn rains and the combined waters of its numerous tributaries, has become a raging torrent, crashing down from the Casentino, bursting its banks and sweeping through the streets of Florence.

One building in Florence, standing on the corner of Via dei Mosca and Via dei Neri, displays two plaques on its wall, so high up that they are rarely noticed by passers-by. They record the high water mark of the two most devastating floods: one occurred in 1333, the other more recently, on 4 November 1966. On that last occasion the flood waters rose to 6m above street level. Thirty five people died, hundreds were rendered homeless and thousands of paintings, statues, frescos and precious books were damaged. More than 20 years later the city still bears the scars in buildings that have yet to be restored and frescos, such as Uccello's *Universal Deluge* in the Santa Maria Novella cloisters, that were damaged beyond repair.

Much, though, was saved and the positive result (apart from flood protection measures designed to prevent a similar disaster from ever happening again) is that many of the city's greatest works of art were subsequently restored. Florence has become an international centre for art restoration, pioneering new techniques for cleaning works of art, removing layers of paint clumsily added by 19th-century restorers and consolidating frescos to prevent further ageing and deterioration. Frescos and paintings once obscure and grimy have been returned to their original incandescent colour, startlingly vivid blues and greens, scarlet, gold and apricot, proving what an extraordinary range of pigments Renaissance artists had at their disposal. Today's visitors can see details that the 19th-century critic John Ruskin, whose *Mornings in Florence* opened the eyes of the world to the city's neglected medieval and Renaissance treasures, could not have seen. Indeed, some of the art which Ruskin praised so highly in Santa Croce church as 'the essential Giotto' has proved instead to be the work of the 19th-century restorer, Bianchi.

The same scientific advances have allowed Piero della Francesca's noble frescos in Arezzo to be restored for the 500th anniversary of the artist's death, celebrated in 1992. *The Legend of the True Cross* in the Church of San Francesco is one of the artistic highlights of a visit to Tuscany, and Arezzo itself is a city of compelling individuality. It was the birthplace of several great cultural figures: Maecenas, the 1st-century BC patron of Virgil and Horace, Guido d'Arezzo, the 11th-century inventor of musical notation, Petrarch, the great 14th-century poet, and Giorgio Vasari (1512–74), whose home in Via Venti Settembre, decorated with fresco portraits of friends and mentors, can be visited.

Vasari is more often than not derided these days, out of fashion with art historians who, despite owing an enormous debt to his *Lives of the Artists*, feel compelled to quarrel with his opinions and accuse him of bias in favour of

UPPER ARNO

Calenzano
Sesto Fiorentino
Fiésole
FIRENZE
Scandicci
Bagno a Rípoli
Dicomano
Sieve
Rúfina
Pontassieve
Consuma
1654 M.Falterno
Stia
Arno
Pratovécchio
Eremo di Camáldoli
Camáldoli
San Piero in Bagno
Bagno di Romagna
Sávio
Vallombrosa
Pratomagno
Poppi
Bibbiena
La Verna
Chiusi della Verna
Pieve Santo Stefano
Impruneta
Incisa in Val d'Arno
Regello
1591
Castel Focognano
Caprese Michelangelo
San Casciano in Val di Pesa
Castelfranco
Loro Ciuffena
Figline Valdarno
Greve in Chianti
Sansepolcro
Subbiano
Tavarnelle Val di Pesa
San Giovanni Valdarno
Terranuova Bracciolini
Anghiari
Monti del Chianti
Montevarchi
Radda in Chianti
Monterchi
Poggibonsi
Castellina in Chianti
Búcine
Arezzo
Sovara
1080
Monteriggioni
Canale Maestro della Chiana
Castelnuovo Berardenga
Castiglion Fiorentino
Monte San Savino
Siena
Cortona
Rapolano Terme
Sovicille
Lucignano
Foiano della Chiana
Asciano
Poggio Pinci
Sinalunga
Tuoro sul Trasimeno
0 10 20 km
0 10 miles

Florentine artists. Vasari is also accused of sycophancy for his series of frescos in the Palazzo Vecchio in Florence. These present Cosimo I as the god-like saviour of Tuscany and gloss over his ruthless brutality in suppressing all opposition to his rule.

After the accession of Cosimo I there was, in the words of American born novelist and critic Mary McCarthy, a 'great diaspora of Florentine artists'. Vasari was one of the few artists who stayed on in the city, working as the Duke's court painter and architect. Harsh judgements about his exercises in grand ducal propaganda should, however, be tempered with due appreciation for his versatility and many achievements.

Vasari designed the Uffizi Gallery in Florence for the Medici art collection. This is uniquely lit by an almost continuous glass wall, thanks to his pioneering use of iron reinforcement. He designed the tomb of his friend, Michelangelo, in Santa Croce church and painted some excellent frescos, including those that decorate the *cortile*, or courtyard, on the ground floor of the Palazzo Vecchio. Though gossip-ridden and opinionated, the *Lives* is a lucid, humorous and illuminating book. Vasari coined the term 'renaissance' or rebirth to describe the extraordinary outpouring of art that occurred in Florence in the 15th century, defined its characteristics and gave us candid insights into the personalities and intentions of the principal artists. All accounts of the city's art ultimately lead back to him and thus, in a very real sense, Florence is Vasari's city; we see it through his eyes.

The friendly centre of Bibbiena, the Casentino's chief town. Although besieged by sprawling modern suburbs, the town's heart retains its old Tuscan identity

AREZZO

MAP REF: 111 D4

Etruscan Arezzo was one of the most important members of the ancient 12-city confederation, the Dodecapolis. *The Wounded Chimera*, an Etruscan bronze of great accomplishment (now in the Archaeological Museum in Florence) was made by local craftsmen in the 5th century BC. The Roman *Arretium* continued the craft tradition, producing highly prized red-glazed Arretine ware. Today the city has a thriving jewellery industry, producing chains, bracelets and rings. A huge antiques fair fills the streets on the first Sunday of every month, and the alleys around the Piazza Grande are full of dark workshops smelling of wood and varnish where aproned artisans restore antique furniture.

The Piazza Grande is also the venue for one of Tuscany's most colourful spectacles, the Giostra del Saracino, the Joust of the Saracen, held on the first Sunday in September. Horsemen from the four quarters of the city ride at full tilt and lunge with their lances at the Saracen's shield, aiming to hit the target in the centre. The spectacle is enlivened by a parade of beautifully costumed knights and ladies, standard-bearers, drummers and trumpeters.

Nearby The church of Santa Maria delle Grazie, located in the city's southern suburbs near the station, is a Renaissance jewel, completed in 1444 and given a pretty *loggia* by Benedetto da Maiano in 1482.

The flower market in Arezzo, one of many in this bustling city

TOWN WALK

Starting from Piazza della Repubblica, walk up the main street, Via Guido Monaco, and turn right at the top for San Francesco Church.

1 Piero della Francesca's frescos round the high altar, recently restored for the 500th anniversary of the artist's death, are the greatest work of an artist who was obsessed with artificial perspective and who wrote a highly influential treatise on the subject. Painted between 1454 and 1466, the frescos depict *The Legend of the True Cross*, a story of fascinating complexity painted in an almost dream-like style that was unique to della Francesca.

The scenes begin on the right with the death of Adam and trace a sequence of events whereby the tree from which Adam and Eve ate the forbidden fruit becomes the Cross on which Christ was crucified, forging a link between original sin and redemption.

Turn right out of the church into Via Cavour, then left into Corso Italia, Arezzo's main shopping street. The church of Pieve di Santa Maria is on the right.

2 The soaring campanile of Santa Maria, built in 1330, is pierced with numerous arches, earning it the name 'the Tower of 100 Holes'. The façade is covered in delicate arcading, though the soft stone has weathered. There are two excellent Romanesque reliefs at the rear of the church and a series of boldly carved capitals in the crypt. On Sunday, the organ recitals given here are well worth attending.

Turn right alongside the towering campanile and walk up Via di Seteria, lined with numerous antique shops, into the Piazza Grande.

3 Vasari's *loggia* (1573) fills the north side of this sloping and irregularly shaped square. To the left is the ornate apse of Pieve di Santa Maria and next door the Gothic-style Palazetto della Fraternità dei Laici, with 15th-century sculptures and a striking Renaissance balcony.

Leave the square by the top left-hand corner, with the Palazetto on the left, and take the first right. The Palazzo Pretorio on the left is covered with stemmi, *the coats of arms of local citizens. Crossing the triangular piazza that leads up to the cathedral, Petrarch's birthplace is on the left, and the extensive public gardens surrounding the Fortezza Medicea are on the right.*

4 Arezzo's vast Gothic cathedral is lit by good 16th-century stained glass. High up on the left of the nave is the tomb of Guido Tarlati, the battling bishop who ruled Arezzo from 1312 to 1327. Bas reliefs on the tomb depict the major events in his life.

From the cathedral steps, bear left down Via Ricasoli, heading for the statue of Ferdinand II of Austria. Turn right in Via del Sasso Verde to reach San Domenico.

5 San Domenico's walls are covered in intriguing fresco fragments; the best works are Cimabue's *Crucifixion* (1260) behind the high altar and an *Annunciation* by the local artist, Spinello Aretino, in the chapel on the right.

From the church exit, walk up the red-paved square and turn right into Via San Domenico. Take the second left, Via Venti Settembre, and Vasari's house, the Museo Vasariano, is a short way down on the right.

6 Vasari was born in Arezzo in 1512 and built this house for himself in 1540. The rooms are decorated with his own frescos, which some visitors find charming, others lifeless.

Continue down the street and turn right at the bottom for Museo Statale d'Arte Medieovale e Moderna.

7 This gallery, housed in a graceful 15th-century *palazzo*, has a worthwhile collection, organised chronologically and ranging from 10th-century sculpture to Renaissance bronzes and ceramics.

From the museum, turn left then first right in Via Cavour, which bends to the left, past the Chiesa di Badia, and back to Piazza San Francesco. Turn right down Via Guido Monaco to return to the starting point. The walk can be extended by taking the third left off Via Guido Monaco, Via Garibaldi, which leads to Piazza Sant'Agostino, the venue for a lively market on Saturday mornings. Turn right in the piazza down Via Margheritone, cross Via Fra Crispi and look for a park entrance on the left.

8 The park contains the substantial remains of Arezzo's Roman amphitheatre, and the entrance to the Museo Archeologico. The museum contains good examples of the locally produced Arretine ware, along with moulds and die stamps. This delicate pottery, covered in red slip and decorated with erotic and mythological scenes, was highly prized by the Romans and was exported throughout the empire. The industry seems to have died around AD 40 when Samian ware from Gaul became fashionable.

BIBBIENA

MAP REF: 111 D4

Bibbiena is the main town of the remote and sparsely populated Casentino region. Though the town itself lacks charm, it is a good base for visiting La Verna; the scenic SS208 road climbs east from Bibbiena through woodlands of astonishing beauty to the Franciscan monastery perched high on a rocky outcrop with far-reaching views.

The summit of the rock, called La Penna, is said to have been torn by a violent tremor at the moment when Christ died on the Cross. The land was given to the Franciscans by Count Orlando in 1213 and in 1224 St Francis received the stigmata here; his hands and feet were painfully marked with the wounds of Christ for the rest of his life. The monastic complex, founded in 1433, has many della Robbia terracottas, but the main attraction is the calm and natural beauty of its setting.

Arezzo is an ancient city, one of the wealthiest in Tuscany

CAPRESE MICHELANGELO

MAP REF: 111 D4

By sheer chance this tiny mountain hamlet witnessed the birth of one of the world's greatest artists. Michelangelo's father was sent here from Florence to serve a short term as *podestà* (mayor) of Caprese and his wife gave birth to Michelangelo in the rustic Casa del Podestà on 6 March 1475. The house, surrounded by battlemented walls, is now a museum containing photographs and copies of his work; the grounds serve as an outdoor sculpture gallery dotted with modern bronzes. The surrounding landscape has an almost alpine beauty; Michelangelo attributed his creative genius to the purity of the mountain air he breathed as an infant.

MOTOR TOUR

The upper Arno Valley, known as the Casentino, is one of the most peaceful and unspoiled regions of Italy. This 50km tour passes through spectacular woodland with plenty of opportunites to stop for a walk or picnic. The tour begins at Poppi.

Poppi
Poppi's fortified Palazzo Pretorio, built in 1274, sits on a plateau high above the town and is visible for miles around. This was once the stronghold of the powerful Guidi family, which ruled much of the Casentino region until it fell under Florentine domination in 1440. The *palazzo* is approached along the attractively arcaded Via Cavour. In Piazza Amerighi, the little domed church of Madonna del Morbo was built in 1631 in thanksgiving for the town's deliverance from plague.

From Poppi follow the signs for Stia. After 1.6km bear left following signs for Florence. At this junction a tall column marks the site of the Battle of Campaldino (1289) in which Dante fought on the side of the Guelf (papal) forces inflicting a heavy defeat on the Ghibellines. After 6.5km, turn right for Pieve di Romena.

The landscape around Caprese Michelangelo, birthplace of a genius

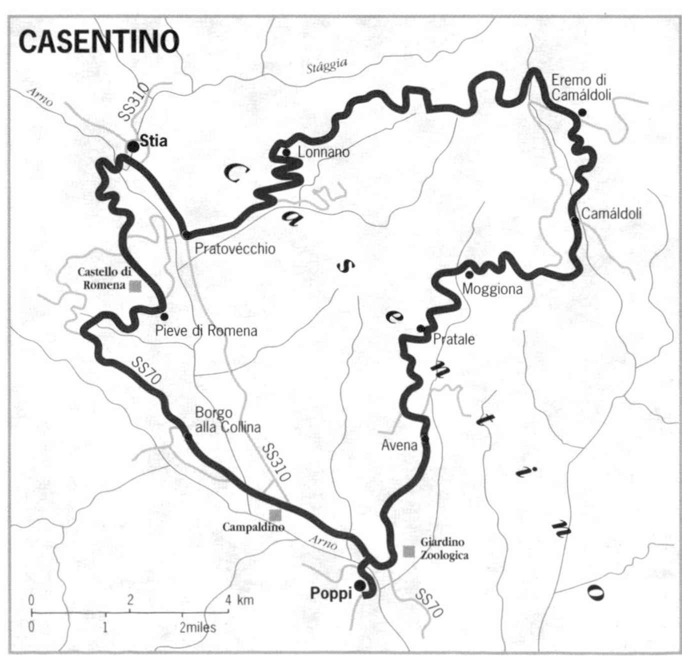

Pieve di Romena
The tiny Romanesque church on the road into Romena was built in 1152 and is the oldest church in the region. Just beyond the church a track to the left leads up to the 11th-century Castello di Romena. The exiled Dante stayed here as a guest of the Guidi family; Canto XXX of the *Inferno* tells the story of a former owner of the castle, the forger Adamo di Brescia, who was burned at the stake for producing counterfeit florins.

Follow the cypress-lined track downhill from the castle to the main road, then turn right for Stia, reached after 3km.

Stia
Stia is located at the confluence of the River Stággia and the Arno; here the Arno is a swift flowing infant, a clean rippling river, unlike its more polluted lower reaches. The source is some 20km away, due north on the slopes of Monte Fatterona. To one side of the arcaded main square is the church of Santa Maria; the off-putting baroque exterior hides one of the best Romanesque interiors in the region, its capitals carved with shepherds and mermaids, wolves and angels. There is a small agricultural museum in the nearby Castello di Porciano, another former Guidi stronghold.

From Stia follow the signs to Arezzo. After 1.5km, in Pratovécchio, turn left following the signs for San Eremo. After 1.5km bear left again. For the next 16km, the road has to be driven with care; there is a speed limit of 40kmh and in many places the road is scarcely wide enough for two cars to pass. The road winds up through glorious chestnut and beech woodland to the Eremo di Camáldoli.

Eremo di Camáldoli
This ancient hermitage is a place of religion and retreat, though there is a small café. Most of the monastic cells date from the 16th century although the hermitage was founded in 1012 when Count Maldolo (hence the name Camaldoli) gave this vast tract of ancient forest to St Romualdo (St Rumbold in English – patron saint of stammerers!). The monks of Camaldoli live as self-sufficient vegetarians and have managed the forest for the past 1,000 years – consequently it is one of the most

ancient and ecologically rich in Europe.

Take the right-hand road from the Eremo, signposted Camáldoli and Bibbiena, to descend through lovely woodland cut by numerous mountain streams. Camáldoli is reached after 2.5km.

Camáldoli
This second monastery of the Camáldolese order has an 11th-century cloister full of flowers and a 16th century pharmacy from which the monks sell herbal remedies and liqueurs. There is a small museum of ornithology opposite the car park and picnic areas with tables are set out in the surrounding woodland.

From Camáldoli, follow the signs for Poppi through Moggiona. After 14km, just before reaching Poppi, look for the signs to the Zoo Fauna Europa; set in a lovely wooded park, the zoo is perfect for children and is devoted to conserving the endangered species of Europe.

CORTONA

MAP REF: 111 D4

Cortona is a town of delightful contrasts, ringed by substantial remains of Etruscan walls and with two good museums. The streets are steep and the main square, the Piazza della Repubblica, is strikingly irregular, neither square nor level and dominated by the outsize tower of the 13th-century Palazzo Comunale. This makes a good starting point for a leisurely walk round the town.

TOWN WALK

With the Palazzo Comunale behind you, take the right hand exit from the square, down Via Nazionale.

1 This street is known locally as Ruga Piana because it is the only one that is level in the whole town. About 100 metres down on the left is the Vicolo del Precipizio (Precipice Alley), one of several steep stone staircases linking the various levels of the town. Via Nazionale leads to Piazzale Garibaldi where there is a balcony and a fine view down on to the Renaissance church of Santa Maria del Calcinaio, begun in 1485.

Return to Via Nazionale and turn right in Via Santa Margherita (signed Via Crucis).

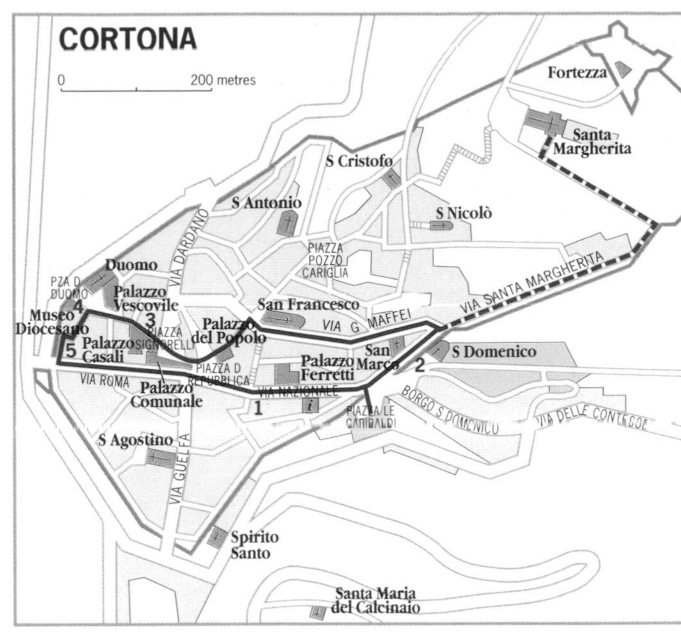

2 This road climbs up past the church of San Marco, with its façade mosaic of St Mark by the Futurist artist, Gino Severini. Visitors with time to spare can follow this road all the way up to the shrine of Santa Margherita on the summit; mosaics depicting the Stations of the Cross line the route, designed by Severini in 1974 as a war memorial. The shrine itself, built in the late 19th century, is graceless, but there are superb views from the terrace, from the 16th-century Fortezza del Girafalco near by and on the downhill route.

Just beyond San Marco, turn left in Via Giuseppe Maffei; keep left at the next junction and continue down between the hospital on the left and San Francesco on the right. Turn left beside the hospital, down a steep flight of steps and through a tunnel to return to the Piazza della Repubblica.Turn right into Piazza Signorelli and the Palazzo Casali is straight ahead.

3 The 13th-century *palazzo* has a graceful courtyard and houses a fascinating museum; the most famous item in the collection is a 5th-century BC Etruscan chandelier, cast in bronze and decorated with grotesque figures. There is a delicate Roman portrait of the muse Polyhymnia, and an eclectic mixture of glass, paintings, carved ivory and costumes.

Turn left out of the museum to reach the cathedral square and the Museo Diocesano on the left.

4 This museum contains several outstanding works, including a Roman sarcophagus depicting the Battle of the Amazons and Centaurs, much admired by Renaissance artists, Signorelli's *Deposition*, and Fra Angelico's beautiful *Annunciation*.

Leaving the square, turn right beside the statue of Santa Margherita down Via del Gesù.

5 This leads through the oldest part of Cortona, past a row of early medieval brick and timber houses with jettied upper storeys; houses like these are familiar enough from medieval paintings but only a handful have survived in all of Italy.

Emerging in the Via Roma, turn left to return to Piazza della Repubblica.

The extraordinarily sited hill town of Cortona

FIRENZE (FLORENCE)

Florence is one of the great cities of the world, a treasure house of art and architecture. The city centre is compact enough to cross in under half an hour on foot but there is so much to see on the way that several days are needed to savour all that Florence (map ref: 110 C4) has to offer. Here the city has been divided into four sections covering the major museums, churches and palaces, plus some suggestions for escaping the city's heat to enjoy the surrounding countryside. The two features on Renaissance art and the history of Florence provide essential background information on a city that has played a major role in shaping Western culture.

ART TOUR

Start at the Piazza del Duomo.

1 The cathedral was begun in 1294 but not completed until 1436, because nobody knew how to solve the technical problems involved in erecting the vast dome. Brunelleschi eventually found the answer by studying the Pantheon in Rome and adapting ancient Roman engineering.

Visitors can climb to the top of the dome for a spectacular view over the rooftops of Florence, or take the easier climb up the gracious campanile at the western end of the church, designed by Giotto who was appointed chief architect in 1331.

2 The baptistry, clad in green and white marble, stands opposite the cathedral portal. The original structure dates from the 7th century. The interior was redesigned between 1270 and 1300 when the Zodiac pavement round the font was laid and the dome was given its mosaics illustrating biblical stories from the

Creation to the Last Judgement. The bronze doors of the south portal were cast by Andrea Pisano in 1339 and tell the story of St John, the city's patron saint. The east doors (1425–52) are the work of Ghiberti and have been hailed as the first truly Renaissance sculptures. Michelangelo called them the 'Gates of Paradise' and the name has stuck. The reliefs illustrate stories from the Old Testament. The north doors (1403–24), also by Ghiberti, illustrate the Life of Christ.

Walk round the north side of the cathedral to the northeastern corner of the cathedral square to reach the Museo dell'Opera del Duomo (9, Piazza del Duomo).

3 The Museo dell'Opera del Duomo (Cathedral Works Museum) was originally a workshop where the sculptures adorning the cathedral were made; Michelangelo carved his mighty statue of *David* in the courtyard in front of the museum. Now the building houses works of art taken from the cathedral and brought indoors to protect them from further erosion. The highlights are Michelangelo's powerful *Pietà* (the head of Nicodemus is a self-portrait); Donatello's anguished *Mary Magdalene* (1455); the lively choir galleries carved with angelic musicians by Luca della Robbia (1431–38) and Donatello (1433–39); and the 14th-century bas reliefs carved by Andrea Pisano for the campanile.

Leave the south side of Piazza del Duomo, down Via dei Calzaiuoli, the principal thoroughfare of medieval Florence, now restored after bombing in World War II.

4 The church of Orsanmichele (a contraction of *Orti* (Garden) *di San Michele*, is just after the fourth turning on the right. The exterior niches are filled with 15th-century statues of the patron saints of the city's guilds. Donatello's famous St George (now in the Bargello) was originally made for this church.

Continue down Via dei Calzaiuoli to Piazza della Signoria.

5 The main square of Florence is dominated by the Palazzo Vecchio with its soaring campanile. Michelangelo's *David* (a copy), Ammannati's licentious *Neptune Fountain* (1563-75) and Bandinelli's *Hercules* (1534) are the most striking works of art

Detail from the bronze doors of the Baptistry in Florence

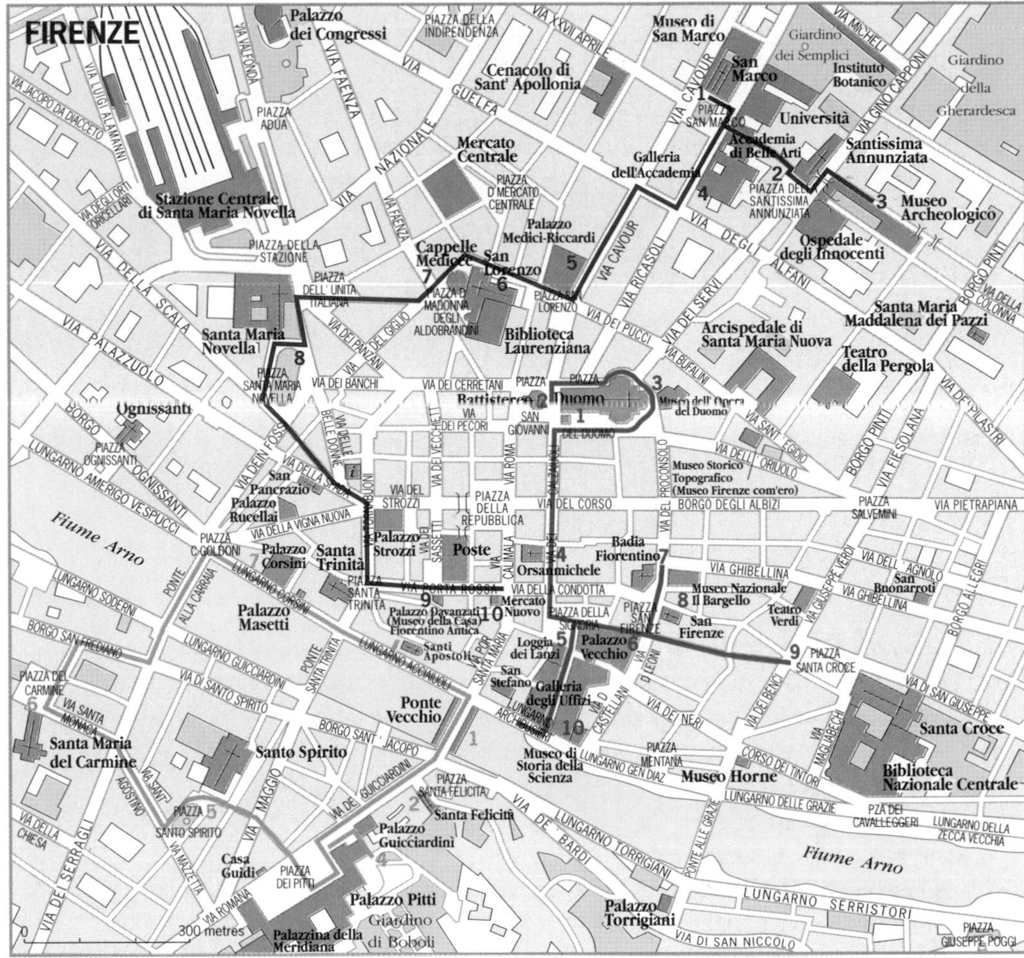

displayed in front of the *palazzo*; further works shelter under the Loggia dei Lanzi, including Giambologna's famous *Rape of the Sabine Women* (1583).

6 The Palazzo Vecchio was begun in 1299 and completely remodelled after Cosimo I established himself as hereditary Duke of Tuscany in 1540. The inner courtyard with its *putto* and dolphin fountain, was frescoed with views of Austrian cities in 1565 when Cosimo's son, Francesco I, married Joanna of Austria. The massive council chamber on the first floor is covered in scenes glorifying Cosimo's military victories over rival Tuscan cities, executed by Vasari between 1563 and 1565. The rest of the palace contains the beautifully decorated and more intimate rooms of the Medici.

Take the alley to the left of the Palazzo Vecchio and turn left in Via del Proconsolo.

7 The first church on the left, the Badia Fiorentino, contains a fresco, *St Bernard and the Virgin* (1485) by Filippino Lippi.

8 The Museo Nazionale Il Bargello opposite, once the main prison, now houses some of the most important sculptural masterpieces of the Renaissance; they include Ghiberti's *Abraham and Isaac* panel (1400) made for the baptistry doors and Donatello's *St George* (1416), both in the hall upstairs. Downstairs, highlights include Michelangelo's drunken *Bacchus* (1497), an early work, Giambologna's airy and athletic *Mercury* and a number of animated bronzes by Cellini.

Turn left out of the Bargello and take the third left, Borgo dei Greci, to reach Piazza Santa Croce.

9 Santa Croce is the burial place of many of Florence's most famous citizens, including Galileo, Machiavelli and Donatello. There is also a grandiose monument to Dante who refused to return to his native city after being sent into exile and was laid to rest in Ravenna. The frescos in the chapel to the right of the high altar were painted by Giotto between 1315 and 1330 and depict the lives of St Francis and St John. The cloister contains many further works of art and the serene Pazzi Chapel, one of the great architectural works of the Renaissance, designed by Brunelleschi (1430).

Return along the Borgo dei Greci to Piazza della Signoria and turn left to reach the Uffizi.

10 The Uffizi, as its name suggests, was built as the offices of the city administration under Cosimo I. Now it houses one of the world's most outstanding collections of art, bequeathed to the city by the last of the Medici line, Anna Maria Lodovica, in 1737. The works are arranged chronologically so as to illustrate the development of art from early Gothic, through the Renaissance period and on to the later Mannerist style. Botticelli's paintings understandably attract the largest crowds but there are treasures to be seen in every room; do not miss Filippo Lippi's tender *Madonna with Angels* (1465) in Room 8, Titian's shocking but influential *Venus of Urbino* (1538) in Room 28, Caravaggio's *Young Bacchus* (1589) in Room 43 and Rembrandt's *Self-Portrait* (1664) in Room 44.

Turn left out of the Uffizi and walk down to the river for a view of the Ponte Vecchio, with its goldsmiths' shops and lively street life. The bridge is a symbol of the city and the oldest of the Arno bridges, constructed in 1345.

THE FLORENTINE RENAISSANCE

The Renaissance was largely created by Florentine painters, sculptors and architects and it is possible to trace the development of this most exciting period in the history of art through the city's unrivalled collection of artistic masterpieces.

Giorgio Vasari, author of the *Lives of the Artists* (published 1550), divided the development of art up to his own time into three stylistic phases. The first was developed by Cimabue, Giotto and the father and son team of Nicola and Giovanni Pisano during the 13th and early 14th centuries. These artists were then rediscovering lost techniques. Cimabue learned how to paint fresco by playing truant from school to watch Greek artists at work in Florence and later supposedly taught Giotto all he knew; similarly Andrea Pisano learned his carving skills from Greek sculptors working on the façade of Pisa's cathedral and passed his skills on to his son.

All four artists developed their own styles, still rooted in Byzantine and Gothic formalism, but enlivened by a greater degree of realism and inventiveness in the composition of their scenes and in their adventurous use of colour. Vasari, in his eulogistic account of Giotto's work, continually praises his powers of observation, saying that 'he was always going for new ideas to nature itself'.

'Realism' at first developed slowly and in relatively small details, such as the use of blue for painting the sky, instead of the celestial gold that is the universal background colour for Gothic religious paintings. Giotto's figures in his great St Francis cycle in Assisi (completed in c1300) still lack the articulation and dynamism that later artists achieved by studying anatomy, but they did, in Vasari's words, 'mark a new beginning, opening the way for the better work which followed'. Even more innovative are the sculptures carved by Andrea and Giovanni Pisano for the Fontana Maggiore (1277) in Perugia, showing the clear influence of antique carving copied from Greek and Roman sarcophagi.

The first truly Renaissance works, belonging to Vasari's second style, were also sculptural. In 1400 the Calimali, the wool importers' guild, announced a competition for the design of new doors for the baptistry in Florence. Five leading artists were invited to submit a bronze relief depicting Abraham's sacrifice of his son, Isaac.

The panels submitted by Ghiberti and Brunelleschi are now displayed in the Bargello (the other three rejected panels were melted down). Ghiberti was chosen as the winner, but both panels have been hailed as marking the watershed between Gothic and Renaissance art. Though the scenes are framed by a Gothic quatrefoil (at the insistence of the Calimali guild) certain key features that define the Renaissance style are already evident: the use of deep perspective, so that the figures seem to occupy a real landscape, accurate portrayal of the human body and allusions to classical sculpture.

The Brancacci Chapel frescos in Santa Maria del Carmine are landmarks in Florentine art

Yet another copy of Michelangelo's masterpiece *David* – in the square named after him

Another milestone was Donatello's statue of St George (1416), commissioned by the Guild of Armourers for the church of Orsanmichele, now also in the Bargello. In return for its money the guild received a statue that was immediately hailed as a masterpiece, the first time since antiquity that any sculptor had achieved a lifelike figure and, moreover, one charged with psychological as well as figurative realism; Donatello's *St George* is no glorified saint or awesome hero but an ordinary man, wearing an uneasy expression, sensing danger and taut with nervous energy.

In fresco, Donatello's equivalent was Masaccio who, tragically, died at the age of 27; the paintings of the Brancacci Chapel in Santa Maria del Carmine give us an indication of what he might have gone on to achieve. Masaccio was just 24 in 1425 when he began work on this cycle, *The Life of St Peter*, as a pupil of Masolino. He was put in sole charge of the work in 1427 and died the following year; in that short time he developed the technique of chiaroscuro (distribution of light and dark masses in a picture) to highlight the faces of Christ and the Apostles, drawing the viewer into the focal point of the picture.

These artists were the pioneers of the second style and their techniques were copied and developed by numerous artists, resulted in a huge outpouring of work during the 15th century. Increasingly, too, artists broke free of purely religious subjects and began to paint portraits, battle scenes, landscapes, nudes and scenes from classical mythology.

Thus, for example, two of the outstanding paintings in the Uffizi, Botticelli's *Primavera* (Spring) and the *Birth of Venus*, both painted between 1465 and 1485, are set in some mythical antique world. Their highly wrought allusions are to the poems of Lucretius and to neo-Platonic philosophy, so far had art been liberated in a very short time from exclusively serving Christianity. Not everyone approved. Savonarola's puritanical reign in Florence, lasting from 1492 to 1498, was marked by the burning of books, paintings, mirrors and clothing on great 'bonfires of vanity' and it is likely that some great works of art were lost in this way because of their pagan or erotic content. Enough remains, however, to indicate what an extraordinary period this was.

It came to an end, as far as Florence was concerned, just after the turn of the 16th century. Vasari's third style, called the High Renaissance by modern art historians, is represented by Leonardo da Vinci, Raphael and Michelangelo. Only the latter spent any significant amount of time in Florence. David, the boy who defeated the tyrant Goliath, was chosen as the subject of his best known work in the city to symbolise the liberation of Florence. Savonarola had been executed, the Medici family had been expelled and a new democratic constitution declared. *David* expresses the optimism of the time and was set up in front of the Palazzo Vecchio as an artistic metaphor for the people of Florence, prepared to defend their liberty against every threat.

Soon, however, the Medici were back, besieging the city with the backing of the imperial army. Michelangelo took part in the defence of Florence, fortifying the walls to the south of the city. He then went into hiding in the New Sacristy behind San Lorenzo where, ironically, he was working on the tombs of two minor members of the Medici family; those tombs are among his last and greatest work in the city. He left for Rome soon after and the history of art thereafter belongs elsewhere.

CITY OF THE MEDICI TOUR

The Medici family had a profound influence on the Renaissance and on the city of Florence through the buildings and works of art they commissioned. Cosimo de'Medici, in particular, had a passion for building, convinced that his works would, like the monuments of ancient Rome, last 1,000 years and immortalise his name. This walk takes in some of the more important monuments associated with the family.

The real thing this time: *David* in its specially built annexe to the Accademia

Start at Piazza San Marco, in the north of the city, where students at the nearby university gather between lectures.

1 The Dominican monastery of San Marco was financed by Cosimo de'Medici and designed by Michelozzi from 1436. Fra Angelico, one of the most influential painters of the early Renaissance, spent most of his life within the cloistered walls, which are painted with his profoundly religious frescos. The background to the *Crucifixion* (1442) in the chapter house is an angry red sky, expressive of the agony of Christ; Vasari reports that Fra Angelico wept as he painted this subject. Fra Angelico's tender *Annunciation* greets visitors at the top of the stairs to the dormitory, where each cell is painted with almost surrealistic frescos designed as an aid to contemplation and prayer. One cell contains mementoes of Savonarola who used the monastery as a retreat.

Take the left-hand street, Via C Battista, out of the square to reach Piazza della Santissima Annunziata.

2 This lovely square is almost completely surrounded by a graceful colonnade. Santissima Annunziata (the Church of the Most Holy Annunciation) stands to the north while to the east is the world's first orphanage, still used as such, the Ospedale degli Innocenti.

Brunelleschi's colonnade, designed in 1419, was the prototype for all similar colonnades in Italy. The spandrils are decorated with glazed terracotta roundels of babies in swaddling clothes, the work of Andrea della Robbia (1487). The museum inside contains Ghirlandaio's radiantly colourful *Adoration*.

Turn right out of Innocenti and take the first right, Via della Colonna, to reach the Museo Archeologico.

3 The archaeological museum, still being reorganised following the disastrous floods of 1966, contains two of the most celebrated masterpieces of Etruscan bronze sculpture: *The Wounded Chimera*, discovered in 1554 near Arezzo and restored by Cellini, and

The Arringatore or Orator, a fine example of Etruscan realism that profoundly influenced Renaissance artists.

Retrace the route to Piazza San Marco and turn left down Via Ricasoli to reach the Accademia, on the left.

4 The Galleria dell'Accademia, founded in 1563 as the world's first school of art, is used to display Michelangelo's *David*. This he carved from a faulty block of marble rejected by other sculptors, demonstrating his principle that the sculptor's job was to release the form already intrinsic in the stone, exploiting naturally occurring faults and cracks. Michelangelo's unfinished *Four Slaves* (1519–36), intended for the tomb of Pope Julius II, is also displayed here and the plaster cast room is packed with miscellaneous nudes and portraits.

Turn left out of the Accademia and walk down Via Ricasoli. Turn right in Via degli Alfani, and left in Via Cavour to reach the Palazzo Medici-Riccardi on the right.

5 This *palazzo* was built for Cosimo de'Medici who took up residence in 1459. The unadorned façade, designed by Michelozzi, was intended to symbolise Cosimo's carefully cultivated image as a no-nonsense man of few pretensions. The Medici Chapel contains gorgeous scenes of the *Journey of the Magi*, painted by Gozzoli in 1459, depicting various members of the Medici family.

At the end of Via Cavour turn right to Piazza San Lorenzo.

6 The street market alongside the Church of San Lorenzo, which continues to operate despite attempts to close it down, obscures the unfinished façade of this church, begun in 1418 and financed by Cosimo de'Medici. The serene interior has two great bronze pulpits covered with crowded scenes of the *Passion* and *Resurrection*, the work of Donatello (1460). The cloister leads to the Laurentian Library, designed by Michelangelo in 1524 to house Cosimo de'Medici's important collection of antique manuscripts, including the famous 5th-century Virgil codex.

Leave the church and circle left, threading through the market, to Piazza della Madonna degli Aldobrandini, where the entrance to the Cappella dei Medici is on the left.

7 The Medici mausoleum, below San Lorenzo, is the burial place of cardinals, dukes and electors palatinate, all descendants of the original merchant family. The Chapel of Princes is a sobering display of costly marble, begun in 1604 and not completed until nearly 300 years later. The New Sacristy contains the outstanding tombs carved by Michelangelo between 1520 and 1533 for two minor members of the family, depicting Night and Day, Dusk and Dawn.

Leave Piazza della Madonna degli Aldobrandini by the western exit, Via del Melarancio, to reach Piazza dell'Unità Italiana, from where there is a view of the Functionalist-style railway station (completed 1935). Walk left down Via Avelli to reach Piazza Santa Maria Novella.

8 This huge square was once the location for chariot races; obelisks surmounted by bronze turtles mark the turning points on the race track. Many distinguished writers stayed in rooms overlooking what in the 19th century was a quiet piazza, including Henry James, Longfellow and Ralph Waldo Emerson. Santa Maria Novella, with its green and white Romanesque façade, was lavishly decorated by Florentines frightened into thoughts of eternity by the Black Death of the mid-14th century. Boccaccio set the beginning of his famous *Decameron* here, the poem in which a group of aristocrats agree to shut themselves away to avoid contact with the plague and amuse each other by telling stories. Outstanding frescos fill the church; Masaccio's *Trinity* fresco, Filippino Lippi's energetic scenes from the life of St Philip, Ghirlandaio's vibrant *Life of the Virgin* (dismissed by Ruskin as verging on the vulgar – he did not seem to like the gaudy colours) and Nardo di Cione's frescos based on Dante's *Inferno* and *Paradiso*, painted in 1351–57. The former refectory is now the Chiostro Verde, named after the predominantly green pigment of Piero Uccello's masterpiece, the *Universal Deluge* (1445), ironically damaged by the 1966 flood. The Spanish Chapel, so called because it was used by Cosimo I's Spanish wife, Eleonora di Toledo, has frescos depicting the teachings of St Thomas Aquinas (1356).

Take the far left exit out of the square, Via del Sole, and continue straight on down Via della Spada, then turn right into Via Tornabuoni, the most elegant shopping street in Florence. Just before the street widens to form Piazza Santa Trinità, turn left down Via Porta Rossa to reach the Palazzo Davanzati, halfway down on the right.

9 The Palazzo Davanzati, or Museo della Casa Fiorentino Antica, provides an opportunity to see inside a 14th-century palace, with its delightful inner courtyard open to the sky, frescoed bedrooms, and bathrooms complete with lavatory and tub. The kitchen is located on the top floor so that smoke and cooking smells would not penetrate the living rooms.

Turn right out of the palazzo to reach the Mercato Nuovo, just after the second turning on the right.

10 A market has existed here since the 11th century. Today it is devoted to the sale of T-shirts, leather goods and souvenirs. To the south of the covered arcade is a bronze boar, known as *Il Porcellino*, a copy of the Roman bronze in the Uffizi, which is itself a copy of a Hellenic original. It is said that anyone who rubs the snout is certain to return to Florence. Coins dropped in the trough below are distributed to city charities.

The interior of Santa Maria Novella is packed full of beauty

FLORENCE AND THE MEDICI

Florence has made an extraordinary contribution to Western civilisation, and not only in the realm of the arts. In politics, science, philosophy and banking Florentines have led the world and the record of achievement continues to this day. Since 1966, when the Arno burst its banks flooding the city and damaging hundreds of thousands of precious books, frescos and paintings, Florence has become an international centre for art restoration.

In earlier times the river contributed to the city's prosperity. The wealth of medieval Florence was built on wool processing and the Arno was once straddled by fulling and dyeing mills. Florentine merchants travelled Europe and the Middle East, buying fleeces and costly dye-stuffs and selling finished cloth.

Banking was a natural extension of the wool trade. Florence began minting its own coins in 1252 and the florin became the first common European currency, widely accepted for its pure gold content. Early Florentine financiers developed credit financing and double-entry bookkeeping, still the fundamental principles of modern banking and accountancy practice.

Dante, born in Florence in 1265, saw the negative side of this nascent capitalism. Florence, to him, was 'a glut of self-made men and fast-got gain'. He had good reason to be cynical. In 1300, he had served on the city executive, the *priorate*. Two years later he was falsely accused of corruption during his term of office, the victim of a mass purge of Ghibellines (supporters of the emperor) by the Guelfs (the papal party). Sentenced to two years' exile, he chose never to return to his native city; his great poetic works, which were to make the Florentine dialect the literary language of Italy, were all composed elsewhere.

When Giovanni di Bicci de'Medici founded the Medici bank at the end of the 14th century, it was just one of a hundred similar establishments in the city. The rapid expansion of the bank resulted from Giovanni's shrewd decision to cultivate a special relationship with the papacy. The family's fortune was made when the bank was entrusted with the collection of papal revenues.

Giovanni's son, Cosimo de'Medici, was the first member of the family to enter public life. He, too, spent time in exile, accused of plotting against the welfare of the city. His 'crime' was to argue for an end to the costly and inconclusive wars that Florence was waging against its neighbours and this made him unpopular with certain rival families whose vested interests were under threat. When Florence was disastrously defeated by the Milanese in 1434, the sentence of exile was revoked and Cosimo came back to run the affairs of the nearly bankrupt city.

Cosimo was the right man for his time. He has gone down in history as a shrewd tactician, carefully cultivating his image; he presented himself as reluctant to take on the responsibilities of government, while all the time manipulating

For a hundred years the Medici virtually ruled Florence from the Medici Palace

behind the scenes with consummate skill. The austere design he chose for the Medici palace was a deliberate ploy to show up his more flamboyant rivals. He presented himself as a devout man who paid for the building of San Lorenzo and the monastery of San Marco.

Yet Cosimo was also a great patron of the arts and under him Florence experienced a golden age. He financed the travels of Poggio Bracciolini who specialised in tracking down lost works by classical authors, such as Cicero. He built up the huge collection of ancient manuscripts now housed in Michelangelo's Laurentian Library, located in the cloister of San Lorenzo. He encouraged the learning of ancient Greek and the translation of forgotten works, including Plato's *Dialogues.* Under the relative stability and patronage of Cosimo's reign, Florence gave birth simultaneously to humanism and the Renaissance. The one fed the other as humanist scholars, rediscovering the richness of antique mythology and epic, threw up new ideas and themes that were rapidly adopted by artists. Art was liberated from religious motifs and Venus became as popular a subject as the Virgin had previously been.

Cosimo's grandson, Lorenzo, was himself a great patron of the humanists and he is often portrayed as the model Renaissance man. He was an outstanding poet and promoted the study of vernacular writers, including Dante and Boccaccio, in the universities. Botticelli's mysterious *Primavera*, whose meaning is still being debated by scholars, was directly inspired by Lorenzo's poetry and his preoccupation with neo-Platonism. Called upon to step into his grandfather's shoes in 1469, he also proved an effective ruler of Florence. As a diplomat on the wider stage he helped to heal old rifts between warring cities and encouraged an alliance between Florence, Venice, Milan, Naples and the Papal States, the five dominant powers of 15th-century Italy.

When Lorenzo died in 1492, aged only 43, Innocent VIII declared 'the peace of Italy is at an end'. He was right. In 1494 Charles VIII of France invaded Italy and besieged Florence. Lorenzo's son, Piero de'Medici, fled the city in panic. Charles moved on to Rome and Savonarola stepped into the vacuum, arguing that Charles VII had been sent by God to punish Florence for its preoccupation with pagan philosophies and profane art. Mirrors, books and works of art were publically burned on 'bonfires of vanity' and Savonarola ruled the city with puritanical zeal in what Harold Acton has called a brief and bloody return to the Middle Ages.

Eventually public opinion turned against Savonarola and he himself was burned at the stake in front of the Palazzo Vecchio in 1498, accused of fomenting civil strife.

Savonarola's lasting contribution was a new republican constitution for the city which was adopted in 1494. For a brief period Florence flourished as an independent republic under the leadership of Soderini and his chancellor, Niccolo Machiavelli. Machiavelli was one of the first victims of the purge that followed when the Medici family were forcibly restored to power in 1512. Dismissed from office, Machiavelli retired to write *The Prince*, a pioneering work of political analysis and a reflection on the characteristics that make an effective leader.

For a period of time Florence was ruled by a series of puppet agents of the Medici popes – Leo X and Clement VII. In 1530, Cosimo I, a distant relative via the female line of Cosimo and Lorenzo de'Medici, was elected Duke of Florence and the city once again had an effective leader, though of an entirely different character to his predecessors. Cosimo was a ruthless militarist who set about systematically subjugating the traditional enemies of Florence – Pisa and Siena in particular – to carve out a Tuscan state under his control. Opponents were publicly executed and the Uffizi was built to bring all the city's administrative functions, such as the judiciary and the guilds, under his direct control.

Despite his brutality, Cosimo I created an effective government machine which lasted until Tuscany became part of the United Kingdom of Italy in 1860.

Cosimo I: the right man in the right place at the right time

OLTRARNO

MAP REF: 110 C4

Oltrarno means beyond the Arno, with the slight suggestion that the south bank and its inhabitants are somewhat inferior to the north. Despite this, Cosimo I and subsequent rulers of Florence chose to live here, in the vast Palazzo Pitti. The noble Medici did not, however, have to mix with the crowds as they travelled between their state apartments in the Palazzo Vecchio and the equally luxurious rooms of the Pitti Palace. Vasari built an aerial corridor, the Corridoio Vasariano, linking the two, high above the confusion of the streets. The walk (below) follows the route of the corridor across the Arno.

TOWN WALK

Start from the Ponte Vecchio, the city's oldest bridge, dating in its present form from 1345.

1 The raised arcade of the Corridoio Vasariano is on the left, high above the jewellers' shops that trade on the bridge. Butchers, tanners and blacksmiths once had workshops here but these noxious trades were banned by an environmentally aware Ferdinand I in 1593 and jewellers have traditionally occupied the quaint and cramped premises ever since.

Continue straight on down Via de' Guicciardini to Santa Felicità, the first church on the left.

2 The Corridoio now forms the upper part of the portico fronting this church, which contains two outstanding works by the Mannerist artist Pontormo, his *Annunciation* fresco (1525–28) and a *Deposition* in oil over the main altar.

Continue down Via de' Guicciardini, past the Palazzo Guicciardini, with its fine courtyard, where Italy's first historian was born in 1483. The corridor now disappears behind this palace. Continue on to Piazza dei Pitti.

3 Robert Browning and Elizabeth Barrett Browning lived in the Casa Guidi, on the opposite side of the square to the palace and the exiled Dostoevsky wrote *The Idiot* near by, at Number 21, his brooding imagination no doubt finding a counterpart in the gaunt and forbidding walls of stone that formed the view from his window.

The Pitti Palace was begun in the 1450s for the banker, Luca Pitti. His aim was to outrival the might of the monumental Medici Palace; instead the scale of the work bankrupted the Pitti family and they were forced to sell the palace to Eleonora di Toledo. She persuaded her husband, Cosimo I, to move here in 1550 and for the next 200 years it served as the home of the Medici Grand Dukes. It now houses several museums.

The Palatine Gallery consists of a series of state rooms frescoed by Pietro da Cortona between 1641 and 1665. The walls are hung with masterpieces from the Medici art collection, including such famous works as Raphael's *Madonna della Seggiola* (1515) and Rubens' allegorical *Consequences of the War* (1638), depicting the famine and misery of Europe during the Thirty Years' War. The rooms above contain the Galleria d'Arte Moderna; the best works, in rooms 23 to 26, are Impressionist-style paintings by members of the Macchiaioli group. The Argenti (Silver) Museum contains *objets d'art* from the Medici collection – everything from antique vases collected by Lorenzo de'Medici to the baubles and jewel-encrusted toys of later dukes.

Turn right out of the Pitti Place to find the narrow gate that leads into the Giardino di Boboli (Boboli Gardens).

4 Just inside the gate is a reproduction of a statue by Valerio Cioli of Pietro Barbino, Cosimo I's court dwarf, sitting astride a turtle. Further up the path is a grotto created by Buontalenti; hidden in the dark recesses is Vincenzo de' Rossi's lifesize erotic sculpture, carved in 1560, of Paris making love to Helen of Troy. The path climbs to the grand terrace behind the Pitti Palace, dominated by Francesco Susini's great fountain of 1641. Stone for the Pitti Place was excavated from this site and the resulting amphitheatre, with

The impressive view of Florence from the Piazzale Michelangelo

its steps and terraces, was used for masques and firework displays.

A series of terraces leads upwards from here to the Neptune Fountain (Stoldo Lorenzi, 1565–8), the frescoed rococo Kaffeehaus (café open in summer) and to the Giardino del Cavaliere with its museum of fine porcelain and views over to the Church of San Miniato. Returning to the rear of the palace, the east wing, called the Palazzina della Meridiana, contains an excellent museum, full of sumptuous court and theatrical costumes that reflect the fashions of the 18th to early 20th centuries.

On leaving the Boboli Gardens, cross Piazza dei Pitti and continue down the little alley, opposite the palace steps, called Sdrucciolo dei Pitti (literally 'Pitti Slide'). This leads to Via Maggio, a street lined with antique dealers' premises. Cross Via Maggio and continue straight on to Piazza Santo Spirito.

5 This quiet tree-planted piazza differs markedly from the palace-lined streets north of the Arno. The parish of Santo Spirito, with its neighbour, San Frediano, is an area of low houses where wool-dyers and leather-workers once carried out their trade and where the traditional Florentine lifestyle still thrives. Santo Spirito church is a minor masterpiece by Brunelleschi, built on the basilican plan from 1436, though the classical simplicity of Brunelleschi's design is spoiled by the ugly baroque *baldacchino* that dominates the eastward view.

Follow Via Sant'Agostino and Via Santa Monaca to reach Piazza del Carmine.

6 The original church of Santa Maria del Carmine was destroyed by fire in 1771; fortunately the famous Brancacci Chapel frescos survived. Three artists had a hand in these scenes from the life of St Peter; Masolini and Masaccio began the cycle in 1424 and it was completed by Filippino Lippi in 1485. Masaccio's work has been hailed as an outstanding contribution to the development of early Renaissance art.

Cross Piazza del Carmine with the church behind you. Turn right in Borgo San Frediano, and first left into Piazza N Sauro. This leads to the Ponte alla Carraia, a modern reconstruction of the original 14th-century bridge, reputed to have been designed by Giotto. Cross the bridge and turn right along Lungarno Corsini.

7 This embankment is lined with fine palaces. The Palazzo Corsini, distinctive for its villa-like form and classical statues lined along the parapet, was built between 1650 and 1717. Further along, the Palazzo Masetti, now the British Consulate, was once home to the widow of Bonnie Prince Charlie. He fled to Italy after his defeat at the Battle of Culloden and ended his days in Florence calling himself the Count of Albany (Albion being an archaic name for Britain). His widow held fashionable salons in the palace, frequented by writers and artists such as Byron and Shelley. The next bridge, the Ponte Santa Trinità, is graced with statues of the Four Seasons, carved by Ammannati in 1593. The bridge was blown up by retreating Nazis in 1944, but the statues were dredged from the river and the bridge restored to its former glory.

More street than bridge, the Ponte Vecchio is covered with shops and houses along its entire length

Continue along the embankment and take the second turning left after the Ponte Santa Trinità, a narrow alley that leads to Piazza del Limbo and the Church of Santi Apostoli.

8 This is one of the city's oldest churches, a tiny Romanesque gem that was probably built in the 10th century (despite the inscription claiming that Charlemagne – *Karolus Rex Romanus* – founded it). The green marble columns of the interior were reused from the nearby Roman baths. Piazza del Limbo itself was once a burial ground for unbaptised infants.

Walk back to the Arno embankment and turn left to return to the Ponte Vecchio.

A rather neglected 16th-century Neptune fountain, in the Boboli Gardens

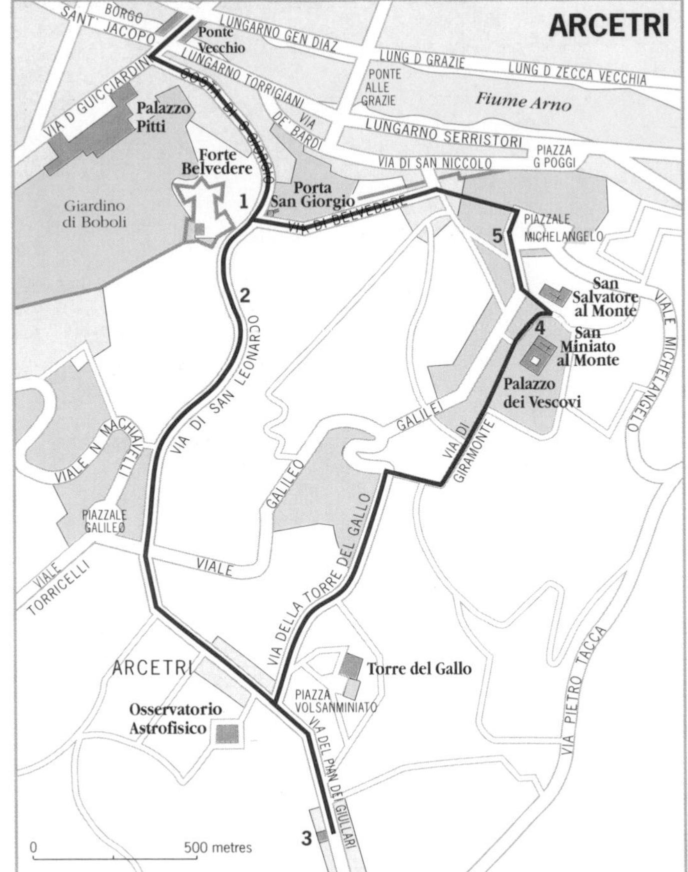

COUNTRY WALK

One of the great joys of Florence is the ease with which visitors can walk from the city into the countryside. This leisurely stroll is popular with Florentines on Sunday afternoons.

Start from the Ponte Vecchio. Walk south towards the Pitti Place and take the second left, beside the Church of Santa Felicita, to reach Costa di San Giorgio, a steep lane that climbs steadily up to the Porta San Giorgio.

The magnificent panorama of Florence that is revealed to the observer from the church of San Miniato

1 Built in 1260, this is the oldest surviving gate in the city walls. To the right is the massive bulk of the Forte Belvedere, built in 1590 as part of the city's defences and today used as an outdoor sculpture gallery and cinema in summer.

Turn right and follow Via di San Leonardo.

2 This rural lane winds uphill between wisteria and rose-covered villa walls. Tchaikovsky and Stravinsky both rented villas in this lane; before the 1917 Revolution, Florence was a popular winter resort for Russians escaping the rigours of their own climate.

Cross Viale Galileo Galilei and continue along Via di San Leonardo to Piazza Volsanminiato in the village of Arcetri, then turn right and follow the Via del Pian del Giulari.

3 Galileo lived at Number 42, Via del Pian del Giulari, from 1631 until his death in 1642, under virtual house arrest after being excommunicated for insisting that the sun, rather than the earth, was at the centre of the cosmos. There are fine views from the village.

Backtrack to Arcetri and turn left, following Via della Torre del Gallo down to the Piazza degli Unganelli; here take the right-hand track, Via di Giramonte, which winds downhill to the Basilica di San Miniato at Monte.

4 San Miniato is a gem of a church, covered in delicate green and white marble in the Pisan Romanesque style. Work began in 1018 and it was completed in 1207, since when little has changed. The interior is adorned with 13th-century intarsia worked panels, mosaic pavements and pulpit decorations illustrating the signs of the Zodiac and mythical beasts. Reused Roman columns support the crypt. The cemetery north of the church is worth a visit for its 19th-century funerary monuments.

From the church, a series of terraces and staircases lead down to the Piazzale Michelangelo.

5 The Piazzale, laid out between 1865 and 1873, offers outstanding views over the city and cathedral, and is decorated with reproductions of Michelangelo's most famous works.

Follow Via di Belvedere left out of the Piazzale. This tree-lined lane runs along the foot of the 14th-century city walls back to Porto San Giorgio, from where Costa di San Giorgio leads back to the Ponte Vecchio.

FIÉSOLE

MAP REF: 110 C4

Hilltop Fiésole, less than 6km from the centre of Florence, is a favourite summertime retreat, especially during the Estate Fiesolana festival held from July to August. The Roman amphitheatre, able to seat 3,000, is the venue for the festival's open-air concerts, films, dance and theatrical performances and there is a superb view over open countryside from the tiered stone seats. Fiésole was once an important Etruscan city and the excellent Museum Faesulanum, within the amphitheatre grounds, houses archaeological finds dating from the Bronze Age through to the 13th century. Near by, in Via Dupre, the Museo Bandini displays paintings, Byzantine carved ivories, furniture and majolica.

TOWN WALK

From Piazza Mino, the broad main square crosses to the rather forbidding cathedral, over-restored in the 19th century. Look for Via San Francesco, which begins across from the cathedral façade. This climbs steeply to a lookout point with memorable views over Florence, provided that the city is not enshrouded in haze. Continue up to Sant'Alessandro.

1 The neo-classical façade of this basilica hides a more attractive interior with reused Roman columns of *cipollino* (onion-ring) marble.

Continue to the top of the hill where San Francesco stands on the site of the Etruscan acropolis.

2 Apart from far-reaching views, San Francesco has a charming cloister and a small museum displaying objects brought back by Franciscan missionaries.

Retrace your steps to Piazza Mino and turn right to follow the narrow Via Vecchia Fiesolana. After 0.5km this passes the Villa Medici.

3 Built in 1458, this villa with its outstanding garden was a favourite retreat of Lorenzo de'Medici and the childhood home of Iris Origo, author of *The Merchant of Prato*.

Continue down Via Vecchia, past several more handsome villas,to reach San Domenico after 1km.

4 Fra Angelico was prior of this Dominican convent before moving to San Marco. His *Madonna with Angels* (1430) is in the church and the chapter house contains his *Crucifixion* (1430).

Opposite San Domenico, Via della Badia descends to the Badia Fiesolana.

5 Founded in the 9th century, the Badia served as Fiesole's cathedral until 1028. The original façade is an exquisite work of inlaid grey, green and white marble, framed by the rough stonework of the enlarged 15th-century church. The monastic buildings house the European University Institute, founded in 1976. There is another outstanding view over Florence from the terrace in front of the church.

Return to San Domenico where there is a stop for the Number 7 bus back to central Florence.

Tacky 'art' on sale in the Piazzale Michelangelo

THE VILLAS OF FLORENCE

The northern suburbs of Florence contain several Renaissance villas that once stood in open countryside. Those described below are all open to the public.

The Villa Stibbert, Via Stibbert 26 (bus No 1), is a vast house stuffed with antiques of every kind, including an important collection of armour dating back to Etruscan and Roman times.

The Villa Careggi, Viale Pieraccini 17 (bus No 14C), is now a nursing home but the grounds are open. Under Medici patronage, in the 1460s, this was the meeting place of the Platonic Academy, whose members included all the greatest scholars of the day; hence it is regarded as the birthplace of humanism.

The Villa della Petraia, Via Reginaldo Giuliano (bus No 28), has an exceptionally garden and park. The main courtyard, glassed over by Vittorio Emanuele II to serve as a ballroom, is covered in 17th-century frescos detailing the history of the Medici family.

The Villa di Castello, a short walk downhill from La Petraia, has another outstanding garden, created for Cosimo I from 1537. Terraces, lavish fountains, and a shell-encrusted grotto full of realistic statues of birds and beasts, all contribute to the ostentatious but enjoyable theatricality.

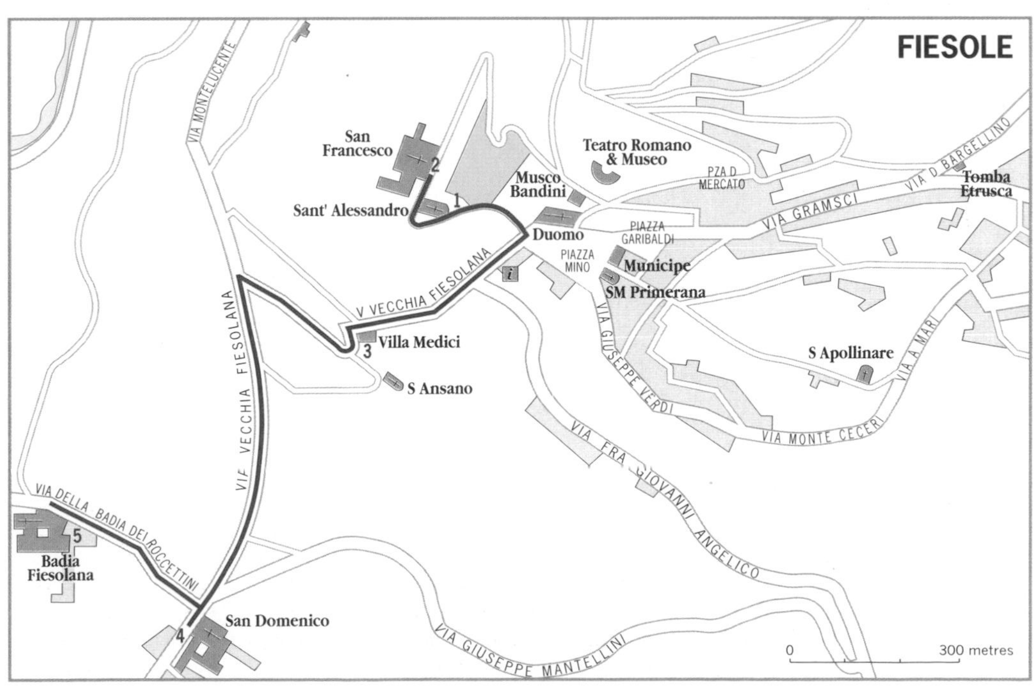

MONTE SAN SAVINO

MAP REF: 111 D4

Monte San Savino stands on a spur above the broad Val di Chiana, today an area of rich farmland but once an inhospitable and malaria-ridden swamp. The town still has the air of a remote and slumbering outpost although it has seen its share of ugly strife; Arretine forces destroyed the city in 1325 and the town's disused synagogue stands as a silent memorial to the small Jewish community, massacred in anti-Semitic riots in 1799.

Today Monte San Savino prides itself on being the birthplace of the High Renaissance sculptor, Andrea Sansovino (1460–1529). The Church of Santa Chiara contains his altarpiece and glazed terracottas made jointly with Andrea della Robbia. Some also credit him with the design of the handsome classical Loggia dei Mercanti in the main street, Corso Sangallo, while others attribute it to Antonio da Sangallo, who built the Palazzo Comunale opposite (1515), the most handsome of several Renaissance palaces in the town. Sant'Agostino, again credited to Sansovino, has a lovely cloister and frescos by Vasari.

Nearby The maze-like streets of Lucignano form a series of concentric rings, an unusual plan that makes exploring fun because every turning holds a new surprise. The circular theme is picked up by the staircase fronting the Collegiata, built in 1594. The Palazzo Comunale contains a collection of School of Siena religious paintings and a finely worked reliquary made by local goldsmiths in 1350.

SANSEPOLCRO

MAP REF: 111 D4

Sansepolcro (home of the world-famous Buitoni pasta factory) suffered heavy bombing during World War II and is not one of Tuscany's more appealing towns. Even so it remains a must for art lovers, especially fans of Piero della Francesca. The *Resurrection* fresco (1463) in the Museo Civico is regarded as his finest work – Aldous Huxley went as far as to call it the greatest painting in the world. It is partnered by his inscrutably mysterious *Madonna della Misericordia* and frescos of St Julian and St Louis of Toulouse.

Nearby The della Francesca trail leads south to Monterchi where, on the edge of the village in the unlikely setting of a cemetery chapel, there is another great fresco, the *Madonna del Parto*, painted in 1445 and recently restored to its original freshness. This fresco has fascinated countless visitors, including the many women who come here to pray for help with childbirth. Within the intimate confines of the chapel painted angels draw aside a pair of curtains to reveal the heavily pregnant Virgin, her dress unbuttoned to afford some relief from the burden in her womb. She wears an ambiguous expression that sums up all her conflicting emotions: the secret pride of impending motherhood, the weariness of pregnancy and the sorrow born of the consciousness that hers will be no ordinary child.

The Annunciation by Piero della Francesca in Galleria Nazionale dell' Umbria, Perugia

PIERO DELLA FRANCESCA

Piero della Francesca was born in Sansepolcro sometime between 1410 and 1420. His greatest works were painted in the 1450s and 1460s, before blindness put an end to his career. He wrote several treatises on Euclidian geometry and the mathematics of perspective. On one level his paintings demonstrate a preoccupation with space, ratio and proportion, a quest for the theoretically perfect forms that students of Euclid believed provided a key to the whole pattern of creation. Yet this philosophical approach does not account for the unique magnetism of his work or the extraordinary psychological depth of a painting like the *Madonna del Parto* in Monterchi. Struggling to define the effect, art critics use words like hypnotic, mysterious, timeless and elemental. Sir Kenneth Clarke warned us that, as with all great art, della Francesca's paintings embody 'values for which no rational statement is adequate'. Writing of the *Resurrection* fresco in Sansepolcro, Clarke went on to say: 'This country god, who rises in the grey light while humanity is asleep, has been worshipped since man first knew that seed is not dead in the winter earth, but will force its way upward through an iron crust'.

VALLOMBROSA

MAP REF: 110 C4

The famous monastery at Vallombrosa (Vale of Shade) was founded in 1038 by the Florentine religious reformer, Giovanni Gualberto Visdomini. The new Vallombrosan order practised a more austere form of the Benedictine rule. The imposing abbey buildings were substantially enlarged and remodelled in the 15th and 17th centuries, reflecting the growing wealth of the order, which grew too powerful and was suppressed in 1866. In 1963 the order was reinstated and a handful of monks now maintain the buildings, which are less remarkable than the magnificent woodlands that surround it. The slow journey to the monastery up winding roads is worth the effort just for the scenery. The poet Milton stayed at the monastery in 1638 and the trees inspired a passage in *Paradise Lost* when the fallen angels, gathering to hear the evil plans of Satan, are described as swarming:

'Thick as autumnal leaves that
strow the brooks
In Vallombrosa, where
th'Etrurian shades,
High-overarch'd, imbower.

Besieged by woodland, the Vallombrosa Monastery

•UMBRIA•

The 19th-century Italian poet, Giosuè Carducci, called Umbria 'the green heart of Italy'. That resonant phrase has now been adopted by the Umbrian Tourist Authority and, for once, it is an accurate description of the region. Umbria lies at the geographical heart of Italy. It is a verdant region of densely wooded hills and high mountain pastures. Red squirrels, wild boar, porcupine and even wolves are found in Umbria's four national parks, officially protected nature reserves. The environment so loved by St Francis of Assisi, proclaimed patron saint of ecology in 1979, has survived relatively untouched by industry, pollution and modern agricultural practices.

Long regarded as second best to Tuscany, Umbria has now come into its own; ruinous farmhouses are being converted into second homes for wealthy Romans, pilgrims arrive in Assisi by the coachload and Nórcia is developing into a popular ski resort. Yet visitors only have to step a little way off the beaten track to find deserted roads, little-visited hilltop towns and Romanesque churches whose walls glow with the colours of medieval and Renaissance frescos.

The ancient walls that surround these towns encapsulate Umbria's history; their lower courses, constructed of monolithic boulders, were built by the ancient Umbrians; neater courses of Roman masonry rise above to meet a jumble of medieval stonework, patched and repaired after each attack by mercenary armies fighting in the name of the Holy Roman Emperor or the pope.

The ancient Umbrians migrated to the region before the 10th century BC; some scholars say they came from Anatolia or Greece, others claim from as far away as India. The River Tévere (Tiber) formed the approximate boundary between Etruscan and Umbrian territory; Perugia, today the capital of Umbria, was originally an Etruscan town and Perugians still speak with a different accent to the people of Assisi, Gúbbio, Todi, Terni or Narni, all towns founded by the Umbrians.

The empire-building Romans conquered Perugia in 309BC, and it was not long before the whole region acknowledged Roman rule. The Via Flaminia was built in 220BC to provide a swift route from Rome to the northern frontiers of the expanding republic. That road, the N3, still forms Umbria's main transport artery. New towns were founded along the Via Flaminia as retirement settlements for army veterans and their prosperity soon began to eclipse that of the ancient hilltop towns.

By the 6th century, however, Umbrians were once again seeking shelter behind their walls as wave after wave of Teutonic invaders pushed southwards to plunder Rome. Umbria was the buffer zone that bore the brunt of attacks by Totila the Goth (who was finally killed beneath the walls of Gualdo Tadino by the Roman commander, Narses, in AD552) followed by the Lombards, who conquered the region and made Spoleto their capital.

By then the power that had once been wielded by the Roman emperor had passed to the papacy, which claimed that the first Christian emperor, Constantine the Great, had bequeathed the empire to the Church. The so-called *Donation of Constantine*, purporting to be the emperor's will, was produced to back the Church's claim to territorial power in Italy. The Lombards stood in the way, so Pope Stephen II invited the Franks to expel them, and the Frankish leader, Charlemagne, was crowned Holy Roman Emperor in AD800, as a reward for his success.

Thus was sown the seed of future conflict, for Charlemagne's successors were themselves to challenge the right of the Church to exercise temporal power. Frederick Barbarossa, crowned Holy Roman Emperor in 1152, invaded Italy soon after and destroyed cities like Spoleto that did not bow to his might. His grandson Frederick II, born outside Assisi and baptised in the cathedral in the same font as St Francis, continued the campaign. He very nearly succeeded in breaking the power of the Church and creating a united Italy under his rule; he blamed his ultimate failure on St Francis whose example had done so much to rekindle support for the Church.

Mighty fortresses and towers dot the Umbrian landscape as a legacy of this strife-torn era. The situation was exploited by *condottieri*, or mercenaries, men like Fortebraccio (Strongarm) who ended up as ruler of Perugia, and Gattamelata (the Honey Cat), born in Narni and honoured with an equestrian statue by Donatello in Padua. They had much to gain from perpetuating the conflict and they were prepared to fight on behalf of anyone willing to pay their price.

The mightiest of them all, however, proved to be a cleric, the Spanish papal legate, Cardinal Gil d'Albornoz, who built the mighty *rocca* in Spoleto. Beginning in 1354, this was the base from which he slowly brought Umbria under papal control. There was no decisive end to the age-old conflict, which continued for another 200 years, but Albornoz did bring a measure of stability to the region in place

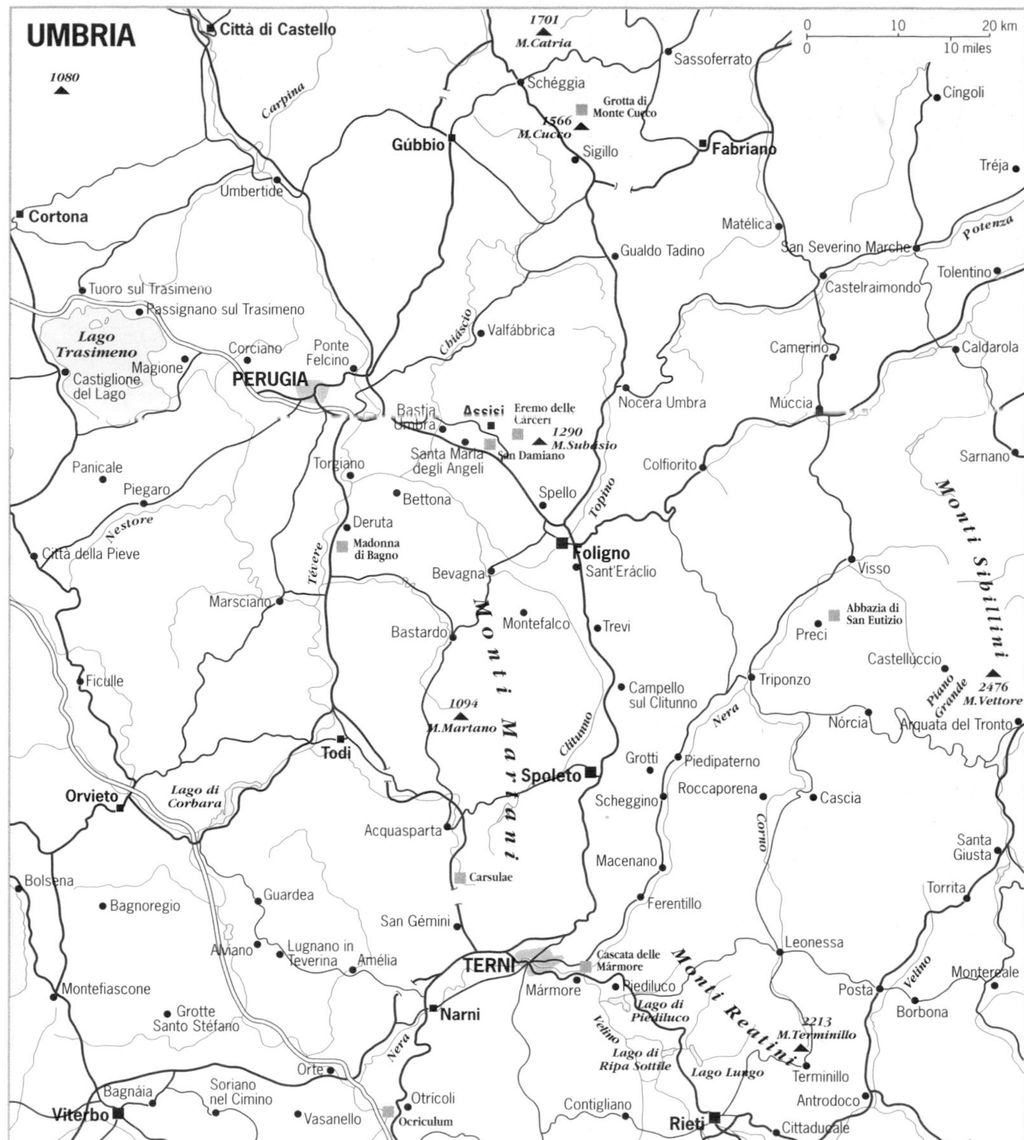

of the former anarchy, and from the mid-14th century until the mid-19th, Umbria was part of the central Italian Papal States, ruled from Rome.

Once peace returned, powerful families and wealthy merchants, organised into guilds, were able to commission the public buildings, fountains and frescos that draw admiring visitors to the region today. Every Umbrian town of importance has its *palazzi* built for local government executives (the *priori*), for the chief executive and judge (the *podestà*) and for the head of the army-cum-police force (the *capitano del popolo*). Umbrian artists, such as Perugino and Pinturrichio, and Florentines, such as Fra Lippo Lippi, Luca Signorelli and Benozzo Gozzoli, were commissioned to decorate the region's cathedrals, producing great masterpieces and all acknowledging their debt to Giotto's pioneering St Francis fresco cycle in Assisi. Most of these frescos survived the Counter-Reformationary zeal of the 17th century when so many churches were remodelled along baroque lines.

Napoleon invaded in 1796 and looted the best of the region's more portable treasures, but he also succeeded in unifying Italy for the first time since the Roman era. Umbria reverted to Church control after the collapse of the Napoleonic regime but was in the forefront of the struggle to create a permanently unified Italy under a secular government. That dream was not finally realised until Rome, the pope's last stronghold, finally fell to Italian troops in 1870, though Umbria itself was liberated by Garibaldi's partisans in 1860.

Umbria then began its slow emergence from a peasant economy. The rivers around Terni and Narni were harnessed for hydroelectric power to supply steel, chemical and armaments factories, the reason why this area was heavily bombed in World War II. Even so, the region's economy was, and remains, based on agriculture and foodstuffs. Fast roads built after the war have connected Umbria to Rome and the prosperous north, so that Gúbbio, once known as the 'City of silence' because of its remoteness, is now close to a major highway. Co-operatives were formed to distribute the region's produce – truffles, bottled water, salami, prosciutto, pasta, tobacco and confectionery – to wider markets.

The roads have also brought visitors and tourist revenue to this picturesque province. Quieter, gentler and more rural than its neighbour Tuscany, Umbria is equally rewarding. Perugia, with its fine museums, Assisi, with its Giotto frescos, Orvieto and Spoleto, with their outstanding cathedrals; while these may be the stars of the region, nearly every hilltop town, gleaming in the sunlight, hides artistic and architectural treasures within its walls, and the Apennines, forming Umbria's eastern border with the Marches, offer some of Italy's most dramatic scenery.

·ASSISI·

The name of Assisi is inextricably linked with that of St Francis and the double Basilica di San Francesco is the town's greatest glory. A dramatic view of the basilica greets visitors on the approach road to the town. It was begun in 1228 and completed in 1253; the majestic series of 53 arches in two tiers, which supports the whole complex, was added in 1474 to shore up the subsiding structure.

The crypt-like lower church is covered in frescos whose fresh colours are only revealed when the eye adjusts to the gloom. The earliest, on the left-hand wall facing the altar, include St Francis preaching to the birds (1236). The first chapel on the left contains Simone Martini's lively scenes from the life of St Martin (1322–26) drawing parallels with the life of St Francis. Midway down, on the right, steps descend to the crypt where St Francis is buried.

The monumental Basilica di San Francesco

The vaults over the high altar are painted with four allegorical scenes (mid-13th century) of the founding principles of the Franciscan order. Chastity is portrayed as a maiden in a white tower, Poverty is a bride being given to St Francis in marriage, Obedience is a seated figure placing a yoke on the neck of a kneeling friar, and an enthroned saint represents the Glory of St Francis.

The left-hand transept contains Lorenzetti's damaged, but dramatic, *Crucifixion* (1320) and his *Madonna and Child*, called the Madonna of the Sunset because the evening sun enters through the window opposite to illuminate the gentle face of the Virgin. Cimabue's portrait of St Francis in the right-hand transept is considered a faithful likeness, corresponding to the description of his friend and biographer, Tommaso da Celano: 'a straight thin nose, ears jutting outward'.

The upper basilica, bright and well-lit, has a forceful impact after the gloom below. Cimabue's frescos in the apse now look like photographic negatives because of the oxidisation of the lead-based pigments, but his *Crucifixion* is still highly theatrical, contrasting the brutality of the crowd on the right of the cross with the grief of those on the left.

Giotto's frescos fill the lower walls on both sides of the nave. The 28 scenes, completed in 1300, tell the story of Francis's path to sainthood and are regarded as the mature work of an innovator who transformed the emphasis of Western art from iconographic representation to realism.

Assisi's main street, the Via di San Francesco, leads from the basilica to the main square, the Piazza del Comune, occupying the site of the Roman forum. Remains of the Roman basilica can be seen in the Museo Romano in the crypt of San Nicolo church (Via Portica 2). Above ground, the *pronaos*, or porch, of the Roman temple of Minerva, with six elegant Corinthian columns, stands on the left. Opposite is the Palazzo del Priori, the medieval palace of the governing council, still used as the town hall.

Via San Rufino leads from the square to the cathedral of San Rufino, a superb example of Umbrian Romanesque, dating from 1140. The façade is covered in lively sculptures and the central typanum shows Christ in Majesty flanked by St Rufino and the Virgin suckling the infant Christ. The font in the cathedral was used to baptise three future saints – Francis, Clare and her sister, Agnes – and Frederick II, the future Holy Roman Emperor, who was born prematurely outside the town in 1194.

Nearby Three Franciscan sites are an integral part of any visit to Assisi. San Damiano, where St Francis heard Christ speak from the cross, stands in olive groves 1.6km south of the town. This simple cloister was the home of St Clare for most of her life and the spot where she died is always marked by a vase of white flowers. A remarkable *Crucifixion* in the chapel, by Innocenzo di Palermo

(1637) has three expressions: anguish when the face is viewed from the left, tranquillity face-on and death when seen from the right.

Santa Maria degli Angeli is a vast baroque-domed church in the valley 6km south of Assisi covering the site of the first Franciscan community. The infirmary where St Francis died is now the Capella del Transito and the corridor leading to the cloisters has a small rose garden; these roses dropped their thorns when St Francis threw himself among them in self-chastisement and remain thornless to this day.

The Eremo delle Carceri, 5km east of the town, is a delightful hermitage. St Francis called this his favourite retreat and it remains a tranquil spot set among the holm-oak woods on the slopes of Monte Subásio.

GIOTTO'S FRESCOS

All the great Renaissance artists, from Masaccio on, came to study Giotto's frescos in Assisi and Vasari hailed him as the first to paint from nature. The artist found inspiration for his greatest masterpiece in the life of a saint who himself taught the world to appreciate nature's beauty. Giotto's figures are not as realistic as later artists were to achieve through the study of anatomy, but they are brought to life through expressive gestures: St Francis raising his arms to heaven in a gesture of trust in God, while the Bishop of Assisi hastens to cover his nakedness; the peasant, desperate with thirst, bending to drink from a spring brought forth by the prayers of St Francis. This, and his bold use of colour, made Giotto the greatest of medieval artists and a pioneer of the Renaissance.

TOWN WALK

Busy as it is with visitors, Assisi (map ref: 111 E3) still has many quiet and little-visited corners.

Start from the car park in Piazza Matteotti. Facing the police station, leave the square by the right-hand corner, taking the Via della Rocca, a lane which follows the town walls to the Rocca Maggiore.

1 The Rocca Maggiore, at the highest point of Assisi, commands superb views over the Tescio valley to the north and the Vale of Spoleto to the south. The first castle on this site was built by Frederick Barbarossa in 1174 and his grandson, Frederick II, spent some time here under the care of Duke Conrad of Urslingen. That castle was destroyed in an uprising against the Duke's tyrannical rule and the present structure was built by the papal legate, Cardinal Albornoz, in 1367.

Backtrack a short way down Via della Rocca, then take the first right along Via del Colle, which is no more than a track. Note the backward views to the cathedral and the Romanesque Torre del Comune, framed by groups of slender cypress trees. Take the first left to descend, via a stone staircase, to the Piazza del Comune.

2 The Piazza del Comune is surrounded by austere civic buildings, notably the Torre del Comune (Municipal Tower) of 1275 whose bells would warn of danger to the town, and the battlemented Palazzo del Capitano del Popolo next door (completed 1282), the medieval police and army headquarters. The 14th-century Palazzo dei Priori, opposite, is still the town hall and has a small art gallery on the first floor.

Enter the left-hand tunnel beneath this palazzo (Via Arco dei Priori) to reach the Chiesa Nuova.

3 The Chiesa Nuova was built in 1605 on the supposed site of the house where St Francis was born. Just inside the door is a cell in which St Francis was locked by his father as a punishment for stealing a bale of cloth; the future saint sold the cloth to pay for repairs to San Damiano church.

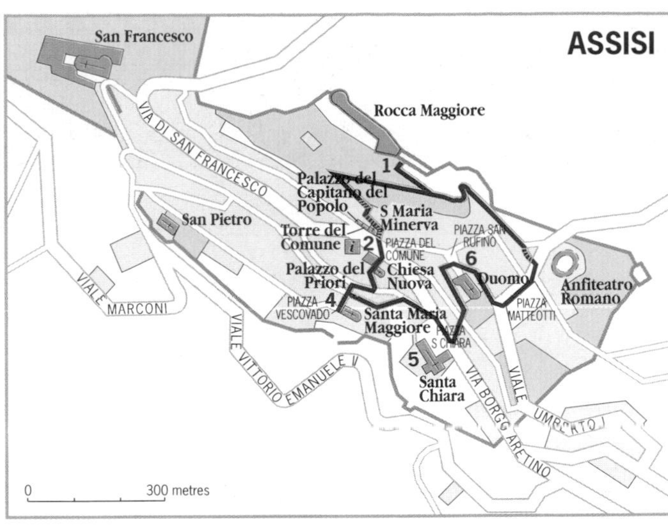

Continue down Via Arco dei Priori, turn right in Via Sant'Antonio and left into Piazza Vescovado.

4 On the left of the *piazza*, Santa Maria Maggiore once served as Assisi's cathedral. Built on top of a Roman temple to Janus, the crypt is early 4th century and the wheel window of the façade is dated 1163. In front of the Bishop's Palace next door, St Francis stripped off his clothes, renounced all possessions and set off into the Umbrian countryside to spark a revolution in the history of Christianity.

Leave the square by taking Via Sant'Agnese, which leads to Piazza Santa Chiara.

5 From the terrace of this square there are wonderful views over Santa Maria degli Angeli and the Vale of Spoleto. Santa Chiara was begun in 1257 and buttressed in the 14th century to prevent the walls from collapsing. St Clare's remains are housed in the crypt and the Capello del Crocifisso contains the 12th-century crucifix that spoke to St Francis, commanding him to rebuild the Church.

From Piazza Santa Chiara take Via Sermei, cross Via San Gabriele and go up Via Dono Doni to Piazza San Rufino.

6 The façade of San Rufino repays detailed study, especially the rose window supported by three comical caryatids, surrounded by symbols of the Evangelists, and the lunette above the central doorway, flanked by marble man-eating lions.

Via del Torrione, to the left of the cathedral, leads straight back to Piazza Matteotti.

·LAND OF SAINTS·

The Via Flaminia, built by the Romans in 220BC (today's N3) links Rome to the Adriatic port of Ancona. Along this road Syrian merchants brought the new religion of Christianity to Umbria, a region that subsequently gave birth to some of the most celebrated saints in Christendom.

St Rita of Cascia, the patron saint of battered wives

St Rufino (martyred in AD238) lies buried in the crypt of Assisi's cathedral and used to be the city's patron saint. His star was eclipsed in 1238 by the canonisation of St Francis, founder of the Franciscan order, patron saint of Italy and, since 1979, of ecology.

Francis was born in 1181, the son of a wealthy cloth merchant. Baptised Giovanni, he was nicknamed Francesco ('little Frenchman') because of his fondness for troubadour ballads (the medieval equivalent of today's pop songs) which he learned from his Provençal mother. He enjoyed fast living and spending his father's money, and he dreamed of gaining glory as a crusader. Illness put an end to his soldierly ambitions and turned him into a recluse. Praying in the church of San Damiano, just outside Assisi, he heard the voice of Christ speaking from the crucifix on the wall, commanding him: *Vade Francisce et repera domum meum* ('Go, Francis, and repair my house'). At first Francis took this command in its literal sense; he stole a bale of cloth from his father's warehouse and sold it to raise funds to rebuild the near-ruinous church of San Damiano. His father, angered by the theft and his son's apparent madness, dragged him before the Bishop of Assisi and demanded that Francis renounce his inheritance or see sense and return obediently to his home. Francis took off his clothes, handed them to his father and began his life as a wandering preacher, begging for alms and distributing them to the poor.

At the age of 29, having gathered a substantial band of followers, he sought permission to found the Franciscan order. Pope Innocent III agreed, but not without reluctance. New movements were springing up all over Europe, threatening the discipline and stability of the Church, and many of them were subsequently suppressed as heretical. The Franciscan emphasis on total poverty and charitable works contrasted unfavourably with the wealth and power of the 13th-century Church.

In fact, even before the end of his life, Francis saw his order split into two camps; those who adhered to the original rule of poverty and those who believed that the objective of succouring the poor was best achieved through an efficient, well-run fund-raising organisation. The latter wing was in the ascendancy, and its leader, Brother Elias, was a shrewd campaigner. Elias knew that Francis was likely to be canonised and that his shrine would become a popular destination for pilgrims; pilgrims meant money and he wanted that revenue to build the worldwide headquarters of a powerful order. Thus when Francis fell terminally ill in Siena,

Elias sent an armed escort to fetch him back to Assisi, where he died in 1226, aged 45, racked by the physical punishments he imposed upon himself in his thousands of miles of wandering in Italy, Spain and Egypt.

Francis asked to be buried outside Assisi on the Colle dell'Inferno, the Hill of Hell, among the graves of the poor and of executed criminals. His wish was granted, but only after Elias secured the hill as the site for his double basilica, intended to be one of the most splendid buildings in Christendom, and changed the hill's name to the Colle del Paradiso – Hill of Paradise. Funds poured in from the sale of indulgences (remission from purgatory 'sold' by the Church) and work on the basilica began in 1228. Three years later, after raiders from Perugia attempted to steal the body of St Francis from its temporary resting place in San Damiano, Elias decided it was time for the official funeral. On the 25 May 1230, crowds flocked to Assisi to watch the cortège, drawn by white oxen and covered in bouquets of wild flowers. Suddenly armed guards seized the coffin, bolted the doors and interred the body in secrecy to frustrate any future attempts to kidnap the holy remains. The exact location of the tomb remained undiscovered until 1818 when, after two months of excavation, it was finally revealed.

Today pilgrims of all religions and none come from the four corners of the world to see the awesome double basilica and to seek inspiration from the life of St Francis, who taught his followers to love all the creatures of God's creation, a message of particular contemporary relevance.

St Clare, another native of Assisi, was an early follower of St Francis. She founded the Poor Clares, a new order of Franciscan nuns, and was fanatical in her pursuit of poverty and privation. Her original rule, later modified as too strict, forbade the wearing of shoes and commanded the Poor Clares to fast permanently, sleep on the bare ground and never to speak except in prayer or to beg alms. She herself was a recluse who rarely left the confines of San Damiano in her 40 years as head of the order. There she received visions, for which she was singled out for a dubious honour; in 1938, Pope Pius XII declared her patron saint of television.

St Clare died in 1253 and the Basilica di Santa Chiara in Assisi was built as her shrine.

Deliberately modelled on the upper church of the Basilica di San Francesco, it was once covered in gorgeous frescos but these were whitewashed in the 17th century because visitors were disturbing the contemplative life of the nuns; some have subsequently been uncovered again.

Nórcia, the birthplace of St Benedict, has nothing but a statue in the main square to commemorate the founder of Western monasticism, a man who has been described as one of the architects of modern Europe. Benedict, born in AD480, kept alive the flame of Christianity and of classical learning through the dark decades of the barbarian invasions, through the monastic communities he founded at Subiaco and Monte Cassino. Pope Paul VI proclaimed Benedict patron saint of Europe in 1964 and said that the Benedictines, through their rule of work and prayer (*Ora et Labora*) had colonised the outer wildernesses of the continent, spreading civilisation from the Mediterranean to Scandinavia, from Ireland to Poland.

Not far south of Norcia, Cascia is another popular pilgrimage centre with a modern shrine, completed in 1947. This houses the uncorrupted remains of St Rita, who died in 1457 but was not canonised until 1900. She was forced into marriage with a man who abused her for 18 years before dying in a drunken brawl. Rita had set her heart on becoming a nun but was rejected because she was not a virgin. Finally the Augustinian order amended its rules, at her persistence, to allow widows to be accepted. Rita is patron saint of infertility, battered wives, parenthood and all those in desperate situations – a wide range of ills that guarantees her a constant stream of pilgrims and petitioners.

As you might expect in the birthplace of a saint, icons and religious statues proliferate

St Francis, the patron saint of Italy

Detail from San Michele, Bevagna

BEVAGNA

MAP REF: 111 E3

This unspoiled gem of a town is where St Francis is said to have preached his famous sermon to the birds on the theme that God provides for the humble sparrow and will look after men and women likewise if they are content with little. Bevagna was also the birthplace of the Roman love poet Propertius who described his native town as 'cloudy Mevania, standing among rain-soaked fields'. Roman *Mevania* was famous for breeding Umbria's sacred white bulls (still seen occasionally), highly prized as sacrificial victims. A well-preserved Roman mosaic of Triton, with an entourage of dolphins, seahorses and a lobster, is preserved in the basement of Via Porta Guelfa 2.

The town's delightful main square, Piazza Silvestri, has changed little in external appearance since the 13th century. A broad flight of steps leads up one side of the Palazzo dei Consoli, the town's most elegant building. Completed in 1270, this now houses the Teatro Tori, recently restored to its 19th-century glory. San Silvestro, alongside, has the date, 1195, and the name of the architect, Binelli, carved in the inscription to the right of the Romanesque portal. The same architect, partnered by Rodolfo, worked on San Michele opposite, with its lively angels thrusting a spear into the mouth of a dragon. The interior, restored in 1954 to its original 12th-century appearance, is pleasing in its ancient simplicity.

CASCIA

MAP REF: 111 F4

An earthquake in 1730 destroyed most of Cascia's ancient buildings but the shrine of St Rita, rebuilt in 1947, is a major pilgrimage centre. Many miracles have been attributed to this 15th-century patron saint of infertility and parenthood. Ten scenes from her life are carved in bold relief round the neo-Romanesque façade of the basilica and the interior is decorated with modern frescos and stained glass.

Nearby St Rita was born in the pretty hamlet of Roccaporena, to the west of Cascia, magnificently sited below limestone crags with extensive views. This hamlet, and nearby Capanne di Collegiacone, are good departure points for gentle walking among the surrounding mountain pastures.

CASTIGLIONE DEL LAGO

MAP REF: 111 D3

A fortified promontory jutting out from the western shore of Lake Trasimeno, Castiglione del Lago (literally, 'the Lion Castle on the Lake') is now a popular holiday resort, with several beaches and lakeside fish restaurants. The ramparts of the medieval castle offer extensive lake views. A long covered passageway leads from the castle to the Palazzo Comunale, once the ducal palace of the della Corgna family who ruled the territory around the lake on behalf of the papacy until the 17th century. Superb late Renaissance frescos of mythological scenes, by Salvio Savini, decorate its ceilings.

Nearby Panicale's charming central piazza and fountain offer a welcome escape from the holiday bustle of Lake Trasimeno. The fountain runs with wine during the Festa della Torta di Pasqua festival in April. San Sebastiano church contains one of Perugino's finest works, a fresco of the martyrdom of St Sebastian (1505).

Elegant buildings surround Bevagna's Piazza Silvestri

Cascia is a major pilgrimage centre

The saint looks rapturously to heaven while the archers strike balletic poses. Viewed through a classical portico, the background to the fresco is one of those beautiful, limpid Umbrian landscapes that are the trademark of this artist.

CITTÀ DELLA PIEVE

MAP REF: 111 D3

More Tuscan than Umbrian in character, Città della Pieve was the birthplace of Pietro Vannucci, better known as Perugino because he spent much of his artistic career working in Perugia. Three of his works can be seen in his native town. The Church of Santa Maria di Bianchi has his *Adoration of the Magi* (1504), one of the artist's best and most characteristic works. The serene pastoral background depicts Lake Trasimeno and the sky is suffused with the first light of dawn. Part of a *Deposition* (1517) survives in Santa Maria dei Servi and San Antonio Abate has *St Anthony with St Marcellus and Paul the Hermit* (1517).

PERUGINO

Although harshly treated by art critics, Perugino is regarded as the greatest of Umbrian painters. Vasari portrayed him as irreligious and mean-spirited; a man who grew wealthy but carried all his money on his person. Later critics say that he painted too long; in the last 20 years of his career (spanning 70 years) he was unable to paint all the works that were commissioned and he would sometimes put his signature to the second-rate work of pupils.

All this obscures the fact that Perugino was a brilliant innovator. He developed techniques for using the minimum amount of pigment, by contrast with his lavishly colourful contemporaries, to capture the limpid ultramarines of the Umbrian sky. Wonderful lighting effects suffuse his landscapes as a symbol of religious spirituality. His greatest work, in the Collegio di Cambio, Perugia, illustrates the continuity between Christian and pagan classical thought.

CITTÀ DI CASTELLO

MAP REF: 111 D4

There is more to Città di Castello than appears from the industrial estates that ring the town. The art gallery is housed in the Palazzo Vitelli from whose upper windows, it is said, Laura Vitelli used to throw rejected lovers to their death. The collection is one of the best in Umbria and includes Signorelli's *Martyrdom of St Sebastian* and Ghirlandaio's *Coronation of the Virgin*.

The Palazzo Albizzini houses the Burri Collection; Alberto Burri, who still lives and works in the town, is Italy's foremost abstract artist. He began making collages from discarded material as a prisoner-of-war. His main aim is to produce aesthetically pleasing objects out of humble materials, including old sacks and plastic.

The Labatoria Tela Umbra in Piazza Costa is a handloom factory set up by an American philanthropist in 1908 to keep alive the skills of local weavers. Città di Castello is also famous for its canoeists. Every April the town hosts an international 8-day canoe race down the Tiber to Rome.

DERUTA

MAP REF: 111 E3

Located south of Perugia, on a picturesque stretch of the Tévere (Tiber) Valley, Deruta is devoted to the production and sale of majolica. The long main street is lined with workshops and showrooms selling reproductions of Renaissance pieces (*reproduzione* or *tradizione*) and contemporary designs (*artistiche* or *moderne*). The history of the local industry is traced in the Museo Regionale della Ceramica in the Palazzo Comunale.

Nearby The walls of the little church of Madonna di Bagno (just south of Deruta) are covered in votive majolica tiles offered by supplicants to the Virgin Mary. This tradition dates back to 1657 when a local merchant offered a tile, painted with an image of the Virgin, and prayed for his terminally ill wife. Her recovery encouraged other miracle seekers to offer painted tiles that illustrate the whole range of human misfortunes, including fire, flood and motor accidents. The tiles provide a fascinating glimpse into everyday hazards and tragedies from the 17th century to the present day, though because of recent thefts this church is often locked when not in use for services.

At Torgiano, 7km north of Deruta, the Museo del Vino is devoted to all aspects of the Umbrian wine industry from Roman times to the present.

Old earthenware pottery from the area around Lake Trasimeno

A worker in majolica ware from Deruta

DERUTAN MAJOLICA

The city of Faenza dominated ceramic production in Italy from the 13th century and sought to keep the formulae for tin glaze applied over bright underglaze colours a secret. Laws forbidding potters to leave the city were often broken, however, as they sought new markets all over Europe. In Deruta they found deposits of the silicate clay they needed for their work and production began here as early as 1387. The earliest pieces show the influence of Faenza in their colours and designs but Derutan potters had developed their own style by the 16th century, specialising in large plates and vases with heavy relief moulding. Grotesque ornaments, fruit and foliage swags are typical Derutan motifs and the predominant colours are a rich deep yellow and turquoise blue. Derutan ceramics have found their way into leading museums, from the Louvre in paris to the Hermitage in St Petersburg.

GUALDO TADINO

MAP REF: 111 E3

Roman *Tadinum* was founded as a staging post along the Via Flaminia, but the town was all but destroyed by Totila the Goth when his forces swept south to Rome. Totila later met his end beneath the ruined walls of the city, killed by the Roman commander Narses in AD552. Not long afterwards the Lombards founded a new city on a hill above the plain and called it Gualdo Tadino, from *wald*, meaning wooded. The town's imposing fortress, the Rocca Flea, was built under the rule of Frederick II and when restored will reopen as a museum and cultural centre. In the meantime the town's artistic treasures are displayed in the church of San Francesco. The *Madonna with Saints* fresco (1477) in the apse is the work of the local artist, Matteo da Gualdo, and the altarpiece (1471) by Niccolò Alunno is regarded as one of his finest works. The town specialises in hand-painted pottery and reproductions of Etruscan black-burnished *bucchera* vases, as well as tasty *soppressata* (compressed sausages).

Nearby The Via Flaminia (N3) north of Gualdo Tadino runs parallel to the plateau-like summit of one of Umbria's highest mountains, Monte Cucco (1,566m). It is possible to drive almost to the summit on the road from Sigillo. The mountain meadows are a popular picnic spot. The same road passes Ranco di Sigillo and the entrance to an extensive cave system. One of the more accessible caves, the Grotta di Monte Cucco, is open on occasions in summer.

MOTOR TOUR

Lake Trasimeno is peninsular Italy's largest freshwater lake. It has an average depth of 8m and survived attempts by Caesar and Napoleon to drain it. Today it is Umbria's summertime playground, ringed by campsites and water-sports centres. This 60km circuit of the lake takes in the most interesting sights and can be combined with a boat trip to Isola Maggiore.

Start at Castiglione del Lago.

Castiglione del Lago
The town's castle and cathedral make an impressive silhouette, jutting out into the lake. The Palazzo Comunale's heroic frescos were painted to glorify the name of the della Corgna dukes who once controlled all the lands surrounding Lake Trasimeno.

Drive north along the SS71 for 8km and turn right to Borghetto, a peaceful fishing village on the Tuscan/Umbrian border. Continue along the country road that runs parallel to the Florence/Perugia autostrada *for 8km to Tuoro sul Trasimeno.*

Tuoro sul Trasimeno
Tuoro is famous for the Battle of Lake Trasimeno in 217BC when Rome suffered the greatest defeat in its entire history, at the hands of Hannibal. The cry of *Hannibal ante portas* (Hannibal at the gates!) rang through the streets of

Rome as the river in the valley below Tuoro ran red with the blood of slaughtered soldiers; thereafter the battle site was known as Sanguineto (the place of blood). History buffs can read an absorbing account of the battle in Livy's *History of Rome*. A 'learning trail', starting in Tuoro, guides visitors round the battleground.

Continue 6km to Passignano sul Trasimeno.

Passignano sul Trasimeno

Passignano is the lake's main watersports centre. White cruisers also leave from here for Isola Maggiore, passing the privately owned Isola Minore on the way. Isola Maggiore's tiny harbour village is home to some of the last remaining lacemakers of the region. The high point of the island is crowned by the 14th-century church of San Michele Arcangelo. Boats also leave from Passignano for Isola Polvese, the largest of the lake's islands, with its ruined castle and fine beaches.

As an alternative to the boat trip, art lovers should visit two nearby churches. Continue round the lake for 4km and turn left for San Vito with its 13th-century Romanesque church. Continue 6km to Castèl Rigone for the superb Renaissance church of Madonna dei Miracoli, with its graceful façade carvings of 1512, the work of Domenico Bertini.

Continue along the SS75bis for 8km to Magione.

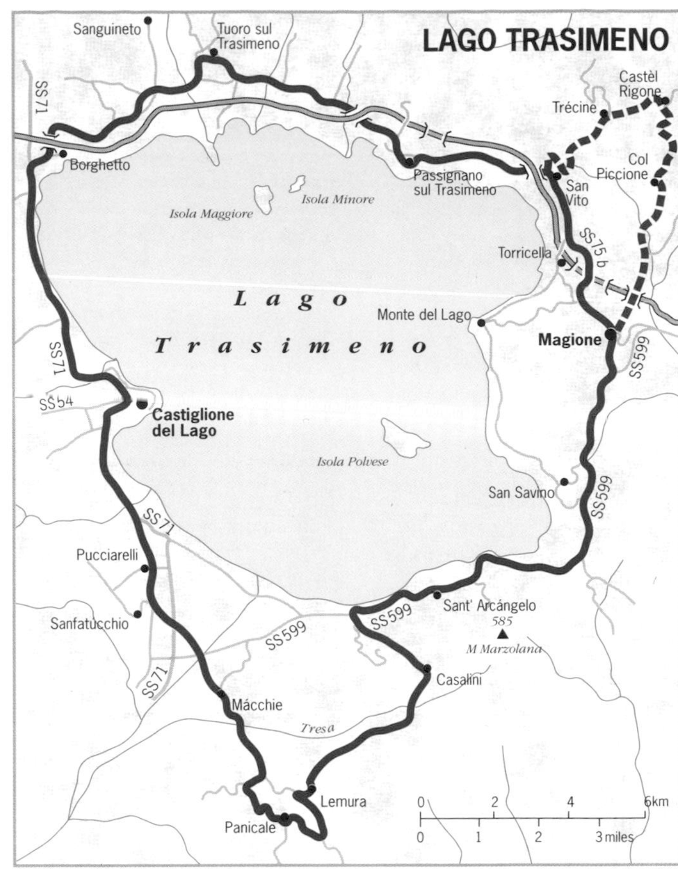

Magione

Magione has two imposing fortifications, part of a chain that once ringed the lake. The Torre dei Lombardi is an unmissable landmark, built around 1200 and now under restoration following an earthquake in 1846. The Castello dei Cavalieri di Malta began as a hospice of the Knights Templar and the original pilgrims' chapel contains School of Pinturicchio frescos. The hospice was fortified in 1420 and turned into one of the most picturesque castles in Umbria.

The 13th-century explorer, Friar Giovanni del Pian di Capine, was born in the town and a fresco in the Palazzo Comunale shows him kneeling before the Emperor of the Mongols. In 1245, Giovanni was sent as papal ambassador to the Great Khan and spent 18 years in Asia. He wrote an account of his travels, the *Historia Mongolorum*, which paved the way for Marco Polo's more famous journey.

Continue southwards on the SS599. After 15km a left turn leads to the tranquil hilltop town of Panicale. From there, follow the signs north for Castiglione del Lago, which will be reached after 20km.

Busy Lake Trasimeno

The beautiful lofty 'town hall' of Gúbbio, the Palazzo dei Consoli, was begun in 1332

GÚBBIO

MAP REF: 111 E4

Gúbbio was once dubbed 'the city of silence' by the poet d'Annunzio because it was so isolated. Now it is bustling, accessible and famous for its ceramics. Of the Roman town of *Iguvium* the well-preserved amphitheatre survives in the plain and is still used for summer performances. The city, refounded higher up the slopes of Monte Ingino after it was sacked by the Goths, is built on a series of dramatic cliff-like terraces, with vertiginous views from the narrow main square, the Piazza della Signoria.

The western side of the square is filled by the noble Palazzo dei Consoli whose vast barrel-vaulted council chamber is used to display ancient masonry fragments. These include medieval toilet seats, as Gúbbio was one of the first cities in Umbria to organise a domestic water supply, piped to individual houses. The famous Eugubine tablets are displayed in the gallery above and there is a stunning view over the rooftops of Gúbbio from the 16th-century *loggia*, reached through a side door off the main hall of the gallery.

A cable car, located alongside the Church of Sant'Agostino, goes to the summit of Monte Ingino (827m) and the Basilica di Sant'Ubaldo. This houses the great wooden candles that are carried in the Corsa dei Ceri (Race of the Candles) festival in May. The route of this endurance test can be traced by returning to Gúbbio on foot down the steep lane called Via Sant'Ubaldo.

TOWN WALK

Begin at the cathedral, on Via Sant'Ubaldo.

1 The serenity of the cathedral is emphasised by the 10 great Gothic arches that focus on the 13th-century stained-glass saints of the east window. The greatest treasure of the church, held in the adjacent Museo Capitolare, is a 16th-century Flemish cope embroidered with scenes from the Passion. It was given by Pope Marcellus, a native of Gúbbio.

2 Next door, the Palazzo Ducale (under restoration) was built in 1476 by Frederico, Duke of Urbino, who was invited to defend the town when its citizens revolted against papal rule. It stands on the site of an earlier Lombardic palace where Charlemagne stayed after being crowned Holy Roman Emperor.

The Giardino Pensile, opposite the palace, offers fine views over the town. Coming out of the garden, turn right in Via Ducale and take the first left down a steep staircase to the Piazza della Signoria.

3 The Palazzo dei Consoli is one of Umbria's more ornate town halls, with its fan staircase and façade arcading. On the right of the façade, however, is a grim iron cage where criminals were once exposed to ridicule and the searing ferocity of the sun.

Walk down Via dei Consoli, to the right of the palazzo, to the Bargello.

4 The 13th-century Bargello served as a prison and it has a *porta del morto* to the left of the façade. Tradition has it that these 'doors of the dead' were only unblocked for the passage of coffins. In fact they originally led to the living quarters; at night the wooden steps could be withdrawn and the narrow entrance firmly barred. Any attacker who entered through the much wider main gate would find themselves in a courtyard where they could be bombarded from above.

The Fontana dei Matti (Fountain of Fools) in front of the Bargello got its name from the belief that a person would go mad after walking round it three times. The young men of the town, calling themselves madmen of Gúbbio, wade around the basin on highdays and holidays.

Take the Via Camignano, alongside the pretty river of the same name, and cross the bridge at the junction with Via Cristini to emerge in the wide, oval-shaped Piazza Quaranta Martiri, named after 40 women and children murdered here in 1944 by the retreating Nazis. .

5 The Loggia dei Tiratori, the Weavers' Loggia, on the north side of the square, was built in the

14th-century to protect cloth, washed in the nearby river, from the heat of the sun as it dried.

6 San Francesco, on the north side of the square, is a delicate 13th-century church built to commemorate one of the miracles of St Francis; he tamed a wolf that had been terrorising the town. Outstanding early Renaissance frescos on the *Life of the Virgin* cover the walls of the north aisle apse, the work of Ottaviano Nelli. The cloister shop displays locally made ceramics, for which the town has been famous since the 16th century when Giorgio Andreoli discovered a formula for making ruby-red glazes.

From San Francesco, cross the wide Piazza dei Mercato to Via Reposati and turn left up Via Cairoli, the main shopping street, where more ceramics shops will be found.

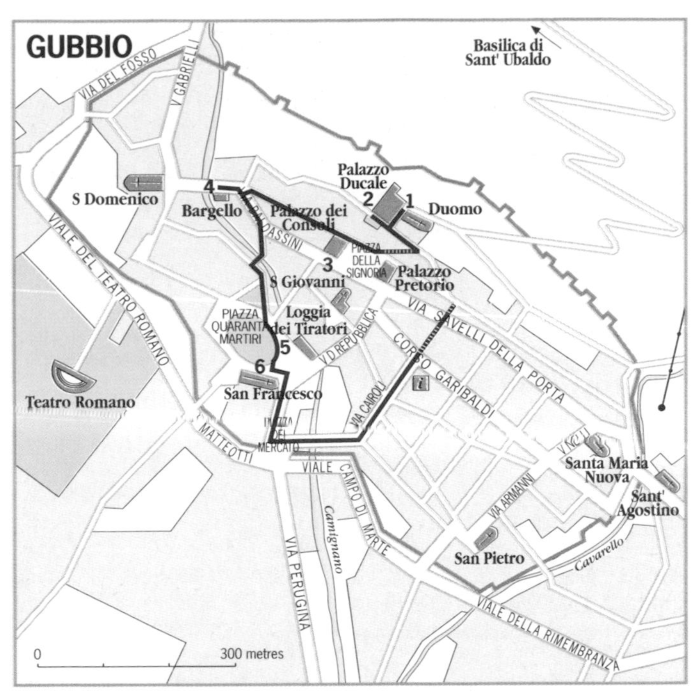

THE EUGUBINE TABLETS

The Eugubine Tablets are the pride of Gúbbio's art gallery. Though not much to look at, these seven bronze tablets, ploughed up outside the town in 1444, contain nearly all we know of the ancient Umbrian language. The earliest of the tablets dates from the 3rd century BC and contains details of the rites observed by a local college of priests, the Attiedi. Together the tablets contain sacrificial instructions, the names of native gods, prayers, and instructions on the correct form of words for casting a curse against enemy tribes.

LUGNANO IN TEVERINA

MAP REF: 111 D2

High above the Tévere (Tiber) Valley, this sleepy town has an outstanding Romanesque church complete with marble *ambones*, pulpits for the reading of the epistle and gospel, and an altar screen carved with the Archangel Michael destroying the dragon. The Byzantine arrangement suggests the influence of Ravenna, on the Adriatic coast.

Nearby To the north of Lugnano lies Guardea, with its castle ruins, once the stronghold of the only English pope, Adrian IV, and the 15th-century castle at Alviano, now a fine museum of rural life. The castle once belonged to Donna Olimpia, sister-in-law of Pope Innocent X. She was so notorious for her sexual appetites and political manoeuvring that her effigy was burned by Protestants all over 17th-century Europe as a symbol of Catholic excess.

To the south of Lugnano is Amélia, ringed by massive walls dating from the 5th century BC. Pliny dated the city's foundation to 1134BC, making it 300 years older than Rome. Tiny gateways pierce the walls leading to steep cobbled alleys that convey a sense of great antiquity. Two of the town's churches – San Francesco and the cathedral – contain 15th-century tombs carved with fine bas reliefs by Agostino di Duccio.

St Francis once rid the tough mountain town of Gúbbio of a plague of wolves, so the story goes

MONTEFALCO

MAP REF: 111 E3

Fine views over the dried-up lake bed of the Vale of Spoleto have earned Montefalco (Falcon Mountain) the nickname *ringhiera* (balcony) of Umbria. The town is equally famous for its full-bodied red wines. The Church of Santa Chiara is dedicated to the local saint (not the founder of the Poor Clares) who died here in 1308. A tree growing in the adjacent convent grew from a staff given to St Clare by Christ in a dream. The nuns make rosary beads from the dried berries.

The artistic highlight of the town is San Francesco, converted to a museum of art. It contains the outstanding St Francis fresco cycle by the Florentine artist Benozzo Gozzoli, painted between 1450 and 1452. Florentine trademarks are the stunning colour and realistic background detail. The Palazzo Vecchio in Florence can be identified as the 'church' in the vision of St Francis below the central window and Montefalco itself features in the scene on the right where St Francis preaches to the birds.

Two *gonfalone* (painted banners for use in religious processions), previously housed in the south aisle, have been moved, along with other free-standing paintings, to a new two-storey gallery wing, adjacent to the church. They depict the Madonna del Soccorso, the Madonna of Emergencies. According to a local story, she came to the rescue of a distraught mother who had wished her child to the devil – who duly turned up and snatched the child. This Madonna is a mighty club-wielding giantess from Umbrian folklore, rather than the tender Virgin that is depicted in most religious paintings: more than a match for any devil,

NARNI

MAP REF: 111 E2

Ancient Narni stands aloof from its industrial offspring, Narni Scalo, located in the valley below.

Entering the town just after the N3 road tunnel, look left for a view of the Ponte d'Augusto, the single remaining arch of the Roman bridge that carried the Via Flaminia. The cathedral stands just off the broad Piazza Garibaldi, on the Via Garibaldi.

Opposite, the Via del Monte leads up through the medieval quarter to the Rocca Albornoz, a papal castle built in the 1370s, with fine views over the Nera Valley.

The Romanesque cathedral is dedicated to St Juvenalis whose feastday is celebrated in May in the nearby Piazza dei Priori by the Festa dell'Anello; costumed horsemen compete to thrust their lances through a metal hoop in a display of skill that dates back to the Middle Ages when the town was famed for its soldiers.

Jousting knights feature on the 12th-century reliefs set into the façade of the Palazzo del Podestà, along with mysterious scenes depicting a beheading and a falconer. The museum on the first floor houses Ghirlandaio's tender *Coronation of the Virgin* (1486) and Lo Spagna's fresco of St Francis receiving the stigmata.

Further down, on Via Mazzini, is the Church of Santa Maria in Pensole, with Christ in Majesty on the façade, dating from 1175, and San Domenico, now a museum that contains Benozzo Gozzoli's charming *Annunciation*.

Nearby Otrícoli lies south of Narni on the border with Lazio. The extensive remains of the Roman river port of *Otriculum* survive just to the south. The ruins were painted by Turner. Pius VI looted the best statues and mosaics for the Vatican Museum in 1776, since when decay has set in. Soon, however, they are to be restored to form an 'archaeological park'.

MOTOR TOUR

This 68km tour of the Nera Valley, or Valnerina, takes in some of Umbria's least visited countryside, including the remote 8th-century monastery of San Pietro in Valle. Some of the fiercest battles of the Middle Ages were fought here between the rebellious peoples of the mountain communes and repressive armies of either pope or emperor. According to one theory, the name of the river Nera comes from the Greek *nar*, meaning fierce or vehement; a word that could apply equally to the region's inhabitants and to the rushing river itself, which has cut several deep gorges through the valley's limestone.

Cerreto, the town at the northern head of the valley, also gave us the word charlatan. The natives of Cerreto, the Cerretani, were originally licensed to sell herbal remedies to raise funds for Church hospitals; by the mid-15th century, the word was being used to describe swindlers of all types, who roamed at large acting as quack doctors and faith healers.

Starting in Spoleto, take the N3 north; just after emerging from the Monteluco tunnel take the SS395 right, up to the Forca di Cerro and down through Grotti to Geppa.

Geppa

Geppa has one of the region's numerous *castelli*, constructed to guard the routes in and out of the valley during the turbulent 13th to

Narni, one of Umbria's most splendid hill towns

15th centuries. Geppa's castle is better preserved than most and there are fine views to the opposite side of the valley, an area of dense woodland and high pasture where Apennine wolves still roam. The area is now protected as a national park.

Continue on the SS395 to Piedipaterno and turn right on the SS209.

Vallo di Nera

Further fortified villages dot the route. Vallo di Nera has a well-preserved *torre* which originally had no ground floor entrance; access was by ladder to a small doorway high above the ground. One of the region's rebel leaders, Petrone di Vallo, came from here. He led the Valnerina's final revolt against papal rule in 1522. It took a force of 7,000 troops to defeat his small band of followers, and Petrone's head was paraded through Spoleto on a pike as a warning to other would-be revolutionaries.

Continue on the SS209 south through Scheggino, home of the Urbani family whose truffle-processing business supplies 40 per cent of the world market. Eight kilometres after Scheggino, turn right up a cypress-lined avenue to San Pietro in Valle.

San Pietro in Valle

The monastery is set in an idyllic location below the wooded summit of Monte Fironchi, reputed to be the site of the first legendary city of the ancient Umbrians, Umbriano. The Lombardic Duke of Spoleto, Faroaldo II, founded the monastery in AD703 and his original church was incorporated into the present building when it was enlarged in the 11th century. The church contains five Roman sarcophagi, carved with mythological scenes, reused as tombs by Lombardic dukes. The main altar is a rare example of Lombardic sculpture, dated AD742; the inscription records that it was carved by Ursus as the tomb of Duke Hildericus Dagileopa; both men are depicted on the altar front beneath a tree of life. The walls of the nave are covered in 12th-century frescos of the Creation and Life of Christ. Art historians regard them as an outstanding example of an emerging Italian – as distinct from Byzantine – style of painting. The main church and frescos were closed for restoration during 1991 and are expected to reopen at the end of 1992.

Return to the SS209 and continue south for 5km to Ferentillo.

Ferentillo

Ferentillo consists of two villages either side of the SS209; Matterella on the right and Precetto on the left. Both sides of the valley are guarded by a medieval curtain wall with lookout towers funnelling all travellers through the valley bottom where the legitimacy of their business could be checked. Some passers-by got no further. The crypt of San Stefano church, in Precetto, contains several mummified bodies, including those of Chinese visitors who died here of cholera, and a stray soldier. Their eerie corpses, like props from a horror movie, date from the 19th century and were preserved by the dessicating effects of the biting winds that howl through the valley in winter.

Continue south along the SS209 for 5km and turn right to Montefranco, worth a stop for the hilltop fortress and wonderful woodland setting. Continue to the summit of this mountain road, turn left then right to descend to the N3, a distance of 8km. On the N3 turn right to return to Spoleto after 17km.

The town of Ferentillo is dominated by twin citadels

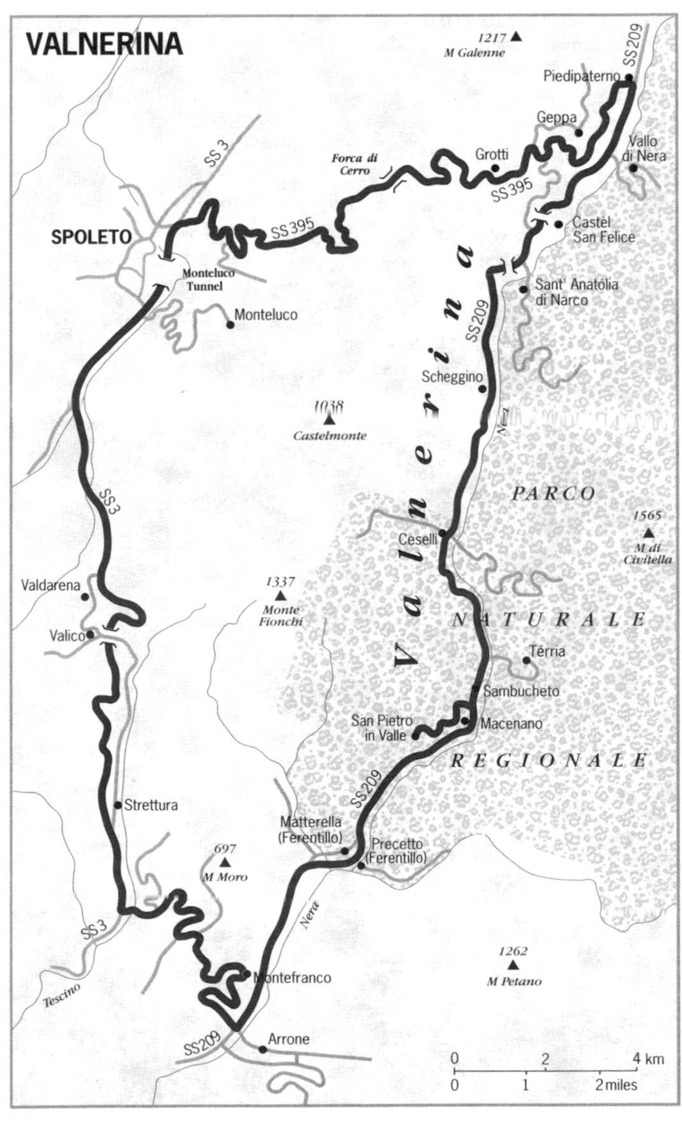

NÓRCIA

MAP REF: 111 F3

Nórcia was the birthplace of St Benedict, founder of Western monasticism. Unlike Assisi, which honoured St Francis with a splendid basilica, Nórcia has nothing but a statue in the main square to commemorate its most famous son. The town is far more preoccupied with its reputation as a centre for the processing and curing of pork. The Piazza San Benedetto is ringed by *norcinerie*, butchers' shops selling locally produced *prosciutto,* and numerous varieties of salami, ranging from strings of tiny sausages to great meat-filled balloons.

The modern appearance of Nórcia owes much to a series of violent earthquakes. After the destructive tremor of 1859 an edict was issued setting a maximum building height of 12.5m. Many buildings still show signs of damage from the last earthquake which occurred in 1979. Others have been modernised recently to provide homes for winter visitors. Nórcia is developing as a ski resort and in a good year snow remains on the surrounding mountains until June (Virgil called the town *frigida Nursia* – icy Nórcia).

The centre of Nórcia has a certain rough charm. The Church of San Benedetto has an elegant Gothic portal and a geometric window inserted after the 1859 earthquake. The crypt is built against the foundations of a Roman temple on the spot where St Benedict is supposed to have been born in AD480. The altarpiece depicts the meeting between St Benedict and Totila the Goth. Next to the church, the Palazzo Communale dates in part from the 14th century. The squat Castellina opposite, built in 1554 as a papal stronghold, contains a small museum with some rare 13th-century wooden figures of saints.

The town's most appealing building is the Edicola on the corner of Via Umberto. This 14th-century tower is carved with masonic tools, the sun, Christ the Lamb, the Instruments of the Passion and complex geometrical patterns. Nobody knows what purpose the building originally served, but it may have been built by a local trade guild.

The Quartiere Capolaterra (Shepherds' Quarter) lies to the north of the Edicola and although many of the houses lining the narrow alleys have been redeveloped, some ancient houses still survive with winter quarters for the sheep on the ground floor and tiny rooms above.

Nearby The Abbazia di San Eutizio, north of Nórcia near Preci, was one of the first Benedictine monasteries and began life as a mountain hermitage. The Romanesque church and campanile, built in 1190, is one of the region's most impressive sights.

Castellúccio is a lonely village of less than 100 inhabitants standing to the east of Nórcia on the rim of the Piano Grande (the Great Plain); Franco Zeffirelli used the village and its dramatic surroundings as the location for his film, *Brother Sun, Sister Moon*, based on the life of St Francis. The empty plain is 8km long, flat as a football pitch and bleak in winter; on the worst days bells are rung in Castellúccio to guide travellers home. In summer the grassland is one continuous flower meadow, and rare alpine plants are found on the surrounding slopes.

The area around Castellúccio is developing as a sports centre, frequented by skiers in winter, hang-gliders and walkers in summer. It is still, though, a working village that seems uncertain whether it wants the attention of tourists. Castellúccio's farmers grow tiny, sweet-tasting lentils that are famous all over Italy; these can be sampled in the simple village restaurant.

The town of Nórcia is crammed with butchers' shops

ST BENEDICT AND TOTILA THE GOTH

The altarpiece in San Benedetto Church in Nórcia, painted by Filippo Napoletano in 1621, illustrates the meeting in AD542 between St Benedict and Totila the Goth, the two greatest men of their age. Totila had heard that Benedict was gifted with prophetic powers. According to the account given by Pope Gregory in his *Dialogues*, Totila first sent one of his soldiers, called Riggo, to impersonate him. Benedict greeted the purple-robed Riggo with the words 'Put off those robes, my son, for they do not belong to you'.

Totila himself then came to see Benedict and prostrated himself before the saint. They spent much time in conversation, during which Benedict tried to persuade the leader of the Goths to abandon his destructive onslaught on Europe. The meeting ended with Benedict's prophecy that Totila would succeed in sacking Rome but would die within ten years and not enjoy his conquest – a prediction that indeed came true.

It is said that San Bernadetto is built on the site of Benedict's birth

THE BUTCHERS OF NÓRCIA

Nórcia has been an important centre of pig-rearing since the Middle Ages and the Nórcians claim to have invented salami. Whether this is true or not, Italian recipe books contain several fine pork dishes bearing the name *alla Nórcina* and pork butchers all over Italy are called *norcini*. The town was also once famed for its surgeons and claims, more controversially, that the word *nursino*, nurse, pays tribute to the medical skills of former inhabitants. Their speciality was castration, the fate inflicted on gifted young boy singers to provide a supply of *castrato* voices for the court choirs of the nobility and papacy.

COUNTRY WALK

The landscape around Castellúccio is one of great natural beauty which invites exploration on foot. This gentle walk from Castellúccio goes northwards to the spring at San Lorenzo and back, a distance of 8km.

Leave Castellúccio on the road east that descends to the Piano Grande. After 200m, beyond a couple of caravans used as as a makeshift café serving coffee to walkers, the metalled road bends right; carry straight on along the unmetalled track, waymarked route number 2. Follow this track for 2.5km, to Capanna Ghezzi. Here the track stops but a footpath to the left, marked *Sentiero* (route) 5, leads for just under 0.7km, through a wood to the San Lorenzo spring, on the right just as you emerge from the wood.

On the outward walk the view is of the Monti Sibillini range, part of the Apennine chain, so called because the prophetic Sybil is said to have retreated from her cave at Cumae, near Naples, to these remote heights. In spring and summer look out for tiny alpine campanulas and other plants where the grass has been cropped by sheep; in the longer grass look for sky-blue chicory, small pink convolvulus, perennial sweet pea and pink and white flowered mallows, as well as the butterflies that feed on them. At the woodland margin there may be hellebores and spurges.

Retracing your steps, the view to the left is of Monte Vettore. Rising to 2,476m, its steep escarpment is scored by mountain streams. It forms part of Umbria's eastern boundary with the Marches. Ahead, like a vast amphitheatre, lies the Piano Grande. In early summer this is literally a mass of scarlet poppies, blue cornflower, white campion and yellow hawkweed.

The Piano Grande, a flat meadow above Nórcia

·ORVIETO·

Viewed from a distance, Orvieto (map ref: 111 D2) is a thrilling sight. Brown cliffs rise from the floor of the Paglia Valley to the high volcanic plateau on which the city sits, backed by vineyard-covered hills that produce the region's crisp white wines. The cliffs that fall away from the city walls are eroding to the extent that it is forbidden to build around the *rupe*, or plateau edge. Vehicle vibrations are adding to the problem and there is a plan to ban traffic from the city. Visitors will then park in Orvieto Scalo, the modern lower town, and take a hydraulically operated funicular railway up to the medieval city.

Orvieto's cathedral is the best of its period in Italy. The exterior, of narrow alternating bands of white travertine and dove-grey tufa, is unmistakably Pisan Romanesque style and the work of the Sienese architect, Lorenzo Maitani.

The cathedral was built to commemorate the Miracle of Bolsena and the foundation stone was laid in 1290 at a critical point in the development of medieval architecture. Gothic was just becoming fashionable and work on the cathedral, planned in Romanesque style, ground to a halt until Maitani was brought in to graft a new Gothic design onto the partly built structure.

The skill with which Maitani achieved this is most evident on the magnificent façade. Here he disguised the massive Romanesque piers of the portal by covering them in bas reliefs of astonishing virtuosity. Over 150 different sculptors worked on these intricate scenes starting in 1310 (some of them are covered with perspex because of repeated vandalism). From left to right they illustrate Genesis, the stories of Abraham and David, the life of Christ and the Last Judgement.

The wheel window above, completed about 1380, is surrounded by busts of saints and mosaic figures of the Four Doctors of the Church.

The interior is calm and serene. Pews have been removed to provide an uninterrupted view across the sun-dappled floor of ox-blood covered marble to the 14th century stained glass of the east window. Unfortunately for the visitor, Signorelli's outstanding frescos of the Apocalypse are currently closed off while they undergo restoration. They are due to be reopened at the end of 1992.

A small exhibition in the cathedral reminds visitors of the force of these most extraordinary and frightening scenes, in which Cesare Borgia is portrayed as the Antichrist and metal-winged monsters carry off the damned to a nightmare world of torture and eternal fire. Signorelli painted his cycle betwen 1497 and 1504. Few painters have so brilliantly expressed the sense of the world coming to an end in total chaos, with twisted bodies flying everywhere as if the law of gravity itself had suddenly ceased. Michelangelo was deeply impressed; he copied Signorelli's brilliantly foreshortened perspective to create his own masterpiece, the Sistine Chapel ceiling.

Detail on the cathedral façade

THE MIRACLE OF BOLSENA

The little town of Bolsena stands on the eastern shore of the lake of the same name, 21km southwest of Orvieto. In 1264 it was visited by a Bohemian priest travelling to Rome to resolve his doubts over the doctrine of transubstantiation. Celebrating mass in the town, the communion host turned to flesh and drops of blood fell on the altar cloth. Pope Urban IV instituted the feast of Corpus Christi as a result and Orvieto's cathedral was built to house the precious blood-stained cloth.

The cathedral – one of Italy's finest

TOWN WALK

Begin with the Museo Civico facing the cathedral on the opposite side of Piazza del Duomo.

1 The museum contains some of the best Etruscan material in Umbria, much of it excavated from tombs dug into the soft tufa cliffs below Orvieto. Upstairs, the Claudio Faino collection consists entirely of Greek and Etruscan painted vases. (The Museo dell'Opera del Duomo, alongside the cathedral, contains important sculptures and paintings, but is temporarily closed for restoration).

Take Via Maitani, beside the museum. At the Church of San Francesco turn left in Via Ippolito Scalza to reach San Lorenzo di Arari.

2 Arari means altar, and the altar of this tiny church, set beneath a 12th-century canopy, is a cylindrical stone drum which once served as an Etruscan sacrificial slab. The colourful frescos, dating from 1330, depict four scenes from the life of St Lawrence and his martyrdom by grilling.

Retrace your steps to the cathedral square and turn left to walk up Via del Duomo where galleries selling ceramics, antiques and works of art provide ample scope for browsing. Turn left in the pedestrianised Corso Cavour.

3 Corso Cavour is Orvieto's main shopping street. Where it joins the Piazza della Repubblica there is an elegant 16th-century *loggia* that now serves as a flower market. Close by is the polygonal campanile of the Church of Sant'Andrea. Pope Innocent III launched the Fourth Crusade from here in 1216. The crypt incorporates Etruscan and Roman masonry.

Backtrack up Corso Cavour and take the first left, Via dei Piazza del Popolo.

4 This broad square, spoiled by its use as a car park, has a colourful morning street market. On the north side is the striking Palazzo del Popolo, a 12th- to 13th-century building that shows the transition from Romanesque to Gothic style, built of the local sandy brown tufa.

Take Via della Constuenti to return to Via Cavour. Turn left and continue all the way to Piazzale Cahen.

5 Here public gardens surround the ruins of an Etruscan temple and the remains of the 14th-century Fortezza. Alongside is the Pozzo di San Patrizio (St Patrick's Well – so called because it is said to resemble a cave in which St Patrick dwelled in Ireland).

The well was dug in 1527 for Pope Clement VII who took refuge here after imperial troops sacked Rome. The shaft is 63m deep and is lined with an ingenious double helix staircase; this enabled packhorses to descend to collect water and return by a separate staircase – the idea came from Leonardo da Vinci who invented such a stairway for a brothel! The descent, down 248 steps, is worth the effort for the views through the shaft openings and the strange subterranean lighting effects.

THE WINES OF ORVIETO

Some 16 million bottles of dry white Orvieto wine are produced annually and exported the world over. Orvieto has a down-market image as a consequence, but there has been a recent revival in quality. Some of the best wines are produced under the Antinori label; they are fuller bodied than the more anaemic *secco*. Until the 1960s, Orvieto produced fragrant golden dessert wines and several producers have revived this older style of wine, notably with Pourriture Nobile, produced by Ducagnano dei Barbi, and Vigneto Orzalume, produced by the Bigi estates.

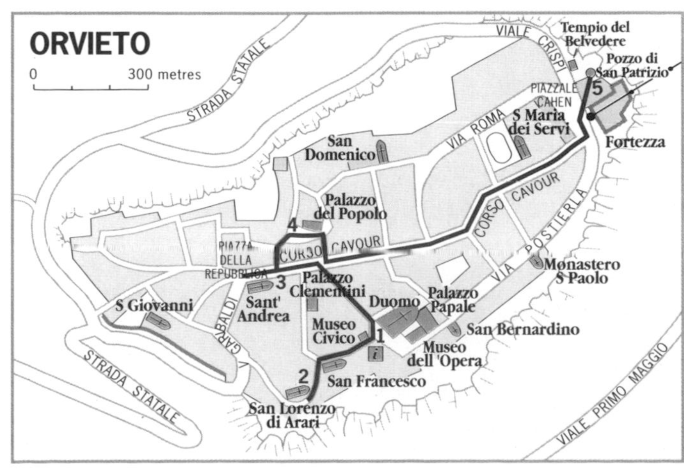

·PERUGIA·

Perugia (map ref: 111 E3), the capital of modern Umbria, is a lively, cosmopolitan city with a large student population. Corso Vannucci is its wide, bustling main street, leading up to the cathedral, whose rough unfinished façade is in stark contrast to the elegant Fontana Maggiore. This fountain, dating from 1277, is an elegant monument to the importance of water to Umbria's hilltop towns. The bas reliefs and statues are the work of Niccolo Pisano and his son Giovanni. They represent an eclectic mixture of religious, secular and mythical subjects, illustrating the Labours of the Months, the Liberal Arts, scenes from Aesop's Fables, Adam and Eve, David and Goliath and personifications of Perugia (a woman holding a cornucopia) and Euliste, the mythical founder of the city.

Within the cathedral, the Cappella del Sant'Anello contains the Holy Ring of the Virgin, locked inside a nest of 15 boxes each with a different key as a precaution against theft (though Perugians themselves stole this relic from Chiusi in 1473). The best fresco, a *Deposition* in the chapel at the rear of the nave, was painted by Barocci in 1559, while under the influence of poison fed him by a jealous rival; the painting inspired Rubens' famous *Antwerp Descent*.

Cosmopolitan Perugia

Opposite the cathedral is a group of buildings that together comprise the 14th-century Palazzo dei Priori. The Sala dei Notari, or lawyers' chamber, is frescoed with the coats of arms of leading citizens. In Corso Vannucci the first door on the right leads to the Sala del Collegio della Mercanzia, lined with 15th-century wood panelling. Next comes the Collegio del Cambio (Bankers' Guild), covered in Perugino's outstanding frescos of 1496, depicting the Liberal Arts, the Nativity and allegories of Prudence, Justice, Temperance and Fortitude (this last is now thought to be the work of Raphael, painted when he was only 17 years of age; note also Perugino's self-portrait painted between these two figures).

The main entrance to the *palazzo* leads to the upper floor and a small collection of Umbrian paintings. These are just a small selection of the huge number currently under reorganisation to form the Galleria Nazionale dell'Umbria.

At the opposite end of Corso Vannucci, below Piazza Italia, are the subterranean remains of medieval Perugia. They were incorporated into the mighty Rocca Paolina, a stronghold built by Pope Paul III in 1535 when his troops crushed the city. The *rocca* itself, a detested symbol of papal rule, was torn down in 1860, but the lower bastion, with its Etruscan city gate and underground passages, has survived.

Further out, along Corso Cavour, is San Domenico, a massive church containing Italy's second largest stained glass window after Milan. There is also the exquisite tomb of Pope Benedict XI, regarded as the finest example of Gothic funerary sculpture in Italy, carved by an unknown hand after the pope died in 1304 from eating poisoned figs. The cloister houses the huge collection of Etruscan and Roman artefacts that makes up the Museo Archeologico Nazionale dell'Umbria.

San Pietro lies further down Corso Cavour, to the left of the courtyard housing the university's faculty of agriculture. Little visited, it contains outstanding 16th-century choir stalls whose arms are carved with a complete bestiary, including elephants, ducks, crocodiles and dolphins.

PERUGIA'S BLOODY PAST

When Pope Paul III ordered his troops into Perugia in 1530, he used brutal tactics to suppress an equally vicious feud that had torn the town apart for 70 years, as the rival Oddi and Baglioni families fought for control and pursued their vendettas with ruthless tenacity. When not fighting each other, the families murdered their own kin. On one occasion, Grifonetto Baglioni had 100 members of his own family slaughtered on the cathedral steps in an attempt to become sole ruler of the city. After this butchery, the cathedral had to be cleansed with wine and reconsecrated.

One of the bloodiest episodes in the Italian War of Independence took place here in 1859, when Pius IX sent the Swiss Guard to quell the city, which they did with such brutality that the event is still known as the 'massacre of Perugia'. Peace finally came in 1860 when Garibaldi's troops entered the city and the papal Rocca Paolina was torn down.

TOWN WALK

From Corso Vannucci take the tunnel that passes beneath the campanile of the Palazzo dei Priori and walk down the characterful medieval street of Via dei Priori. Pass through the Arco di San Luco, once a gate in the ancient Etruscan city walls, to the Piazza di San Francesco.

1 The Piazza is dominated by San Francesco al Prato, huge and ruinous, begun in 1253 and already subsiding by the early 1400s. Alongside is the delightful Oratorio di San Bernardino. St Bernardino of Siena did much to try and end Perugian in-fighting and framed statutes for the city intended to regulate local government. Perugians continued to quarrel all the same but they honoured the saint with this lovely church covered with swirling figures of angelic musicians, carved by Agostino di Duccio in 1451.

Take Via A Pascoli north out of the piazza, which leads to the Via del Acquedotto.

2 The Via del Acquedotto is a picturesque elevated waterway resting on arches that date originally from 1277 when Friar Bevignate took charge of a publicly funded scheme to bring water into the city centre. He designed a system of underground pipes and aqueducts to bring water from Monte Pacciano, 3km away, to the Fontana Maggiore in front of the cathedral. Just to the south is the baroque Palazzo Gallenga, now the University for Foreigners. Alongside is the Arco Etrusco, a 3rd-century BC Etruscan city gate.

Turning your back on this gate, head across Piazza Fortebraccio and head down Corso Garibaldi.

3 A short way down the Corso, on the right, the Church of Sant'Agostino contains beautifully carved choir stalls of 1502. Next door, the interior of the Oratorio della Confraternità di Sant'Agostino is a superb example of baroque plasterwork, more like an opera house than a church. It was created by French artists in the early 17th century.

4 At the end of Corso Garibaldi is the circular Church of Sant'Angelo, dating from the 5th century; the plan emulates the form of early Christian churches in Ravenna and Rome and is built of reused Roman bricks, pillars and capitals. Sant'Agnese, near by, contains a lyrical Perugino painting that depicts two of his cousins, who were nuns at this convent, kneeling either side of the crucified Christ. Good views of the city's medieval walls are to be had from the nearby Porta Sant'Angelo, built in 1326 by Lorenzo Maitani.

The Palazzo dei Priori

Return up Corso Garibaldi to Piazza Fortebraccio, pass under the Arco Etrusco and climb up Via Ulisse Rocchi, known locally as the Via Vecchio (Old Road) because it was the main street of the Etruscan city. This leads directly back to the cathedral, past the Etruscan Well, a massive stone-lined shaft, 35m deep, dating from the 4th century BC.

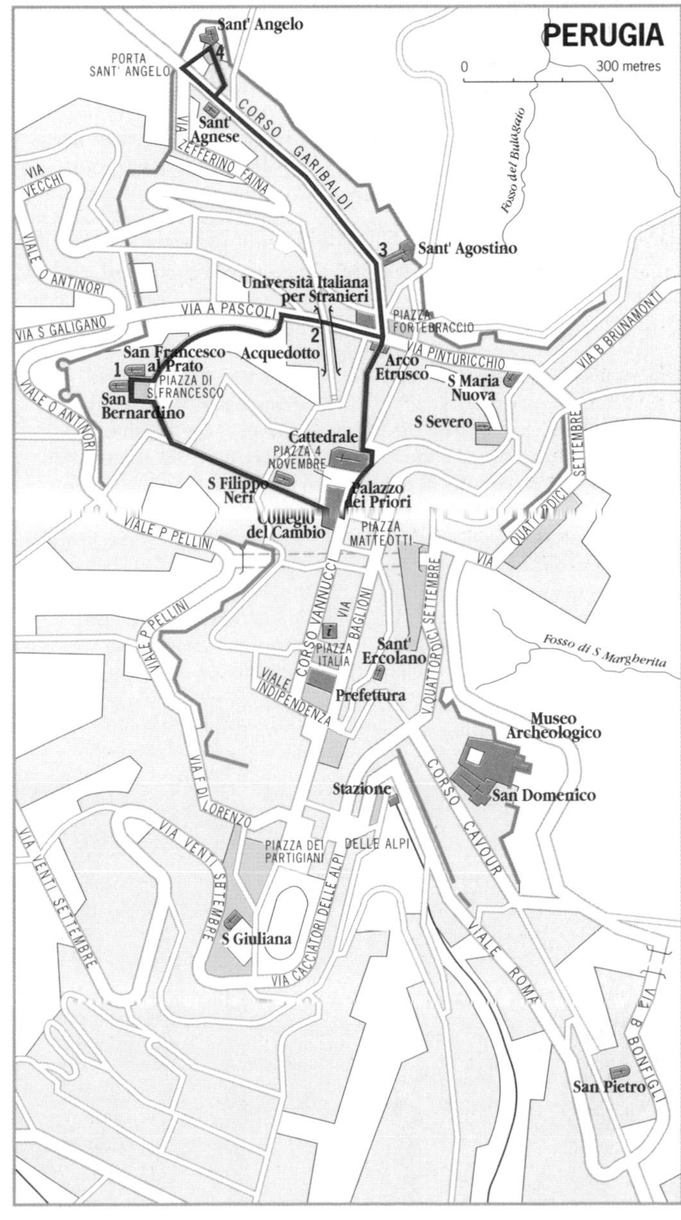

Porta Venere, one of Spello's excellently preserved Roman gateways

SPELLO

MAP REF: 111 E3

Hilltop Spello is little bigger today than the original Roman settlement of *Hispellum.* There are reminders of its Roman origins everywhere, from the encircling walls, built in the time of Augustus, to the reused Roman masonry on the façade of the Church of Santa Maria Maggiore. The dull interior of the church is transformed into a blaze of colour by Pinturicchio's frescos in the Cappella Baglioni. Painted in 1501, they represent the Annunciation, the Nativity, the Coming of the Magi, the Dispute in the Temple and the Sybils who foretold the birth of Christ. Restoration has revealed the true sensuality of the colours and the exotic landscape is full of fascinating detail. The artist's self-portrait hangs on the wall of the house in which the Archangel Gabriel appears to the Virgin.

The floor of the chapel contributes to the rich effect. The 16th-century majolica tiles, made in Deruta and painted with dragons and griffins, show their age, but here and there a patch of colour stands out with the brilliance and intricacy of a Persian carpet.

SPOLETO

MAP REF: 111 E2

Spoleto is a city of extraordinary architectural richness, with monuments dating from all periods in its history; from Roman times to the modern works of sculpture that dot the city as a legacy of its annual Festival dei Due Mondi (see Festivals in Tuscany and Umbria, p73).

Spoleto's graceful cathedral was built on the ruins of the old one, destroyed by the imperial troops of Frederick Barbarossa, and was consecrated by Innocent III in 1198. Eight rose windows, like lace doilies, pierce the façade. The central one is supported by two caryatids, with symbols of the Evangelists carved in the corners. Above is a mosaic of Christ Enthroned with the Virgin and St John, signed and dated 'Solsternus, 1207'.

Pope Urban VIII was to blame for remodelling the cathedral interior in 1644. His architect, Luigi Arrigucci, did at least spare the lovely floor of inlaid marble and Filippo Lippi's sensuous frescos on the *Life of the Virgin* in the sanctuary.

Lippi is buried in the cathedral – his tomb is in the right-hand transept. Designed by his illegitimate son Filippino, himself an accomplished artist, it is carved with an epigram written by the humanist orator, Politian.

THE SEDUCTIVE ARTIST

Filippo Lippi's artistic talent was stimulated by his love of women. As Vasari recounts: 'He was so lustful that he would give anything to enjoy a woman he wanted. . . and if he couldn't buy what he wanted, then he would cool his passion by painting her picture'. Lippi is best known for his sensuous Virgins, many of them portraits of his mistress, the beautiful Lucrezia Buti. Lippi's *Life of the Virgin* cycle in Spoleto was begun in 1468 but he died before he could complete the work. Vasari, who loved gossip, reports: 'they say that, in one of those sublime love affairs he was always having, the relations of the woman concerned had him poisoned'.

Whether this is true or not, the artist died at the full height of his powers and these frescos, recently restored, demonstrate the lyrical charm and vibrant colours that were his trademark. David Sante, the art historian, has summed up their appeal: 'the painter transformed the typical queen-like figure of the Virgin into one of a charming girl'.

The Ponte delle Torri, an aqueduct 230m long, links Spoleto and Monteluco

TOWN WALK

Climb the steps out of the cathedral square and turn left to follow the Via della Rocca to reach the city's fortress.

1 Totila the Goth first built a castle here in the 6th century, using Roman masonry looted from the amphitheatre. The amphitheatre again served as a source for the 14th-century *rocca*, once the most powerful fortress in Umbria, and the base from which papal representatives subjugated the region. It was built in 1355 under the direction of Cardinal Albornez, and, in more peaceful times, was converted into a luxurious palace. For a time it was the home of Lucrezia and Cesare Borgia, and a favourite papal retreat.

More recently, the *rocca* has served as a maximum security prison, holding members of the Red Brigade. Now under restoration, it will reopen as a museum and cultural centre.

Follow the lane round the foot of the castle walls for a spectacular view of the Ponte delle Torri.

2 The Ponte delle Torri is an extraordinary aqueduct that spans the gorge between Spoleto and Monteluco, opposite. The *ponte* was built in 1345, before the *rocca*, but subsequently incorporated into it, to provide a reliable water supply in the event of siege and an escape route out of the city in times of danger. Water no longer flows along its channel (though it can be turned on if necessary) and it is possible to walk across the top of the massive structure, 230m long and 80m high, enjoying the views up and down the Tessino gorge.

Return to the centre of Spoleto by means of Via della Rocca. Just beyond the cathedral steps, in Via Aurelio Saffi, look for a gate in the wall on the right, leading into the quiet courtyard of the 15th-century Palazzo Arcivescovile.

3 On the right of the courtyard is the simple façade of Sant'Eufemia, another of Spoleto's ancient and well-restored churches. Late Roman materials were used to build the current church in the 12th century and the ornate square column on the right-hand side of the nave, carved with vine leaves, may have come from the palace of the 8th-century Lombardic Dukes of Spoleto. The triforium above was added in the 15th century and the *matroneum*, or women's gallery, at the west end, in the 16th.

Emerging from the grounds of the Archiepiscopal Palace, turn right then first left, down to the Piazza del Municipio.

4 On the left of this small square is the Palazzo Comunale which houses the city's picture gallery. The highlights of the collection are two works by Lo Spagno: *The Virtues* (1512) and a *Madonna and Child* (1516). The vaults of the palazzo contain the well-preserved remains of a 1st-century AD Roman house, once claimed to be the home of Vespasia Pollo, the mother of the Emperor Vespasian.

To the left of the Piazza del Municipio is the busy shopping and restaurant centre of the city, the Piazza del Mercato.

5 The *piazza* stands on the site of the Roman forum and the 1st-century AD Arco di Druso closes off the southern exit. This was built to commemorate the Germanic victories of Drusus, son of the Emperor Tiberius. The neglected remains of a Roman temple stand alongside.

SPOLETO'S EARLY CHRISTIAN CHURCHES

Three remarkable churches are located on Spoleto's periphery. San Gregorio Maggiore stands on the west side of Piazza di Vittorio. Following the basilican plan, the altar is raised on a dais 3m above the nave. The vaulted crypt contains a forest of reused Roman columns and capitals and the sarcophagus of St Abbondanza who was massacred in the nearby amphitheatre along with 10,000 companions, causing the Torrente Tessino to run red with their blood.

From the Roman Ponte Sanguinario signs lead the way to the town cemetery and the church of San Salvatore. This has an untouched 4th-century façade and a Carolingian nave, its dusty floor littered with fragments of fallen columns.

San Pietro, south of the city, stands by the side of the Via Flaminia, with a fine view of the 10 massive arches of the Ponte delle Torri. The façade is covered in fine carvings, probably 12th century in date.

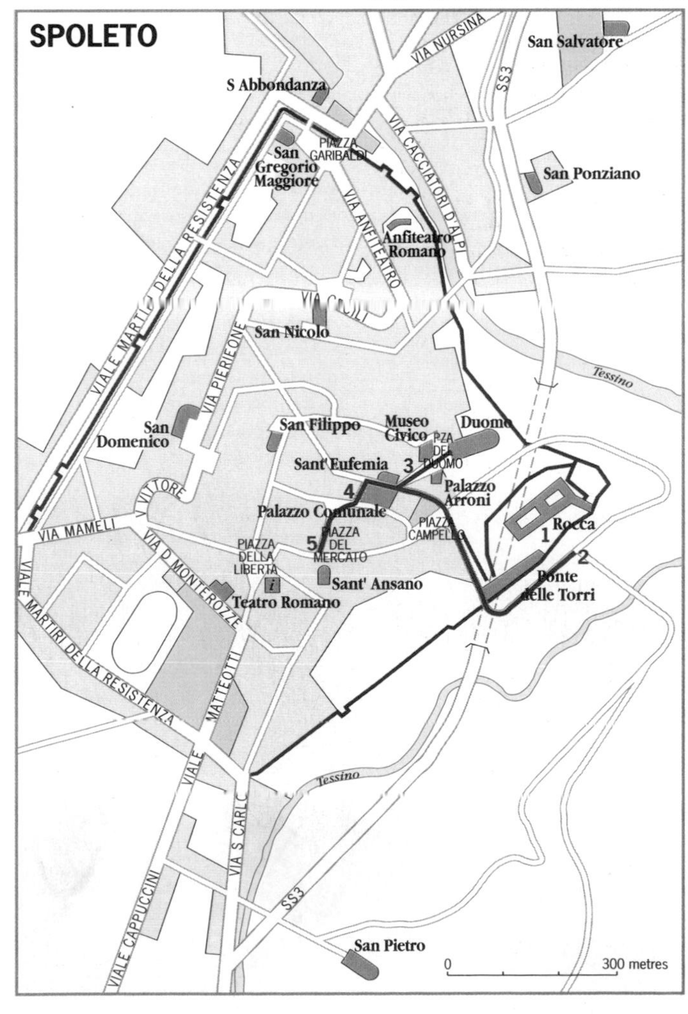

FESTIVALS

Every self-respecting community in Tuscany and Umbria has at least one major festival during the year. Some of them are pre-Christian in origin, though taken over and transformed by the Church. Monte Amiata's *Fiaccole di Natale* (Christmas Torch) festival began as a pagan midwinter celebration; now the torchlight procession and towering bonfire in the main *piazza* have been turned into a Christmas Eve vigil.

Gúbbio's *Corsa dei Ceri* (Candle Race) has been celebrated every 15 May since 1154. The phallic shape of the three candles, heavy octagonal structures of wood over 6m in height, hints at even older pagan fertility rites. The candles have now been sanitised; they are surmounted by statues of St Ubaldo, the town's patron saint, St George and St Anthony, patrons of merchants and farm workers respectively. Teams of Gúbbians set off at timed intervals to race with the candles up the punishingly steep path that leads to the Basilica di Sant'Ubaldo on the summit of Monte Ingino. The race can be over in as little as 15 minutes, but the rest of the day is spent in animated discussion to establish the winner – perhaps the fastest team, perhaps the one that showed the greatest skill.

In Florence, on Easter Sunday, crowds gather in the Piazza del Duomo to watch the *Scoppio del Carro*, the Explosion of the Cart. This 18th-century gilded carriage is drawn by white oxen to the cathedral doors. Flints, taken from the Holy Sepulchre in Jerusalem by crusaders, are used to ignite a dove-shaped rocket suspended on a wire. If all goes well, the 'dove' swoops from the high altar through the cathedral doors igniting the fireworks hidden in the carriage. The Church regards this as a celebration of the Resurrection, but for many a rural onlooker it has a different significance; a successful explosion presages a good harvest.

Orvieto has a similar event, the *Festa della Palombella*, which takes place on Whit Sunday. Here the dove, symbol of the Holy Ghost, descends on a wire from the spire of San Francesco to a tableau representing the Last Supper on the steps in front of the cathedral. The tableau is stuffed with fireworks, and again the fortunes of the city over the coming year are dependent on the success of the explosion. The charred remains of the tableau are

Siena's Palio: on the surface, just a horse race…

presented to a newly married couple, confirming that fertility rites underlie this custom too.

Some festivals are, however, purely religious, with no pagan undertones. Every Christmas Day in Prato, the pulpit in front of the cathedral is used to display the Virgin's Girdle; according to legend, Thomas, the doubting apostle, was given this girdle by the Virgin in a vision to confirm the truth of the Assumption. Perugia displays the Virgin's 'wedding ring' on 30 July, when 15 trusted citizens, each of whom holds a unique key to the nest of 15 boxes in which the ring is normally kept, come together for the ceremony.

Assisi celebrates Easter with a re-enactment of the Passion. Orvieto has a costume procession on the feast of Corpus Christi when its sacred relic, a cloth stained with the blood of Christ, is displayed. Spello celebrates the same feast by filling its streets with splendid floral carpets. Perhaps most touching of all are the living tableaux mounted in many rural churches for Christmas Eve, complete with live oxen, ass and infant. The custom is said to have been introduced by St Francis as a means of communicating the story of the Nativity to the illiterate peasants of Umbria.

Ancient enmities, dating back to the turbulent Middle Ages, lie at the root of many of the region's non-religious festivals. In Arezzo, on the first Sunday in September, costumed knights on horseback charge at a dummy called 'the Saracen' and attempt to spear the ring on his shield. A similar festival takes place in Narni (the *Festa dell'Anello*, Ring Festival, in May). Superficially the jousting recalls the conflict between crusaders and infidel, but the ferocity with which rivals from different sectors of the city support their champions demonstrates that ancient intercommunal rivalries are the real issue.

This is equally evident in the *Calcio in Costume* 'football' match, played on three occasions (17 and 24 June, and 1 July) in Florence; the game, a cross between football and rugby, is played by four teams, representing the four original *rioni*, or districts, of the city. The rivalry is intense and the teams sometimes employ vicious tactics to ensure victory, cheered on by their intensely partisan supporters.

Siena's *Palio* represents the epitome of communal pride and rivalry. On the surface *Palio* is a thrilling horse race that takes place in early July and again in mid-August. Dig deeper and you find that *Palio* is a way of life; each of the 17 *contrade* or districts of the city has an organising committee that makes and maintains the elaborate costumes; children are taught flag-waving and drumming skills from the earliest age and indoctrinated with stories of past triumphs in the *Palio* to cement *contrada*, or communal spirit. That spirit is so strong that Sienese will even think twice before marrying someone from a rival *contrada*, and the Sienese expression, *Il Palio corre tutto l'anno* (Palio runs all year), is no exaggeration.

Sometimes this rivalry is expressed simply through competition to produce the best displays and the most lavish costumes, as at Viareggio's pre-Lent carnival, famous all over Italy for the political and satirical content of many of the carnival floats, or at the *Calendimaggio* festival held in Assisi on 30 April and 1 May.

Other festivals are celebrations of the bounty of nature. The *sagra*, or feast, is a rural celebration of the grape (best in Panicale and Città della Pieve in May when the fountains run with wine), fish (Piediluco in July), truffles (Gubbio in October) or the chestnut (Umbertide in October).

At the opposite end of the scale in sophistication are the region's cultural festivals, of which the most famous is Spoleto's *Festival dei Due Mondi* (Festival of the Two Worlds) held in late June and early July. Founded by the Italian–American composer Gian Carlo Menotti in 1957, it brings together artists from Europe and the Americas and has turned into the best music, drama and ballet festival in Italy.

The region's surviving Roman theatres and amphitheatres are often literally called into play for summer performances; Fiesole's Roman theatre is the venue for the *Estate Fiesolana*, a summer-long festival of opera, music, dance and drama. Churches in Florence play host to performances by international stars during the May *Maggio Musicale* music festival while visitors to Umbria in September are likely to stumble across musicians and choirs performing church music during the *Sagra Musicale Umbria* festival. Far less sedate is *Umbria Jazz*, Italy's major jazz festival which brings Perugia and neighbouring towns alive during July and August, attracting some of the biggest names in Jazz.

...but in fact a complete way of life for all its citizens, as it has been for at least 700 years

TERNI

MAP REF: 111 E2

Industrial Terni, once called the 'Italian Manchester', is worth a brief visit for the Church of San Salvatore, which stands to one side of the vast Piazza Europa at the centre of the city. This tiny and delightful church was originally built in the 3rd century BC as a sun temple; the sun still shines down on the high altar at noon through a porthole in the beehive-shaped dome over the sanctuary.

Terni's art gallery is housed in the 17th-century Palazzo Manessei, located behind the post office in Via Fratini, across the Piazza della Repubblica. The collection includes works by prominent 20th-century artists such as Miró, Kandinsky, Chagall, Léger and shoemaker Orneore Metelli (1872–1938) who painted local industrial landscapes in the naive style.

Nearby The Cascata delle Mármore, 8km east of Terni, is a stupendous man-made waterfall some 162m in height. The fall was engineered under the rule of the Roman consul Curius Dentatus in 271BC to drain the marshy plains around Terni. A new channel was dug to join the rivers Nera and Velino and the combined force of the two rivers, spilling over the side of Mount Mármore, became a powerful cascade.

Since 1938 the waters have been used to drive hydro-electric turbines and the falls are turned on only occasionally, so the best time to see them is at weekends. The dramatic force of the cascade is well summed up in a comment recorded by the painter Sir Joshua Reynolds. Wilson, his companion, stood speechless in admiration for a while before exclaiming 'Well done water, by God!'.

The extensive remains of the Roman town of Carsulae lie 14km northwest of Terni. Founded around 220BC, the town went into decline when the Via Flaminia, which once passed through the town, was diverted to the east. It was finally abandoned at the end of the 1st century AD after an earthquake and rediscovered in the 16th century, since when excavations have revealed the town's temples, amphitheatre and bathhouses. The temple walls retain some of their original pink marble cladding, hinting at the lost splendour of a town which both Tacitus and Pliny described as very beautiful.

TODI

MAP REF: 111 E3

Todi is a delightful sight, clinging to its hilltop with the tower of San Fortunato pointing into the sky and contrasting with the domed bulk of Santa Maria della Consolazione on the hillside below. The town has been 'discovered' by wealthy Romans, many of whom have weekend homes here, and is a perfect place for a leisurely stroll.

The Church of San Fortunato stands at the highest point in the town. This graceful Gothic church was begun in 1292 to honour Todi's patron saint, the appropriately named Bishop Fortunato, who led the town in successfully resisting an attack by Totila the Goth. Delicate carvings, crowded with vignettes illustrating biblical stories, surround the portal. The crypt contains a modest memorial to the Franciscan poet, Jacopone (1250–1306), who composed the *Stabat Mater* but whose zealous attacks on Church corruption led to his imprisonment by Pope Boniface VIII.

To the left of the church, Via San Fortunato leads to the Porto Marzia, the town's one surviving Etruscan gate, through which lies Corso Cavour and the Piazza del Popolo. The *piazza*, surrounded by medieval buildings, is one of the most striking in Italy, designed so that the narrow exits at each corner could be closed off and the square defended. The Palazzo del Popolo, with its Ghibelline fishtail battlements, is one of the oldest surviving public buildings in Italy, begun in 1213. Next door, the Palazzo del Capitano, dating from 1292, is fronted by a fine staircase. The cathedral, at the opposite end of the square, is a blend of Romanesque and Gothic and has choir stalls (1530) covered in scenes of delicate intarsia work (inlaid wood).

Santa Maria della Consolazione stands just outside the town walls. This elegant domed church so resembles the original plan of St Peter's in Rome that it was once attributed to the same architect, Bramante. It is now known to have been begun in 1508 by Cola da Caprorola but many others lent a hand before it was completed in 1607. It has been called one of Italy's finest Renaissance buildings and its setting, in an expanse of green lawn backed by wooded hills, lends it considerable charm – though the lifeless baroque interior may come as a disappointment.

MOTOR TOUR

This tour follows the rim of an extinct lake, which was partially drained by the Romans and completely dry by the 16th century. It starts and ends in Assisi and takes in some of Umbria's finest hilltop towns.

Take the San Vitale road southeast out of Assisi and join the SS75. After 13km turn left for Spello.

14km northwest of Temi lies the ruined Roman town of Carsulae

Spello

Pinturicchio's richly colourful frescos in Santa Maria Maggiore are the highlight of this quiet town.

Continue south along the SS75, bypassing Foligno, whose old core was virtually destroyed by World War II bombing. At the intersection with the N3 follow signs south towards Spoleto. About 3km from the intersection, turn left on the SS77; immediately after turn right following signs for 6km to Abbazia di Sassovivo.

Abbazia di Sassovivo

This peaceful Benedictine monastery was founded in 1070. It stands amidst woodland high above the Vale of Spoleto and has a gracious Romanesque cloister.

Retrace the route back to the N3 and drive south for 10km to Trevi.

Trevi

The narrow streets of this hilltop town are a minor work of art, paved with pebbles set in frames of stone to divide the surface into patterns of squares, diamonds or herringbone. Massive corbels (*sporti*) support the upper stories of sombre *palazzi* which seem to meet across the sky to shade the alleys from the heat of the sun. There are no great buildings of note here, but winding streets and flower-filled courtyards offer surprises at every turning.

Return to the N3. After 4km look for an easily missed sign pointing right to the Tempio di Clitunno.

Tempio di Clitunno
Known locally as the *tempietto* this little church looks like a mini-Acropolis; it was built in the 4th century as a shrine to the early Christian martyr, San Salvatore. Frescos inside of Christ with St Peter and St Paul date from the 8th century and are some of the earliest in Italy to have survived.

Approximately 1.6km further south on the N3 turn right for the car park of the Fonti di Clitunno.

Fonti di Clitunno
These delightful crystal-clear springs were sacred to the Romans. Umbrian white bulls were purified here before proceeding to Rome for ritual slaughter and the river god Clitunnus issued oracles from the bubbling waters that spill from clefts in the rock into a willow-fringed pool. Virgil, Byron and the artist Corot were among the countless visitors to have been enchanted by the idyllic scene.

Take the N3 south for 12km to Spoleto.

Spoleto
Spoleto's many attractions demand at least half a day (see pages 70 and 71), so on this tour it is best just to concentrate on the magnificent view of the Ponte delle Torri aqueduct to be had from the N3. Just after the aqueduct, pull off to the left to park in front of the Church of San Pietro, from which can be seen the massive arches of the aqueduct and Spoleto's *rocca* crowning the hill to the left of the Tessino gorge. The lively 12th-century carvings on the façade of San Pietro are worth studying in detail.

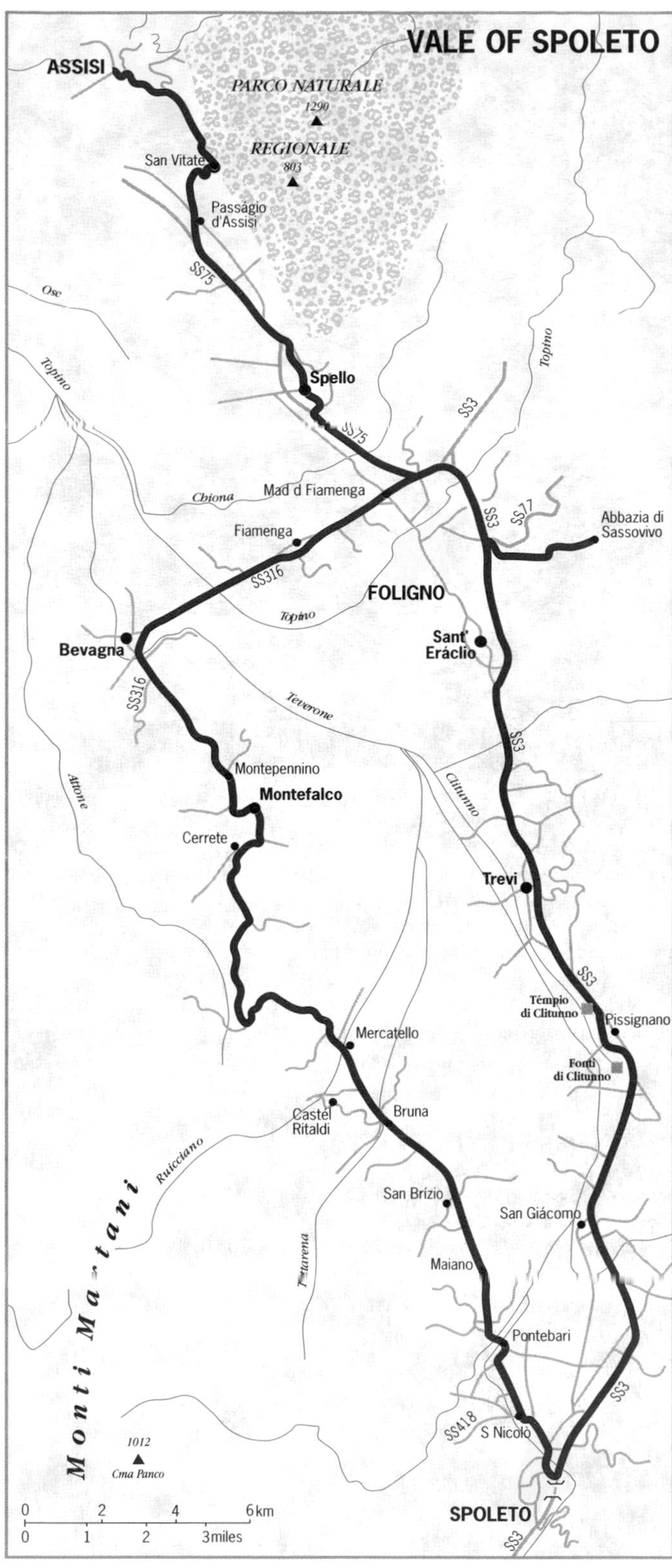

Drive back northwards along the N3 and turn left after emerging from the road tunnel to skirt Spoleto's old town. Head for Spoleto's railway station but turn left just before the station itself, on the well-signposted road through the suburbs towards Montefalco. After 13km drive past the romantic castle ruins of Castel Ritaldi on the left, and Montefalco itself is reached after another 13km.

Montefalco
On a clear day the extensive views from the town walls explain why this quiet town is called the balcony of Umbria. The Church of San Francesco has been turned into a museum and features Gozzoli's highly enjoyable St Francis fresco cycle (1450–52).

Take the road due north of Montefalco for 8km to Bevagna.

Bevagna
Tiny sleepy Bevagna has a perfect ensemble of medieval buildings on its main square, Piazza Silvestri. When so many 12th-century buildings are the work of anonymous architects, it is unusual to have the names of two masons, Binelli and Rodolfo, carved on the façades of the two superb Romanesque churches facing each other across the square.

To return to Assisi, take the road east across the bed of the former lake for 8km to Foligno and turn left on the SS75 northbound. Assisi is on the right after 16km.

CENTRAL TUSCANY

Central Tuscany, with Siena as its focal point, is *the* Tuscany of the popular imagination. Its photogenic landscapes and historic hilltowns, such as San Gimignano, Monteriggioni or Montalcino, are those that spring to mind whenever the name of Tuscany is mentioned, our mental image of the region fed by the tempting pictures in holiday brochures and newspaper travel supplements. Yet the landscape of central Tuscany is extremely varied, consisting of several distinct regions, each with its own character.

Stretching south from Florence right to the suburbs of Siena is a range of hills called the Monti del Chianti – mountains in name only, since few peaks exceed 850m and most are less than 500m high. This is the Chianti region, famous for its wines and baronial castles. Its cultivated landscape of vine-clad hills and silvery olive groves is varied by large stretches of oak, chestnut and beech forest. Over the last 20 years, something like 100,000 isolated and abandoned farm buildings have been bought up by incomers, seeking the good life of long lazy lunches on the terrace or round the swimming pool amidst stunning scenery, a convalescence from humdrum realities. The term 'Chiantishire' has entered the language, with the implication that the region has been transformed into an enclave of Englishness, where middle-class English refugees struggle to create herbaceous borders around their converted stable, barn or farmhouse.

In fact, there are just as many French, German, Swiss, American and Dutch people living in the region and they are not all here on holiday; some run successful commercial enterprises – shops, restaurants, hotels, vineyards or dairies producing *pecorino* cheese. Whilst the idea of bucolic self-sufficiency is one that is often satirised, these incomers, with their willingness to undertake the labour-intensive work involved in the production of olive oil, cheese and wine, have helped to maintain the region's economy at a time when many farming families were abandoning the land in favour of a shorter working day, a more comfortable routine and a more stable income in factory or office employment.

South of Siena, the landscape of the Crete area is different again. Here it is easier to cultivate the soil using machinery and to grow crops that attract European Community farm subsidies. In winter tractors crawl across the endless succession of low hummocks characteristic of the Crete, ploughing up the glistening heavy brown clay to create a monotonous landscape. This changes in spring to the vivid greens of maize, wheat and rye, while in summer the sunflowers with their vast yellow heads shimmer in the heat.

Travelling eastwards towards the Umbrian border, hills give way to the flat plains of the Valdichiana, stretching from Sinalunga to Chiusi. This was once a huge inland lake, drained by the Romans to create rich wheatfields, and destroyed by Hannibal on his march against Rome so as to deprive the city of a major source of food. Today the farmers of the

The pretty town of Certaldo, where even the pavements are brick

Valdichiana specialise in the rearing of Chianina cattle, a prized and ancient breed that supplies the restaurants of central Tuscany with the raw ingredients for succulent *bistecca alla Fiorentina (steak Florentine)*.

If there is one unifying element in these different landscapes, one that makes them quintessentially Tuscan, it is the ubiquitous presence of noble cypress trees. They point skywards, like church steeples or still tongues of flame, grouped on top of hills and mounds; they line country roads and they surround lonely villas and farmhouses. All of them were planted deliberately by hundreds of anonymous landowners for purely altruistic reasons, for while they do provide a degree of shade, their purpose seems more aesthetic, to punctuate the view and turn the landscape itself into a work of art.

Much of central Tuscany was once under the sway of Siena, the one city of any size in what is predominantly an agricultural region. As the capital of a thriving republic in the 13th and 14th centuries, Siena was a major artistic centre that rivalled Florence and Pisa. At the same time as Giotto was painting his influential frescos in Florence and Assisi, Sienese artists were the acknowledged masters in Italy of the international Gothic style. The works of Simone Martini, Pietro and Ambrogio Lorenzetti and Duccio di Buoninsegna form the highlights of a visit to the city, and their radiant, delicate portraits of the enthroned Virgin, Siena's patron, are enlivened by incidental details drawn from the surrounding landscape. Sienese architecture is also determinedly Gothic and continued to be so even in the 16th century, as if the city deliberately chose to ignore the Renaissance style of the old enemy, Florence. Yet the region also gave birth to two men who played a major role in the development of humanistic and Renaissance ideas. Angelo Ambrogini, better known as Poliziano or Politian, was born in Montepulciano in 1454, the son of an influential lawyer who was murdered by political rivals because of his support for the Medici. The Medici acted as patrons to the fatherless boy, paying for the best education that money could buy. By the age of 18 he was regarded as one of the most learned men in Europe, an indefatigable translator of ancient Greek and Latin texts, a composer whose musical drama, *Orfeo*, is regarded as the precursor of modern opera, a gifted poet and orator, and a great influence on intellectual life at the Florentine court.

Another towering figure of the time was Aeneas Silvius Piccolomini, born in Corsignano (later renamed Pienza), where his parents, Sienese aristocrats, had sought refuge during one of the many periods of political strife to which the city was prey. Piccolomini grew up to be an extraordinary polymath: poet, geographer, historian, ambassador and patron of the arts. He travelled widely, visiting Scotland as papal ambassador to the court of King James II, was crowned poet laureate by the Emperor Frederick III and acted as matchmaker between Frederick III and his bride to be, Eleonora of Portugal.

Surprisingly, he combined all these talents with skill as a cleric. As Pope Pius II he brought the intellectual daylight of humanism to bear on Church reform and, for a brief moment in history, the papal chair was occupied by a man with an intellect worthy of the position. Something of the esteem in which he was held can be gauged from the fact that he was one of the few popes of that era who died a natural death: he fell ill of fever and died in the port of Ancona in 1464, just as he was about to embark on a crusade against the Turks.

Pienza, which he sought to rebuild as a model Renaissance city, and the Piccolomini Library in Siena's cathedral, frescoed with scenes from his remarkable life, are two of the major highlights of this infinitely rewarding region.

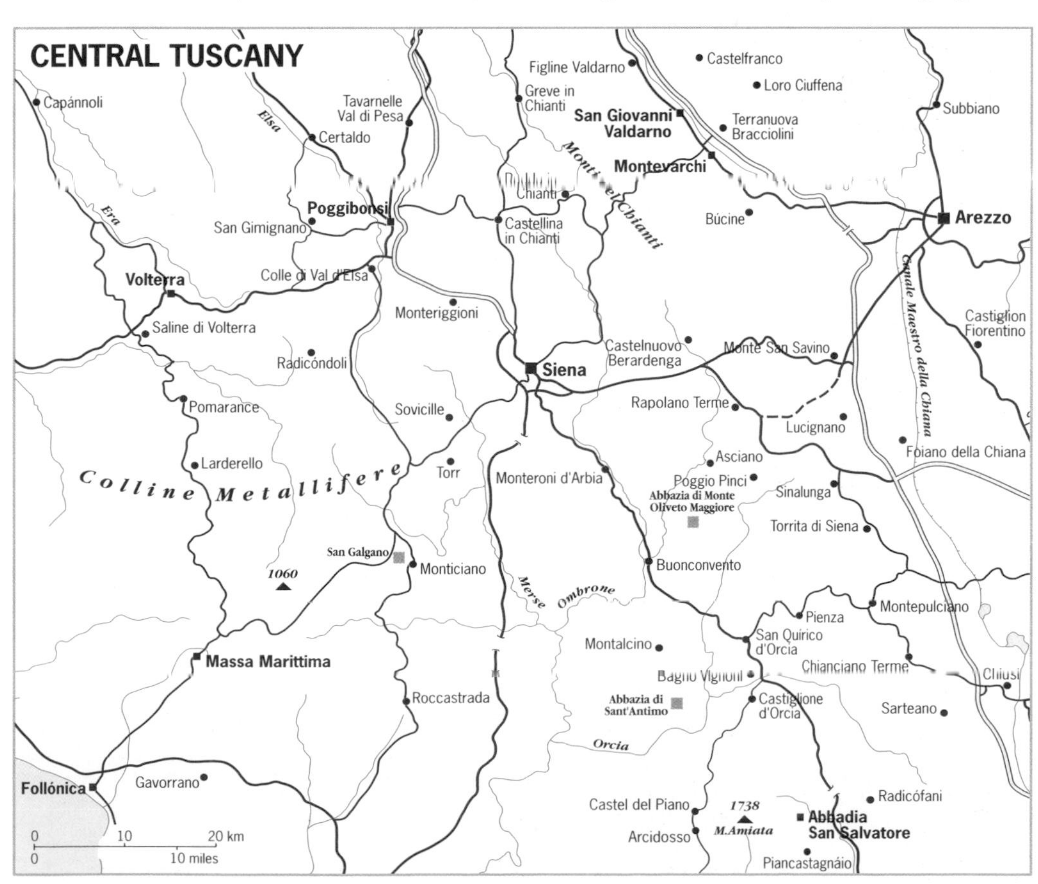

St Benedict guides the faithful in the Abbey of Monte Oliveto

ASCIANO

MAP REF: 110 C3

The little hilltop town of Asciano came under Sienese control in 1285 and stout walls built by the Sienese in 1351 still surround the town. Corso Matteotti, the main street, is lined with solid *palazzi* and leads to the Romanesque Collegiata, built in the 11th century. Alongside, the Museo d'Arte Sacra contains a small but notable collection of Sienese art. Among its pictures is a *Nativity of the Virgin* by an unknown 15th-century painter called the Maestro della Osservanza; it shows what childbirth was like in an aristocratic household of the time, with St Anne, the mother of the Virgin, attended by a clutch of midwives bearing towels and hot water. San Bernardino, also on Corso Matteotti, is now used to display finds from the Etruscan necropolis at Poggio Pinci, 5km to the east.

BUONCONVENTO

MAP REF: 110 C3

Buonconvento stands on the western edge of the Crete area, with its eerie empty landscape. The town has had a bad press from disappointed travellers. In 1817 Lady Morgan complained of spending the night in a room blasted by winds from the manifold chinks in the wall. Tobias Smollett, in 1761, fell out with the local innkeeper and concluded that all Italian innkeepers were 'greedy, impertinent and provoking'.

Today Buonconvento treats guests differently; the town is noted for restaurants serving game and truffles. The walls surrounding the medieval core have two sturdy gates with their original iron-bound wooden doors surviving from 1366. A small but good collection of Sienese School paintings is housed in the Museo d'Arte Sacra.

Nearby The Abbazia di Monte Oliveto Maggiore, 8km northeast of Buonconvento, is a spiritual retreat surrounded by gentle woodland. The abbey was founded in 1313 as the headquarters of the Olivetan order, dedicated to restoring the original simplicity of the Benedictine rule. The severity of the buildings, dating from the 15th century, is relieved by the warm colour of their brickwork and the statuesque cypresses that line the approach road.

The monks who tend the monastery specialise in restoring old books. The signs requesting silence and the atmosphere of aloof dignity contrast with the flamboyance of the frescos in the Great Cloister depicting scenes from the life of St Benedict. They were begun by Luca Signorelli and completed after 1505 by the idiosyncratic Giovanni Antonio Bazza, better known as Il Sodoma. Il Sodoma was excessively fond of male flesh (hence his nickname) and kept a menagerie of badgers, squirrels and ravens. Both his loves find their way into his enjoyable frescos, though these suffered the same fate as Michelangelo's work in the Sistine Chapel; the outraged monks ordered the naked bodies to be clothed, although the cheeky Il Sodoma did not entirely do as he was told. He also left a self-portrait, which includes his pet badgers, in the scene where St Benedict mends the broken sieve.

Besides the frescos, the abbey church contains choir stalls decorated with *trompe l'oeil* scenes in inlaid wood (intarsia work) dating from 1505 and considered among the finest in Italy.

A pleasing use of brick in Certaldo

THE CRETE AREA

The area known as Le Crete stretches southeast from Siena down towards Pienza to form the strangest landscape in Tuscany. Trees are conspicuous by their near absence – a double row of cypresses marching across the low rounded hills demarcates a highway or a private road leading to an isolated villa; otherwise the landscape is bare and bleak, dotted with the clay hummocks that give the area its name. The hummocks, denuded of topsoil by centuries of heavy autumnal rain, are especially striking in summer when their bare subsoil contrasts with the green of surrounding crops. They may look barren, but their numerous hollows and miniature ravines harbour foxes, badgers and even porcupines and wild boar.

Until recently the land was farmed by Sardinian shepherds renowned for their *pecorino*, or sheep's milk cheese. Now much of the pasture has been ploughed up to create vast wheatfields and to the agri-business farmer the hummocks are a nuisance – *maligne crete*; as long as they survive, however, they contribute to a striking and much-photographed landscape of almost primeval emptiness.

An industrious carpenter's shop in Certaldo

CERTALDO

MAP REF: 110 C4

Giovanni Boccaccio (1313–1375), the Chaucer of Italy, spent the last 13 years of his life in Certaldo and is buried in the local church. Certaldo also claims to be his birthplace, but this is disputed by both Paris and Florence.

Boccaccio is best remembered for the bawdier tales in his *Decameron*, but he was also a man of immense learning, revered as one of the founding fathers of Italian vernacular literature.

The old part of Certaldo, known as Castello, is pleasing for the harmony of its brick, used for paving and for palaces alike. Boccaccio's house, Via Boccaccio 18, has been restored as an international centre for medieval studies. His tomb in the church of Santissimi Michele et Iacopo is a modern work, but surmounted by a bust of the author carved in 1503 by G F Rustici. The original monument, which Boccaccio designed himself, was destroyed in 1783 by prudish vandals fired by disapproval of his work. It is not clear whether they disapproved of the low-life humour or the portrayal (*Decameron: Sixth Day, Tenth Story*) of the people of Certaldo as gullible victims of a fraudulent friar who conjured sacred relics from feathers (the wing of the Archangel Gabriel) and charcoal (left over from the roasting of St Lawrence).

One of the town's most attractive buildings is the 15th-century Palazzo Pretorio, in Piazzale del Vicariato; the walls are covered in stone *stelli*, the coats of arms of former deputies who ruled the region on behalf of Florence. Inside is a pretty courtyard and small museum.

CHIANCIANO TERME

MAP REF: 111 D3

Chianciano is really two towns; medieval Chianciano Vecchio is a typical Tuscan town with a 13th-century church and a museum of religious art housed in the 18th century Palazzo del Arcipretura.

Another world away, but geographically just to the south, is Chianciano Terme, one of Italy's biggest and most prosperous spa towns. The curative powers of the local waters were known to the Romans but today's town, with its 1950s architecture, is the product of rapid development over the last 50 years. Signs all over the town promise visitors a healthy liver – *fegato sano* – but the hot mineral springs are used to cure just about every known ailment. People of every European nationality – except the sceptical British – come here for the good of their health and the town has a phenomenal number of hotels. It also boasts some of the most expensive and exclusive shopping in Italy; between saline baths and mud-pack treatments, rejuvenated visitors spend their time shopping for furs, jewellery and designer clothes.

Nearby Sarteano, 8km south of Chianciano, is another spa town but with more historic character. Narrow alleyways, *vicoli*, thread the compact heart which is dominated by the 13th-century *rocca* and surrounded by Etruscan and medieval walls.

The Church of San Martino in Foro contains an endearing *Annunciation* attributed to the Sienese architect, Domenico Beccafumi.

CHIUSI

MAP REF: 111 D3

The little town of Chiusi is famous for its painted Etruscan tombs, rivalled only by those at Tarquinia, over the border in Lazio. The Etruscan city of *Kamars* was ruled by Lars Porsena who, in 508BC, dared to lead an attack on Rome itself, only to be stopped by the heroic Horatio who defended the last bridge into the city against impossible odds.

Modern Chiusi appeals to the imagination rather than to the eye. Though not beautiful, its streets read like a layer-cake of history, with medieval buildings superimposed over the street plan of Roman *Clusium,* which itself overlies a labyrinth of subterranean galleries dug by the Etruscans.

Chiusi's cathedral is a venerable Romanesque building whose antique patina is reinforced by the large quantities of Roman and Etruscan masonry recycled for its building. The campanile is built over a large Roman cistern. The Museo Nazionale Etrusco is packed with funerary urns, sarcophagi, painted vases and beautiful black burnished *bucchero* ware, whose clean lines and sensuous forms seem modern; altogether this is one of the most varied collections of Etruscan art in Italy. Guided tours to nearby tombs can be arranged at the museum. The Tomba della Scimmia (Tomb of the Ape) is the most rewarding; the paintings on its walls depict wrestling, chariot-racing, domestic scenes and the monkey after which the tomb is named.

Castellina in Chianti

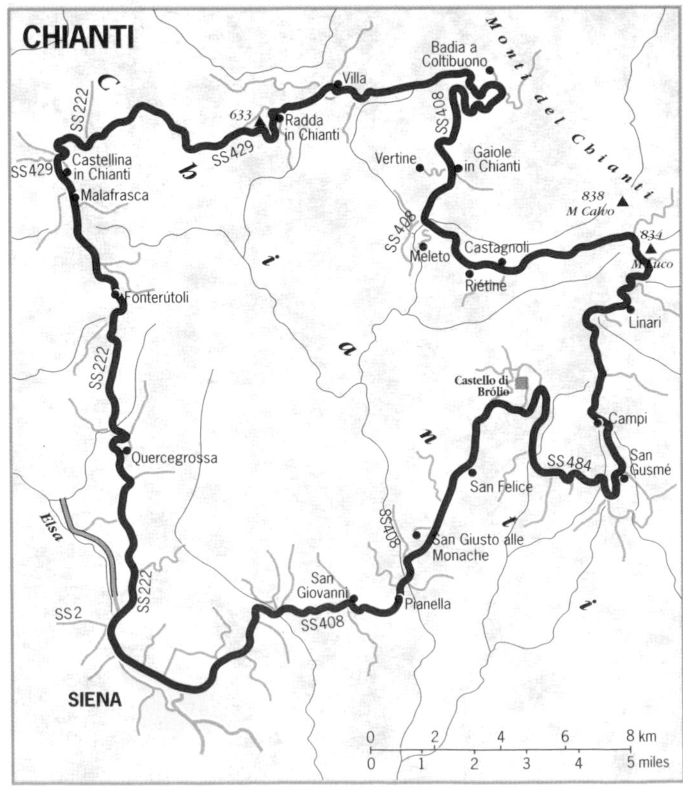

MOTOR TOUR

The name Chianti conjures up visions of straw-wrapped flasks of soft and highly palatable red wine – though these days the wine comes in plainer bottles. Thanks to the novels of John Mortimer and others, the name also evokes a feudal landscape where the rich but decadent Tuscan aristocracy fight a war of attrition against impoverished but genteel English retirees. 'Chiantishire' is, however, more of a myth than a reality. The Chianti region, situated between Florence and Siena, remains quintessentially Tuscan and the people warmly hospitable depending, as they do, so much on tourism. The region's *fattorie*, or wine estates, supplement their incomes by doubling as hotels and restaurants with leisure facilities such as riding stables attached, and those that announce *vendita diretta* welcome the trade of passing oenophiles.

*Take the Florence road out of Siena and, about 1.6km from the city centre, take the right-hand road, signposted Castellina in Chianti. Follow this road for 18km to Castellina. Vineyards line the route and signs continually remind the visitor that this is the land of the Black Cockerel (*Siete nel mondo del Gallo Nero*), the symbol of the best Chianti Classico wines.*

Castellina in Chianti
As its name suggests, Castellina is built around a splendid *castello*, which survives at the centre of the town, restored to pristine condition in 1927. The town also retains its walls, all part of the medieval defences strengthened under Florentine rule in the 15th century as part of a defensive chain linking the valleys of the Elsa and Arno. The Bottega del Vina Gallo Nero (Via della Rocca 10) is a showcase for the region's wines and olive oils, and offers advice on local vineyard tours and tastings.

Leave Castellina following the signs for Radda in Chianti, taking the right-hand turning at the junction 1.6km out of Castellina. For the next 10km the road passes through the beautiful woodlands of the Parco Naturale della Viriglia, proof that not all of Chianti is one vast vineyard.

Radda in Chianti
After the freneticism of Siena, Radda is a place for soaking up the slow pace of village life. Visitors

may relax in one of the prettiest villages in the Chianti region, sampling wines with Tuscan snacks such as *crostini* in the local *enotece* (wine bars). Medieval streets radiate from the central *piazza* with its stately Palazzo del Podestà. Nearby Volpaia, 6km to the north, is regarded as even more picturesque, with its pristine towers and castle.

From Radda follow the signs to Montevarchi. At a crossroads after some 6km take the leftmost road, signposted Badia a Coltibuono.

Badia a Coltibuono

This monastic complex, whose name means Abbey of the Good Harvest, dates from the 11th century and the church is a lovely example of the Romanesque style. Unfortunately it is only open during services, but there is a good restaurant alongside (which also sells wine, olive oil and honey) and its situation alone makes it worth a stop; the views from the abbey look over castle-topped hills to the Pratomagno mountain range rising steeply above the Arno Valley to the west.

Return to the crossroads and take the Siena road to reach Gaiole in Chianti after 5km.

Gaiole in Chianti

The village of Gaiole has a stream running along its main street. Wines can be bought at the local co-operative, the Agricoltori Chianti Geografico, Via Mulinaccio 10. A road to the right of the church leads to the 11th-century church at Spaltenna, with restaurant attached, and on to Vertine, a tiny walled village sitting on top of a vineyard-covered hill.

Continue along the Siena road and turn left after 3.5km. Chianti castles and fattorie *now come thick and fast; first Meleto with its sturdy castle, then Riétine and Castello di Castagnoli. Continue on following the signs to Monte Luco; the summit of this pine-covered hill is reached after 8km. Turn right at the summit following signs to Siena; far-reaching views open up on all sides as the road descends to the walled hamlet of San Gusmé after another 8km. Just beyond San Gusmé, take the right-hand road, signposted Gaiole; after 8km, this leads to Castello di Brólio.*

Castello di Brólio

The *castello,* regarded as the birthplace of the modern Chianti industry, offers guided tours, a well-stocked shop and the chance to learn all you want to know about local wine production. The Ricasoli family can trace its ownership of this estate back to 1167 and wines have been produced here since well before that date. Barone Bettino Ricasoli, who also served as Italy's second prime minister, established the formula that has been used since 1870 for making Chianti Classico. He specified the precise blend of juice from white and red grapes and confirmed the ancient practice of adding dried grapes to the vat to cause a second fermentation; it is this that gives Chianti its characteristic flavour and softness.

Ancient Chiusi

To return to Siena, take the San Marcellino dei Monti road, which joins the SS408 after 8km; turn left and follow the signs to Siena, which is reached after 16km.

Charming Castellina looks today much as it did 400 years ago

FOOD AND WINE

Florence likes to think that it gave birth to French cuisine. In 1533 Caterina de'Medici was married, at the tender age of 14, to Henri de Valois, soon to become King Henry II of France. Horrified by both the table manners and by the food of the French, she introduced her own chefs and recipes. The result is that several dishes are common to both Tuscany and France: hare stew, the Tuscan *lepre in dolce e forte*, is *dolce forte* in French; *canard a l'orange* is the Tuscan *papero alla melarancia* and *vol au vents* are sold in Tuscan pastry shops as *turbanate di sfoglia.*

These Renaissance dishes are not the staple of modern Tuscan cuisine, however; with few exceptions, the restaurateurs of Tuscany and Umbria have no time for fussy food, preferring to make homely and inexpensive dishes based on simple, fresh ingredients. Their philosophy is well summed up by the Italian saying: *piu se spenna, peggio se magna* (the more you spend, the less well you will eat). There are, as always, some exceptions to this rule. Tuscany, and Florence in particular, prides itself on its *bistecca alla Fiorentina*, tender beefsteak brushed with virgin olive oil, grilled over the scented embers of a chestnut wood fire, seasoned with herbs and served with a wedge of lemon. This is an expensive dish; the price on the menu is per 100g of raw meat and no self-respecting Italian gourmet would order less than half a kilo; it is also an addictive dish that, once tasted, prevents steak being fully enjoyed if prepared any other way.

Umbria's equivalent at the luxury end of the scale is the truffle (*tartufo*). Black truffles are the most common and least expensive, and they are usually grated over pasta dishes or used as a garnish. The rarer, more expensive, *bianchetto*, the white truffle, has a much more pronounced flavour and a little goes a long way; it is usually served as a sauce ingredient for pasta, sometimes combined with other wild mushrooms, mashed olives and garlic, or in an omelette with cheese and *prosciutto*. Truffles are more abundant in late autumn and winter; out of season they will have been preserved by freezing, canning or vacuum packing, with an inevitable loss of flavour.

For everyday eating, both Tuscany and Umbria are blessed with an abundance of good raw ingredients that are combined with honest simplicity. *Antipasti* range from robust wild boar ham or fennel-flavoured salami (*finocchione*) to a colourful plateful of appetising *crostini*, bite-sized pieces of toasted bread, dribbled with olive oil and topped with anchovy, liver or tomato paste, or crushed pinenuts flavoured with cheese and basil.

New World ingredients, introduced from the Americas by Florentine merchants in the 16th century, were adapted with relish, and roasted aubergines or peppers, bathed in thick emerald green olive oil, make a refreshing

The people of the region like their cakes, desserts and pastries

and simple beginning to the meal. A fondness for beans, served in thick soups or with tuna, has earned Tuscans the nickname *mangiafagiole* – the bean eaters.

Peasant thrift is evident in the number of soups that use up left-overs; *pappa al pomodoro* is a rich thick soup of tomatoes poured over yesterday's bread, and *acquacotta* takes care of any spare vegetables. Egg is stirred into this filling dish just before it is served. Best of all is the fish soup served in coastal restaurants, especially around Livorno, called *cacciucco*; this is the original *bouillabaisse* if local chefs are to be believed, and it uses scores of tiny and otherwise inedible fish as the base for a rich stock to which shellfish are then added – every restaurant has its own secret recipe.

The pasta course often presents a bewildering variety of choice. The local version of this Italian staple is rolled and pulled out by hand rather than extruded through a machine: *fatt in casa* indicates that it is homemade and the best variety is *umbrici*, a thick form of spaghetti, particularly popular in autumn served with sauce made from pungent wild mushrooms.

Meat for the main course is most commonly spit roasted or grilled over an open fire (*alla griglia*, or *alla cacciatore* – hunter's style). Pork and lamb are the year-round staples, flavoured with rosemary and pepper. In autumn, with the opening of the game season, wild boar, hare, rabbit, pheasant, partridge (and, sadly, songbirds such as thrushes) will be offered as the house speciality, casseroled with olives, roasted with a wrapping of bacon and herbs or made into a rich gamey stew.

Fish is plentiful, even in landlocked Umbria, where the clean fast-flowing rivers yield wild trout and crayfish (a particular speciality of the Valnerina). Lake Trasimeno is the source of eels (*anguille*), pike (*luce*) and carp (*carpe*), served in tomato sauce or fried in olive oil. The coastal towns of Tuscany, such as Orbetello and Livorno, are renowned for swordfish and tuna steak, and *fritto misto*, deep-fried pieces of the 20 or so varieties of fish caught in the Tyrrhenian Sea. The meal usually ends with *formaggio*, *frutta* or *dolci* – cheese, usually *pecorino*, made from sheep's milk, fresh fruit or sweetmeats that will vary depending on the season. Typical of the region are tarts and cakes made from nuts, candied fruit, honey and spices, or pasta – again – served cold with chopped nuts, cinnamon, lemon, sweet ricotta cheese or a liqueur-enriched sauce.

Such robust food demands equally full-bodied wine as an accompaniment, and there is no lack of choice: Chianti, Montepulciano and Montalcino in Tuscany, along with Montefalco and the Torgiano region in Umbria, all produce superior quality red wines based on the versatile Sangiovese grape. Certain label markings help to identify the best: *classico* attached to the name of any wine indicates that it comes from a long-established area; *riserva* indicates a wine that has been aged for at least three years in wooden casks producing a bigger wine than *normale*. The Gallo Nero (Black Rooster) label on bottles of Chianti Classico signifies that the wine has been produced according to the methods approved by the Consorzio Chianti Classico, founded in 1924 to control production. Neighbouring regions, outside the Classico zone, have a similar *consorzio* and their wines carry the Chianti Putto label, with its *putto*, or cherub, symbol.

These simple classifications disguise the sheer bewildering breadth of wines on offer, differing markedly in style and quality. Wine *aficionados* will enjoy experimenting; those with no pretensions to wine expertise should trust the restaurateur's recommendations, and not be put off if he recommends a *vino da tavala* (table wine). Many small vineyards that do not qualify for a quality designation, and some big producers who have decided to go their own way, unhindered by consortium rules, produce plain *vino da tavala* of exceptional quality.

Celebrated Orvieto, chief of the Umbrian wines

Tuscan Chianti grapes

COLLE DI VAL D'ELSA

MAP REF: 110 C4

The prosperous lower town, or Colle Bassa, is Italy's main centre for the production of crystal glass and there are plenty of shops offering fine examples of this local craft. Colle Alta, the upper town, stands high above the valley floor. Steep stone staircases link the two but it is easier to drive out of the lower town on the Volterra road and park beneath the walls of the upper town. From here a path leads to the impeccably maintained Via del Campana, lined with imposing *palazzi* displaying rusticated door and window surrounds. From here it is apparent that Colle Alta, which looks large and complex from below, in fact consists of one long main street which follows the undulations of the ridge on which it stands.

Turning left up the hill leads to a viaduct with open views either side over the Elsa Valley. In 1269 the valley was the site of a fierce battle in the long-running feud between Siena and Florence. One of those who watched the battle from a tower near this spot was Sapia, a Sienese noblewoman who had been sent into exile. Bearing a grudge against her native city, she revelled in its defeat at the hands of Florence; later, Dante finds her weeping with remorse in purgatory (*Purgatorio*, Canto XIII, 106–123). Straddling the viaduct is the delicate Palazzo Campana, built in 1539 by Baccio d'Agnolo. Its typically Tuscan archway, with a teardrop-shaped keystone, forms a splendid overture to the Via del Castello. Lined with medieval buildings, this has shops selling antiques and crystal glass, and several small museums. The walls of the Museo d'Arte Sacra, Via del Castello 27, feature 14th-century frescos of hunting scenes by Taddeo di Bartolo. The Antiquarium, next to the cathedral in Piazza del Duomo, displays Etruscan finds and material documenting the life of Arnolfo di Cambio, the architect of the Palazzo Vecchio in Florence, who was born here sometime in the 1230s. His supposed birthplace, Via del Castello 63, is a well-preserved example of a 13th-century tower house.

Sant'Antimo, south of the walled village of Montalcino

MONTALCINO

MAP REF: 110 C3

This beautiful town stands above vine-covered slopes that produce one of Italy's finest wines, the noble Brunello. This, and other local wines – such as the lighter Rosso di Montalcino and the fragrant Moscadello di Montalcino – can be sampled in the *enoteca* located in the 14th-century *rocca* that dominates the town and the views for miles around. From the airy heights of the park surrounding the fortress views stretch unbroken over miles of countryside; this productive landscape is the source of the culinary and herbal delights sold in the shops lining the route to the fortress – local honey, dried lavender, sheep's-milk cheeses, olive oil and succulent hams.

At the entrance to the *rocca* itself, a plaque records the town's resistance to the 'Medici thief' and the ancient battle standard inside is revered by Sienese patriots with long memories. Montalcino gave sanctuary to a group of Sienese refugees when the city finally fell to Florence in 1555; here they set up a Sienese government in exile, ever hopeful of wreaking revenge on Cosimo I and restoring their native city to its proud independence. Instead, Cosimo took Montalcino in 1559 and extinguished the flame of Sienese republicanism forever. Even so, the *Palio* in Siena (see page 95) is still preceded by a procession of citizens from all the towns that once belonged to the republic. Montalcinese flag-bearers lead the parade, accorded the place of honour in gratitude for the role they played four centuries previously.

For art lovers, Montalcino has several high spots: the Museo Civico e Diocesana, below the *rocca*, displays 15th-century painted wood statues of saints and several good Sienese School paintings, such as Girolamo di Benvenuto's *Adoration*. Madonna di Soccorso, an unusually delicate baroque church, is worth seeking out if only because it offers more sweeping views over the adjacent park.

Nearby Even if you are suffering from cultural indigestion, the exquisite Romanesque abbey of Sant'Antimo, 10km south of Montalcino, is guaranteed to revive the spirits. The delicate beauty of the travertine-built church, set against the deep green of the surrounding hills, has enraptured countless visitors. The contemporary English poet,

A summit madonna at Monte Amiata welcomes all visitors

Charles Tomlinson, captured the serenity of the place when he described the wind-blown cypresses chasing their sinuous shadows 'to and fro across the still stone tower'. The abbey was founded in the 9th century – by Charlemagne, according to local legend. The present buildings, in Lombardic style, date from 1118. The interior of the church is radiant with the translucent tones of locally quarried alabaster, and visitors can climb to the *matroneum*, the women's gallery, for an unusual view of the whole church.

MONTE AMIATA

MAP REF: 110 C3

The heights of Monte Amiata (1,738m) are covered in snow for several months of the year and dominate the skyline of southeastern Tuscany. Visiting in 1462, Pope Pius II fondly described the 'sweet shade and silvery springs' of the summit as fit for nymphs, fauns and poets. Today skiers crowd the upper slopes in winter and hikers circumnavigate the tree-covered cone of this extinct volcano in summer. It is also possible to drive to the summit for outstanding views from Abbadia San Salvatore or Castel del Piano. The towns that cluster round the foot are linked by scenic roads that pass through chestnut woods, best seen in the full blaze of their autumn colour. Abbadia San Salvatore, founded in AD743 and once one of the most powerful monasteries in Italy, is now hemmed in by the suburbs of the town which bears its name; all that remains of architectural interest is the 8th-century crypt with boldly carved capitals. Piancastagnáio, to the south, is [illegible], with its newly restored *rocca* standing among chestnut groves.

Breathtaking views of southeast Tuscany from the heights of Monte Amiata, an extinct volcano

Pienza, birthplace of Pope Pius II

MONTEPULCIANO

MAP REF: 111 D3

Montepulciano is a town where fun meets high seriousness. The citizens call themselves *Poliziani* after the town's Latin name, *Mons Politianus*. It is a matter of intense pride that the great humanist and poet, Angelo Ambrogini, better known as Politian, was born in the town and that the town's annual arts festival, founded in 1975 by the composer Hans Werner Henze, attracts leading contemporary dramatists, choreographers and composers. The *Poliziani* also know how to enjoy life, especially at the *Baccanale* festival in August, held to honour their Vino Nobile; this full-bodied wine has been described as full of autumnal fragrance and was 'ennobled' by a 16th-century pope who thought it the most perfect of all wines. Vino Nobile can be sampled in the Cantine Cantucci in the Piazza Grande, but it should be treated with respect; Henry James over-indulged and sourly decided that Montepulciano (rather than he himself) was 'parched and brown and queer and crooked'.

The Via di Gracciano del Corso is more winding than crooked and lined with fascinating buildings that blend Florentine and Sienese styles along with a few idiosyncratic quirks. One of these is the Palazzo Bucelli, whose façade is studded with Etruscan and Roman cinerary urns and reliefs. The Church of Sant'Agostino, on the opposite side of the Corso, has a pleasing terracotta lunette above the portal depicting the *Virgin and Child with Saints John and Augustine*, designed, like the church, by Michelozzo in the 14th century.

The extensive views from the Piazza Grande compete for attention with the varied architecture of the cathedral, palaces and *loggie*. The *Assumption* altarpiece in the cathedral, by Taddeo di Bartolo (1401) has been called the greatest work of the Sienese School, partly because of its astonishingly vibrant colours. The Palazzo Comunale, clearly modelled on the Palazzo Vecchio in Florence, offers the chance to climb the tower for views over miles of unspoiled countryside. Perhaps the greatest of the city's buildings, however, lies outside the town on the Pienza road. The church of Madonna di San Biagio is a masterpiece of Renaissance classicism, built by Antonio da Sangallo in 1518. The church, of honey-coloured travertine, approached by an avenue of cypresses, seems perfectly in harmony with its setting.

MONTERIGGIONI

MAP REF: 110 C4

Superbly situated high above the N2 Siena road, Monteriggioni is a stirring sight. It still has its complete ring of walls and towers, and nowhere else in Italy can visitors experience the purity of an intact medieval town uncompromised by encircling modern suburbs. Monteriggioni was built as a fortress in 1213 to guard the northern limits of Sienese territory; as such it was frequently attacked by Florence, so that its survival is all the more remarkable. In fact, little has changed since Dante's time; the poet compared 'Montereggion's ring-shaped citadel', with its 'circling rampart crowned with towers' to the abyss at the heart of his Inferno, guarded by 14 giants (*Inferno*, Canto XXXI, 40–43). Nothing so horrifying greets today's visitors; the sleepy town has a few souvenir shops and a restaurant or two for leisurely indulgence before or after a relaxed stroll round the 560m circuit of the walls.

PIENZA

MAP REF: 110 C3

Pienza is an exquisite town that reflects the ideals of the humanist age. Until the mid-15th century Pienza was a small town of 2,000 people called Corsignano. Its fortunes changed when Aeneas Silvius Piccolomini, who was born there in 1405, was elected to the papacy. As Pope Pius II he decided to transform his birthplace into an ideal city. Bernardo Rossellino was commissioned as the chief architect, but the pope's visionary plans were never realised. Only the central *piazza* was completed before it became clear that even the papal purse was not deep enough to see the project through. Rossellino had cheated his patron all along, siphoning off funds for his own ends and spending more than twice the original budget. Pius I forgave him because, despite his deceit, Rossellino had 'built these glorious structures which are praised by all except the few consumed by envy'.

These glorious structures consist of the buildings around Piazza Pio II. Reactions differ to the measured simplicity of the cathedral façade, the well and the Palazzo Piccolomini; some find the buildings elegant, others cold and austere. The buildings remain frozen in time; in 1462 the pope changed the name of the town to Pienza by papal bull and ordered that nothing should be changed. The command was respected by humankind at least; nothing has been added to or removed from the cathedral, but nature has caused the east end to subside, and despite buttressing the problem is getting worse. Surprisingly, the classicism of the façade is not carried through to the interior, which is Gothic in inspiration and filled with Sienese School altar paintings. Light floods the church through tall windows in accordance with the pope's own wishes; he wanted a *domus vitrea*, a house of glass, symbolic of the intellectual enlightenment of humanism in contrast to the

San Biagio, Montepulciano

shadowy mysticism of the medieval church.

The Palazzo Piccolomini, now a museum, is filled with the pope's personal possessions and is modelled on the Palazzo Rucellai in Florence. From the library, visitors can step out on to the three-storey *loggia* at the rear to enjoy stunningly framed views.

Pienza caters for the body as well as the soul; it is the self-proclaimed 'capital of sheep's cheese', renowned for its delicate *pecorino*, while plenty of shops offer local crafts.

The old core of Corsignano survives to the west of Pienza and the 11th-century Pieve, where Piccolomini was baptised, is worth seeking out for its portal curiously carved with dragons and mermaids.

MOTOR TOUR

This 50km round tour from Pienza takes in the uniquely dramatic landscape around La Foce.

From Pienza follow the signposts to Montepulciano for 10km.

Montepulciano
The hilltop town is complemented by the towering Renaissance church of San Biagio, the masterpiece of Antonio da Sangallo. The winding Corso and the spacious Piazza Grande are the main focus of architectural interest in the town and there are shops selling good local ham, cheese and Vino Nobile.

Follow the signs for Chianciano Terme, which is reached after 8km. Turn right in the centre of this modern spa town, following the signs for La Foce/Siena. After climbing for 5km you will reach the top of a ridge; ignore all side turnings and carry straight on to descend the hill and look for the car park on the left, opposite the Oasi La Foce restaurant.

La Foce
The landscape that unfolds below the car park is stunning; to the left an ancient Etruscan road zigzags up the hill marked out by a double row of cypress trees spaced at precise intervals. To the right is an area of clay hummocks typical of the empty Crete landscape, like a mass of giant anthills. It is a scene of bizarre contrasts between the chaos of nature and the precise geometry of the cypress trees. Walk from the car park back uphill and left (signposted

Pienza's *pecorino*, a sheep's cheese

Montepulciano) to the hamlet and castle of Castellúcio. This is the home of Iris Origo, author of *The Merchant of Prato*, who sheltered refugees from Nazi persecution here during World War II and wrote of her brave resistance to tyranny in *War in the Val d'Orcia*. Scores of pathways thread through the oak woods surrounding Castellúcio and nature lovers will find a mass of bulbs and hellebores in flower in spring, rock roses, broom and juniper in summer and carpets of cyclamen in autumn.

Continue downhill from the car park. In dry summer weather with a sturdy vehicle it is possible to drive along the cypress-lined and unmetalled Etruscan road over the hill to the right; otherwise it is necessary to drive two sides of a triangle to La Vittória (5km) and turn right, following the Siena signs. The road follows the broad Val d'Orcia, with clear views of Monte Amiata ahead, for the next 8km. Take the next right turn, signposted to Pienza, which is reached after another 8km.

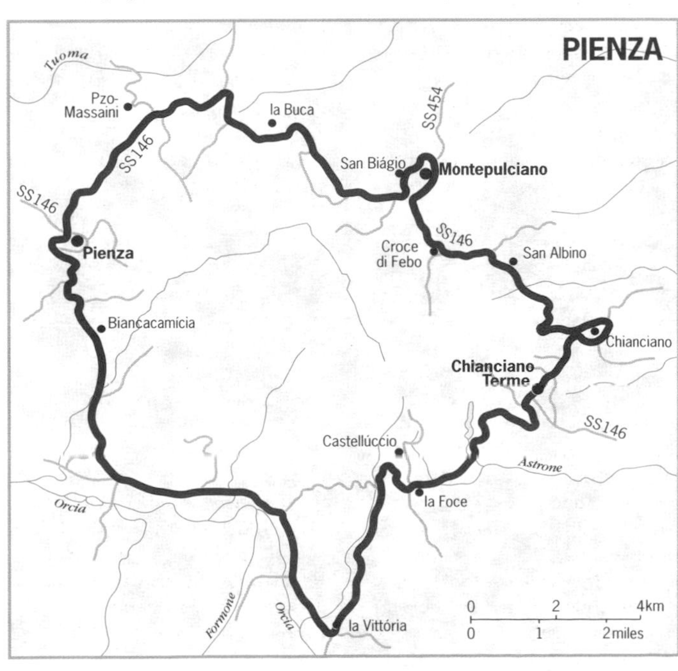

SAN GIMIGNANO

MAP REF: 110 B4

Despite over-exposure (San Gimignano features on countless posters and postcards) this 'city of the beautiful towers' is one of the highlights of a visit to Tuscany. Nor is the city's appeal limited to its dramatic skyline. San Gimignano's churches and museums contain charming medieval frescos, the streets are lined with art galleries and shops selling jewellery, ceramics and local Vernaccia wines, and there are several fine restaurants to choose from. Inevitably a city of so many attractions suffers from overcrowding and visitors may have to queue patiently to park; follow the car park direction signs left round the city walls and aim for the third and last car park, which is also the largest and most likely to have free space.

TOWN WALK

From the car park, cross the road and enter through the gap in the city walls; turn right following Via Folgore da San Gimignano and Via XX Settembre into Via San Matteo.

1 Entering Via San Matteo is like stepping back 600 years in time; only the occasional modern shop sign intrudes on the prospect of medieval palaces and towers. The same ornamental motifs are repeated in endless variations on the façades; window arches are decorated with a frieze of arrow heads and the doors are framed by typically Tuscan arches, with a keystone shaped like a teardrop. The designers of these 13th-century palaces all took their cue from the façade of the Church of San Bartolo, halfway up the street on the left, a tiny Romanesque building of rose-pink and yellow brick.

Continue up Via San Matteo to enter the Piazza del Duomo.

2 'New York in stone' is how numerous commentators have described this tower-filled square. The beauty is sculptural and elemental, but the original purpose of these towers was grim. In the ups and downs of medieval interfamily conflict, the towers were both a status symbol and a fortress from which enemies could be bombarded. Noble families, the *magnati*, crowned their palaces with these symbols of their wealth, aiming to build higher than their neighbours; several of San Gimignano's towers exceed 50m. Fourteen towers survive of the original 70 that were once packed into this tiny city. The towers are windowless and impenetrable, designed as a refuge in time of danger. To the governing authorities they represented a nuisance; civil warfare would remain a constant threat while these private fortresses remained in the city. In Florence and Siena laws were passed first limiting the height of the towers and then forbidding new ones from being built. Whenever a family fell into disgrace or was sentenced to exile, their towers would be demolished as a sign of defeat. Many more were demolished from the 15th century onwards as the *magnati* replaced their medieval palaces with new ones in the Renaissance style, and few towers now remain in Tuscany. San Gimignano's towers survived only because the city became a forgotten backwater, of little economic importance, once Florence gained control of the whole region in the 16th century.

Walk across to the left-hand corner of the Piazza del Duomo to descend into the Piazza della Cisterna.

3 This is another delightful square, named after the pretty 13th-century well at the centre, whose graceful buildings harmonise despite their disparity; brick and stone, Romanesque, Gothic and Renaissance are all intermixed, creating wonderful contrasts.

Leave the square by the right-hand corner, passing under the 14th-century Arco dei Becci. From here you can walk all the way down Via San Giovanni, which has some of the city's best shops, to the Porta San Giovanni city gate. Turn right at the gate and right again to climb back to the city centre along Via Berignano, a quiet residential street with unusual views of the towers crowning the highest point of the city. At the end of this street turn right then first left up Via della Costarella. At the top, turn right through the archway that leads into the frescoed courtyard of the Palazzo del Popolo.

4 The *palazzo*, dating from 1323, houses the Museo Civico; this has many excellent paintings by artists such as Gozzoli, Filippino Lippi and Pinturrichio, but by far the most beguiling exhibits are the *Wedding Scene* frescos of Niccolo di Segna, showing the happy

Italy's best-preserved medieval city

couple taking a bath together in a huge wooden tub and the groom stealing into bed alongside his sleeping bride. The energetic can climb the adjacent Torre Grosso for outstanding views.

From the palazzo turn right, then immediately left under an arch into a small courtyard called Piazza Luigi Pecori.

5 The *loggia* to the right, where musicians play to entertain summer visitors, shelters an *Annunciation* fresco by Ghirlandaio (1482). There are two small museums in the square displaying archaeological finds and religious art.

Leave the square and turn left to reach the steps of the Collegiata, in Piazza del Duomo.

6 The interior of this church, modelled on Siena Cathedral with its striped walls and star-covered vaults, is full of enjoyable frescos. *The Last Judgement* scenes by Taddeo di Bartolo (1393–6) are the greatest attraction since they depict an imaginative and grotesque range of punishments being meted out on the damned by devils who clearly relish their task. More beguiling are the scenes from Genesis by Bartolo di Fredi (1367), including a charming depiction of the creation of Adam and Eve. The other highlights include Barna di Siena's scenes from the Life of Christ (1380) and the Ghirlandaio frescos on the Life of Santa Fina (1475) in that saint's chapel.

Turn left out of the Collegiata and left again down beside the church. Follow the path that leads to the 14th-century Fortezza di Montestaffoli, from whose walls there are good views of the city and surrounding countryside. Return to the Piazza del Duomo, turn left to walk back down Via San Matteo. At the Porta San Matteo, turn right down Via Cellolese and left into the Piazza San Agostino.

7 San Agostino (1298) is another fresco-filled church; Benozzo Gozzoli's scenes in the choir (1465), illustrating the life of Saint Augustine, are fresh and vivid, full of the gentle landscapes that this painter so loved to paint.

To return to the car park, leave the square beside the Church of San Pietro and walk back down Via Folgore da San Gimignano to the exit gate in the city walls.

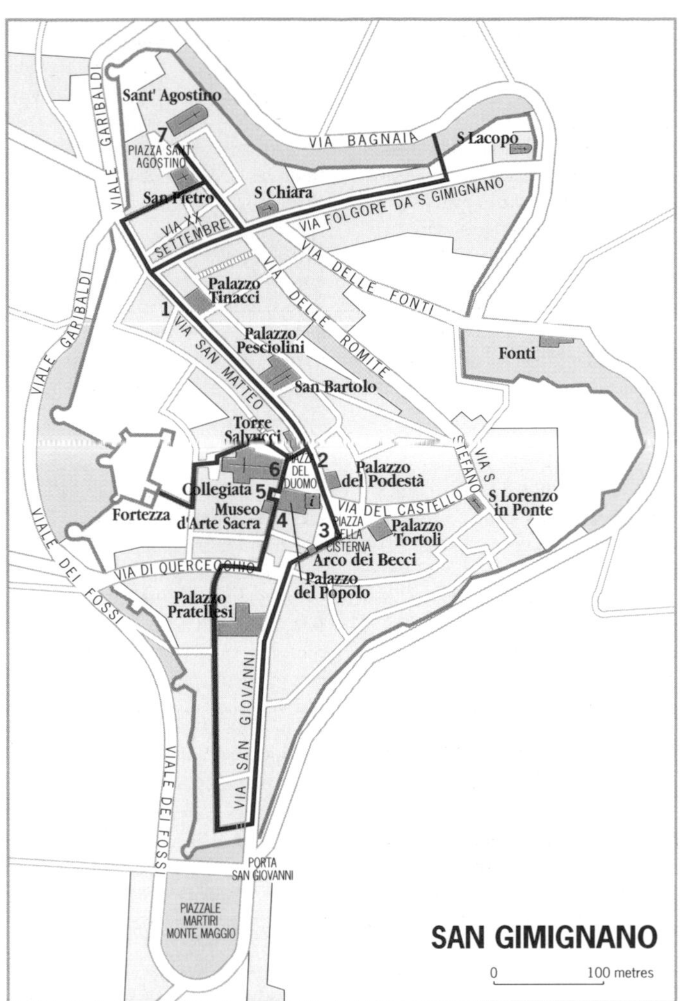

SAN QUÍRICO D'ORCIA

MAP REF: 110 C3

The busy N2, which now bypasses San Quírico, was once a pilgrimage route linking Rome and northern Europe. This explains why the humble agricultural town has such a fine Romanesque church, with three carved portals. The church, begun in 1080, commemorates the 3rd-century infant Saint Quiricus who, according to legend, declared himself a Christian as soon as he could talk and was promptly martyred with his mother. Inside the church is Sano di Pietro's radiant *Resurrection* triptych, and the delicately crafted inlaid wood choir stalls by Antonio Barili (1453–1516). High above the town are three medieval castles which are dramatically spotlit at night: Rocca d'Orcia, Ripa d'Orcia and Castiglione d'Orcia. A walk or drive to their windy heights is rewarded with sweeping views.

Nearby At the heart of Bagno Vignoni is a stone *piscina*, a large pool of bubbling hot sulphurous water in which many illustrious bodies have bathed: St Catherine of Siena to chastise her body with the heat and the arthritic Lorenzo de'Medici for the good of his health. Until recently it remained a favourite night-time bathing place for *spumante*-drinking young sophisticates but swimming under the stars has now been forbidden; modern baths have been built further down the hill where local people gather for summer festivities. The town's spa hotel is renowned for treating all kinds of 'traumatic illness'.

San Gimignano attracts the tourists

WRITERS IN TUSCANY

Dante Alighieri, poet

Few regions of the world have inspired so many classics of literature as Tuscany. Of native writers, everybody has heard of – though few have actually read – Dante's *Divine Comedy*, the poems of Petrarch and Boccaccio's *Decameron*. These works helped to establish the Tuscan dialect as the language of educated Italians and encouraged an outpouring of vernacular poetry from the 14th century onwards. Everyone in Renaissance Tuscany, it seems, wrote poetry. Even the puritanical Savonarola wrote lyrics (rather in the style of today's evangelical hymns) to be sung to the tunes of popular carnival songs, while Michelangelo, Politian and Lorenzo de'Medici all left humorous, erotic and philosophical sonnets of great accomplishment. The list of Florentine classics that remain in print and are read to this day includes Machiavelli's *The Prince*, Cellini's *Autobiography*, Vasari's *Lives of the Artists* and Galileo's scientific *Dialogues*.

Shelley lived in Livorno

Foreign writers began to record their impressions of Tuscany from the beginning of the 18th century when Florence became a stopping-off point on the Grand Tour. In this age when all things classical were admired, a traveller like Goethe could dismiss the Basilica di San Francesco in Assisi as a 'Babylonian pile' but be enraptured by the far-from-complete remains of the town's Temple of Minerva. Like many northern European visitors, the Protestant Goethe found Catholic Italy distasteful; his notebooks are full of observations on how he would improve everything, from local farming methods to the weather.

Extreme censoriousness also characterises the work of Tobias Smollett, whose *Travels in France and Italy* is one long catalogue of complaints. His account of Siena is typical: 'we were indifferently lodged in a house that stunk like a privy and fared wretchedly at supper'. He regarded Italian men as savages and Italian women as immoral for their habit of taking to bed with their *cicisbei* (toyboys in modern parlance). Even so he still found time to write his masterpiece, *Humphrey Clinker*, while living in a villa near Livorno in 1769.

Other writers, attracted to Italy by cheap villas and a sunny climate, were more passionate about the landscape than Smollet but did not mix with native Tuscans, leading Charles Greville to say that their descriptions of the region suffered from 'no foundation of natives'. Shelley celebrated the views from his villa near Livorno in *To a Skylark* but he and Mary lived 'in utter solitude'. Others created a mini-England in Florence or Bagni di Lucca, complete with tea-time salons. So great was the number of English exiles living in Florence that Horace Mann, British Consul to the Medici court, feared he would be bankrupted by the duty of entertaining them all to dinner.

The Napoleonic Wars brought a temporary halt to travel in Europe, but after Waterloo the momentum picked up again as Russian, English, American and French visitors flocked to the city described by Shelley as 'a paradise of exiles'. Florence Nightingale was born and educated in the city after which she was named. Tennyson and Wordsworth had their romantic imaginations stirred by their Tuscan experiences, and wrote some appalling verse as a consequence, such as Tennyson's:

'*O love, what hours were thine and mine,*
In lands of palm and southern pine;
In lands of palm, of orange blossom,
Of olive, aloe and maize and vine'.

Only too often English writers seem to have found themselves so paralysed by the poetry of Tuscan landscapes and art that they became prosaic in their own work. George Eliot's *Romola*, carefully researched and set in Renaissance Florence, is her least successful novel, and Elizabeth Barrett Browning's reputation as a poetess is not helped by verse such as:

I found a house at Florence on the hill
Of Bellosguardo. 'Tis a tower which keeps
A post of double observation o'er
The valley of the Arno . . .

The Brownings famously eloped to Florence in 1846 and Elizabeth's health improved dramatically when Robert succeeded in weaning her off opium, substituting the rather less harmful red wine as her nightly soporific.

Robert Browning's own dramatic monologues, based on Vasari's *Lives*, are among the better works to come out of mid-Victorian Florence, but generally it was American writers who wrote best of the region, least hampered by romantic rapture. Henry James looked down on his 'detested fellow pilgrims'; his own works, *The Aspern Papers* and *Portrait of Places*, are subtle and more sensitive than the outpourings of what he called the 'dilettante scribblers of Little Tuscany'. Mark Twain, too, was refreshingly irreverent; *Innocents Abroad* is full of witty invective, such as his description of the Arno: 'they all call it a river, and they honestly think it is a river, do these dark and bloody Florentines. They even help out the delusion by building bridges over it. I do not see why they are too good to wade'. Another famous Twain outburst expresses well what all visitors come to feel from time to time when saturated with too much art: 'Enough. Say no more! Lump the whole thing! Say the creator made Italy from designs by Michelangelo!'.

Tuscany continued to be celebrated in the 20th century by a bevy of penetrating observers; E M Forster's novels, *Where Angels Fear to Tread* (set in San Gimignano, which he calls Monteriano) and *A Room with a View*, head the list of classics. Virginia Woolf's diaries are full of poignant observations; Dylan Thomas, predictably, headed straight for the cheap wine, 'drinking Chianti in our marble shanty, sick of *vini* and *contadini* and *bambini*'. D H Lawrence allowed his own zealous philosophising to obscure fact in *Etruscan Places*, but he still makes compelling reading.

The history and art of the region has inspired some masterpieces of historical narrative, notably Iris Origo's *The Merchant of Prato*, J R Hale's *Florence and the Medici* and Harold Acton's *The Last Medici*. As an antidote to what Mary McCarthy calls the 'tooled-leather idea of Florence', a city of 'old maids of both sexes, her ever-lively book, *The Stones of Florence*, is an entertaining and informative read.

Tuscany continues to be a place that foreigners find conducive to artistic endeavour, offering an inspirational environment. Muriel Spark, Germaine Greer, the poet Peter Porter and the actress Miriam Margolyes are among the better known habitués, while John Mortimer's humorous account of shady dealings in Chiantishire (*Summer's Lease*) is necessary reading for idling away the hours around a villa pool.

The poets Robert Browning and Elizabeth Barrett Browning honeymooned in Florence

·SIENA·

Siena, the city of rose-pink brick, has been celebrated in literature as the feminine counterpart to the masculine Florence. Siena is Gothic, its art sweet and decorative, while Renaissance Florence is a city of classical reserve and fortress-like palaces. Such descriptions of Siena whet the appetite, but it is as well to be aware of the mundane realities; traffic is excluded from the historic centre and the supply of parking space is limited, so be prepared for a long walk from the suburbs, where street parking is easier.

For orientation it helps to know that Siena (map ref: 110 C4) is shaped like an inverted Y, with the famous Campo, the city's main *piazza*, sitting at the intersection of the three arms. Each arm climbs to the summit of one of the three hills on which Siena is built.

Once practical issues are resolved, most visitors to Siena head straight for the Campo, as if drawn by an irresistible force. The shape of the huge sloping Piazza del Campo has been compared to a fan, an amphitheatre, an oyster, a cockle or scallop shell. The Sienese see it as the protective cloak of the Virgin.

The curved side of the Campo is ringed with pavement cafés and restaurants, perfect for contemplating the public buildings, ranged like a theatrical set, on the opposite side of the Campo. The scene is even more pleasing at night when the buildings are spotlit.

The surface of the Campo is paved in the same pinkish brown brick as the surrounding civic buildings, the colour known to artists as burnt Siena. The surface is subdivided by blue bricks into nine fields, symbolising the *Governo dei Nove*, the Government of the Nine, which ruled over the city during its golden age – the period which began in 1260 and ended in 1348 when the Black Death brought a sudden halt to the city's booming economy.

All over Siena, statues of Romulus and Remus being suckled by a she-wolf serve as a reminder that, according to legend, the city was founded by Senius, the son of Remus. By 1260 the city was rich, powerful and determined enough to inflict a decisive defeat on Florentine troops at the Battle of Montaperti. Florence had invited the disaster by arrogantly demanding the submission of Siena; instead, Florence found itself facing imminent destruction and was spared only through the intervention of Florentine exiles serving in the Sienese army.

Filled with a new sense of civic pride at the defeat of so powerful a rival, Siena embarked on a huge programme of building. At the same time, Sienese artists found ready patronage among the wealthy wool merchants and bankers of the city, and the result was an outpouring of religious paintings and sculpture. The Black Death, which came to Tuscany in 1348, carried off one-third of the city's population and Siena's fortunes quickly went into reverse. The city slid into political turmoil, with first the nobility and then the wool workers staging revolts against the government of the day. Torn by factional violence and heading for bankruptcy, the city was easy prey for the Hapsburg Emperor Charles V, who swept through Italy in 1530, taking Siena before moving on to besiege Rome.

In 1552 the Sienese revolted against the Spanish garrison installed by Charles V. This gave Cosimo I of Florence the

No traffic in central Siena

The huge Piazza del Campo

opportunity to take long overdue revenge for his city's earlier defeat. In alliance with the Spanish, Cosimo launched a long and bitter war against Siena, which began in 1554 and ended in April 1555 when the starved and besieged city finally surrendered. By the end, some 8,000 Sienese had lost their lives, reducing the population to a mere 6,000; the war was so brutal that, to this day, [illegible] foot in Florence.

As a defeated member of the new Grand Duchy of Tuscany, Siena was singled out for particular repression; its banking and wool industries were suppressed because they posed too much of a threat to Florentine traders. Tourists visiting Siena in the 19th and early 20th century wrote disparagingly of a city in near-terminal decay; 'crumbling and rotting' as Henry James described it in 1909. The only happy outcome of this tragic decline was that Siena was preserved from change: its medieval buildings and its works of art have since been restored and Siena, having regained its long-lost civic pride, now prospers from tourism. It also continues to act as a foil or counterpoint to the old enemy, Florence; Siena's graceful Gothic buildings appeal especially to those with a romantic soul.

The Palazzo Pubblico

Siena's Palazzo Pubblico stands at the focal point of the Piazza del Campo, surmounted by the soaring Torre del Mangia, the second tallest medieval campanile in Italy after Cremona. Standing 102m tall, the tower is symbol of the city that is visible for miles around. Its curious name, translated as Tower of the Wastrel, derives from *Mangiaguadagni* ('eat the profits'), the nickname of one of the early bellringers whose job it was to toll the curfew and call citizens to public meetings.

The Palazzo, built between 1297 and 1342, still serves as the town hall but the frescoed upper rooms house the Museo Civico. Siena's most famous painting, Simone Martini's *Maestà* (1315), is in the Sala del Mappamondo, where fragments also remain of Lorenzetti's cosmological map after which the room is named. Better preserved is Lorenzetti's *Allegory of Good and Bad Government* (1338–1340) in the Sala della Pace (also known as the Sala dei Nove – meeting room of the Council of the Nine). Good Government depicts an ideal city and countryside, full of cheerful, well-dressed and busy people. Bad Government (though damaged) is a far more convincing and familiar picture of daylight robbery and of urban and rural decay.

Anyone with the energy to climb to the top of the Torre del Mangia is rewarded by glorious views; the second-best option is to climb the staircase from the *palazzo* entrance up to the *loggia* where Jacopo della Quercia's original relief carvings made for the Fonte Gaia (1409–19), the fountain at the centre of the Campo below, are displayed.

Nearby In the countryside south of Siena there are two atmospheric abbeys. Torri is located off the SS73, approximately 8km from the city; here the simple Romanesque church has a three-storeyed cloister with delightfully varied columns.

Twenty-two kilometres further south along the same road is San Galgano, a romantic abbey with the sky for a roof, grass for a floor and glassless windows through which the swallows skim. The ruined abbey, dissolved in 1652, was once the chief Cistercian house in central Italy. It was begun in 1180 on the site of San Galgano's lonely hermitage. On the hill above the abbey is the circular Romanesque Cappella di Montesiepi, begun in 1185. Inside is a sword miraculously encased in stone. San Galgano, in reverse of the Arthurian legend, thrust his sword into the stone as a sign that he was renouncing his dissolute and violent life as a soldier. This and other episodes from the saint's life are depicted in Ambrogio Lorenzetti's frescos on the chapel walls.

TOWN WALK

Facing the Palazzo Pubblico, walk to the right-hand corner of the Campo and climb the steps of the Chiasso del Bargello; take the first left, Via di Città, past the 14th-century Palazzo Chigi-Saracini, a miniature version of the Palazzo Pubblico, the venue for summer concerts by members of the renowned Accademia Musicale Chigiana. At the next junction, turn left in Via San Pietro to reach the Pinacoteca Nazionale.

1 This picture gallery, housed in the graceful 15th-century Palazzo Buonsignori, contains an outstanding collection of Sienese School paintings, organised chronologically. Pictures of the enthroned Virgin, patron and protectress of the city, predominate – more than half the pictures commissioned by Sienese patrons between 1350 and 1550 were of this subject. Outstanding are the works of Guido da Siena, the 13th-century founding father of the Sienese School, Simone Martini, Ambrogio Lorenzetti and Duccio di Buoninsegna.

Turn right out of the museum and walk back up Via San Pietro; at the junction, continue straight up Via del Capitano, which leads to the cathedral.

2 Siena's cathedral is beautiful or outlandish, depending on personal taste – Ruskin called it a costly confectionery; Wagner was reduced to tears by its beauty. It is certainly striking with its frilly façade covered in saints, prophets and philosophers (these are mostly reproductions, the originals being in the Museo dell'Opera del Duomo) and its zebra-striped tower. These stripes are even more emphatic inside, where they cover every surface to dizzying effect. The cathedral was begun in 1186 and took 300 years to complete; the dome was finished in 1264 but the façade was not begun until 1284. In 1339 the Sienese decided that their still incomplete building should be expanded to create the biggest church in Christendom. The bare ruined nave to the right of the cathedral shows how far construction had proceeded before the Black Death struck the city. Abandoning this grandiose

Fussy, like a huge iced cake...

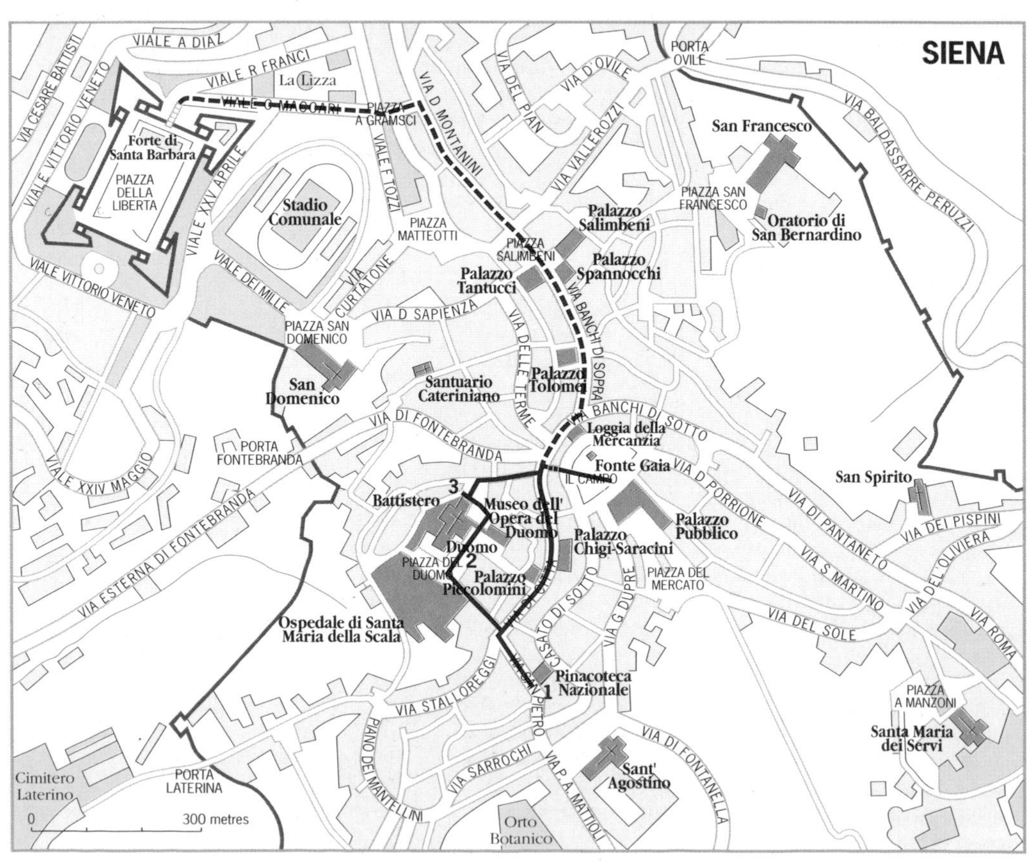

...and elaborate, the cathedral façade

scheme, the Sienese finally completed the cathedral in 1382. Part of the skeletal nave, to the right of the campanile, has been bricked up to form the Museo dell'Opera del Duomo; this contains Duccio's *Maestà* (1308–11), a seminal Siena School painting of the enthroned Virgin, and figures carved by Giovanni Pisano for the cathedral façade (1284–96).

From the Museo, turn right down a steep flight of marble stairs and left to the rear of the cathedral, where the baptistry is located.

3 The baptistry's unusual position, in the crypt below the cathedral apse, makes it seem like something of an afterthought, and its Gothic façade, begun in 1390, was never completed. Even so, it houses an outstanding font decorated with bronze reliefs (1411–30), the collaborative work of three great Gothic and Renaissance artists: Jacopo della Quercia, Donatello and Ghiberti.

From the baptistry, walk down the steps and turn right into Via dei Pellegrini, which leads back to the Campo. To explore Siena in more depth, turn left in Via di Città and keep walking uphill along the main shopping street, Via Bianchi di Sopra. This leads to the Palazzo Salimbeni, a handsome 14th-century building, now the headquarters of the Monte dei Paschi bank, one of the city's biggest employers. Continue along Via dei Montanini; from here it is a short walk left to the Forte di Santa Barbara, built by Cosimo I after he conquered the city and now devoted to the happier pursuit of wine sampling. The Enoteca Italia Permanente (National Wine Library), located in the fortress, has a wine bar where the best of the region's products can be sampled, and there are fine views over the city from the fortress, especially at sunset.

SIENA CATHEDRAL

The ceiling of Siena's cathedral nave is painted to represent the starry heavens; below is an outstanding marble pavement covering the entire 3,716 square metres of the cathedral floor. The engraved *sgraffito* scenes sum up the whole complex system of medieval and Renaissance beliefs; alongside biblical prophets the scenes depict the Seven Ages of Man, the Wheel of Fortune and Hermes Trismegistus, the mythical author of the Hermeneutic books upon which the sciences of astrology and alchemy were based. The prominence given to Hermes is an indication of the respect accorded to pagan precursors of Christian thought.

To the left of the nave is the Piccolimini Library, a monument to Aeneas Silvius Piccolimini, later Pope Pius II, who devoted much of his life to the grand humanistic enterprise of reconciling pagan and Christian teaching into one unified world picture. The library was commissioned by the pope's nephew, Pius III. Though the precious collection of classical manuscripts has gone, the walls are covered in enjoyable frescos by Pinturicchio (1502–5) on the life of Pius II and the pope's favourite sculpture takes pride of place: *The Three Graces*, copied from the antique original of Praxiteles. Elsewhere in the cathedral the eye is delighted by a wealth of detail, not least Nicola Pisano's pulpit (1280) and Duccio's 13th-century stained glass.

PALIO IN SIENA

All round Siena modern posters and ancient stone carvings depict the symbols of the city's 17 *contrade* – an eagle, a wolf, a caterpillar, snail or rhinoceros. Each *contrada* is a subdivision of the city, roughly equivalent to a parish. The *contrada* is a unique club, entered by virtue of being born within the *contrada* area, and it combines social, religious and charitable functions. The *contrade* are most evident during Siena's world-renowned *Palio*, the bareback horse race that takes place in the Campo twice a year: on 2 July and 16 August. The mechanics of this race are easily described; 10 jockeys from the 17 *contrade* compete in each *Palio* – the seven who did not run in the previous race and three chosen by lot; the horses are also allocated at random. All the noise and flag-waving of the rival *contrade* stops for the race itself; three turns round the soil-covered Campo. It is quickly over and the victor is presented with the *palio*, a banner embroidered with the image of the Virgin. It all sounds simple, except that huge sums of money are bet on the outcome and bribery, nobbling, drugging and kidnap – of horses and riders – are commonplace. Luck, skill and skulduggery are integral to the whole proceedings or, as John Mortimer put it in *Summer's Lease*, 'in the *Palio* it is less important to win than to see your enemy lose

Striped pillars and Gothic vaulting are among the cathedral's treasures

·VOLTERRA·

Volterra has a particular atmosphere which many visitors have found unsettling. D H Lawrence described the city as sombre, chilly and grim, and many subsequent writers have perpetuated this image. It is true that Volterra, standing high on the last great plateau before the hills of Tuscany fall away to the coastal plain, is buffeted by winds; it is also true that the high walls encircling the town make Volterra feel withdrawn from the world, but those same walls encompass parks, orchards and olive groves, good museums and fascinating buildings, all of which make the city well worth a visit.

The Fortezza Medicea, at the entrance to the city, was built when Lorenzo de'Medici sought the aid of the Duke of Urbino, Frederico di Montefeltro, in subjugating Volterra; Florence wanted control of the city's alum mines – alum being an important ingredient in the cloth dyeing process. The *fortezza,* dating from 1472, stands as a reminder of the brutality which even the ideal Renaissance princes and patrons of the arts could employ to achieve their ends. The Piazza dei Priori is the city's main square and here, for the first time, the antique grandeur of Volterra (map ref: 110 B4) is fully revealed. Sloping and irregular, the spacious *piazza* is bordered by the Palazzo dei Priori to the left, the oldest public building in Tuscany, begun in 1208, and the prototype for many others. Inside is a picture gallery containing works by Ghirlandaio and Signorelli, amongst others. Opposite is the 13th-century Palazzo Pretorio partnered by the Porcellino tower, so called because of the pig carved in relief at its base, only just visible after centuries of wear. To the right, the Co-operative Artieri Alabastro is a showcase for the local alabaster-carving industry on which Volterra's economy now depends.

Local alabaster carvings

Behind the Palazzo dei Priori is the octagonal baptistry of 1283 and the rewarding cathedral; the most striking of its many works of art is a *Deposition* of painted wood above the high altar. This could easily be mistaken for a contemporary work, but the fluid and dramatic composition actually dates to the 13th century. It is just one of several excellent wood carvings, most of which are displayed in the Lady Chapel to the left (north) of the nave. The 13th-century pulpit also features good Romanesque carvings, including an expressive relief of the Last Supper.

TOWN WALK

This walk reveals the huge scale of Etruscan Volterra, whose walls encompassed an area three times greater than the modern city.

Start at the Piazza Martiri della Libertà and turn right in front of the Albergo Nazionale, down Via dei Marchesi, past the rusticated Palazzo Inghirani. Turn left and climb the steep Via di Castello to enter the Parco Archeologico Enrico Fiumi through a gate on the right.

1 The park is a peaceful spot occupying the site of the Etruscan acropolis. Excavations have revealed the Roman cistern and the foundations of the 5th-century BC temple complex.

Take the left-hand path down to meet the walls of the Fortezza Medicea and leave the park by turning left. Turn right and take the first left, down a steep staircase that descends to Via Don Minzoni. The Museo Guarnacci is immediately opposite.

2 The Museo Guarnacci has one of the best collections of Etruscan art in Italy. Room after room is filled with alabaster and tufa cinerary urns carved with deities, domestic scenes and portraits of the dead. Two exhibits are particularly intriguing: the bronze statuette known as *L'Ombra della Sera* (The Shadow of the Night), an elongated figure dating from the 5th century BC which was used as a fire poker by the farmer who found it in 1879, before it was recognised as a masterpiece of Etruscan art; and the vividly realistic 'Married Couple' urn, dating from the 1st century BC.

Turn right out of the museum and walk down Via Don

Roman remains in an old city

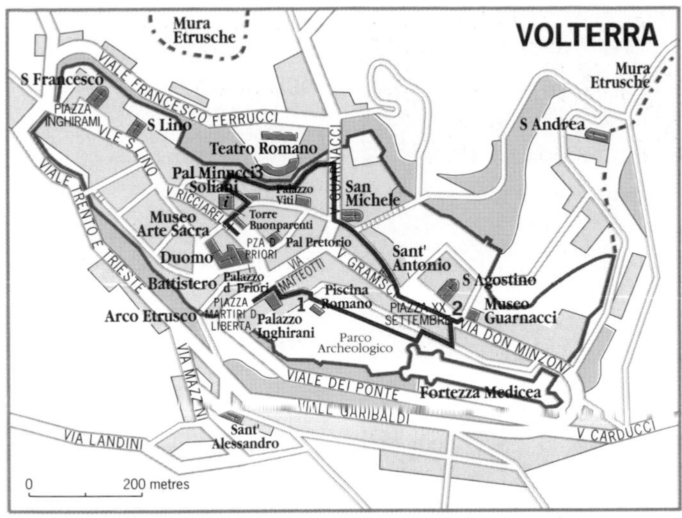

Minzoni, crossing Piazza XX Settembre and taking the street to the right of the Church of Sant'Antonio, Via di Sotto. This leads to a striking corner formed by the Church of San Michele and a group of truncated medieval towers. Turn right in Via Guarnacci and, just before the medieval Porta Fiorentina, turn left in Via Lungo le Mura del Mandorlo.

3 This narrow lane follows the line of the medieval walls and provides a bird's eye view, to the right, over the extensive remains of the Roman theatre and bath complex, currently being excavated and restored.

To the left, in the far distance, is the unmissable bulk of the Church of San Giusto. This stands at the northwestern limits of the ancient Etruscan town, whose walls also encompassed much of the suburbs and open countryside visible below and to the right. *Velathri*, as Etruscan Volterra was named, was a vast and powerful city until it was conquered by the Roman empire in 80BC, with a population of perhaps as many 500,000 people.

Follow Via Lunga le Mura until reaching a small piazza and a covered passageway on the left which leads into Via del Mandorlo. Turn left, then right into Via Buonparenti, with its characterful 13th-century tower houses, to return to the Piazza dei Priori.

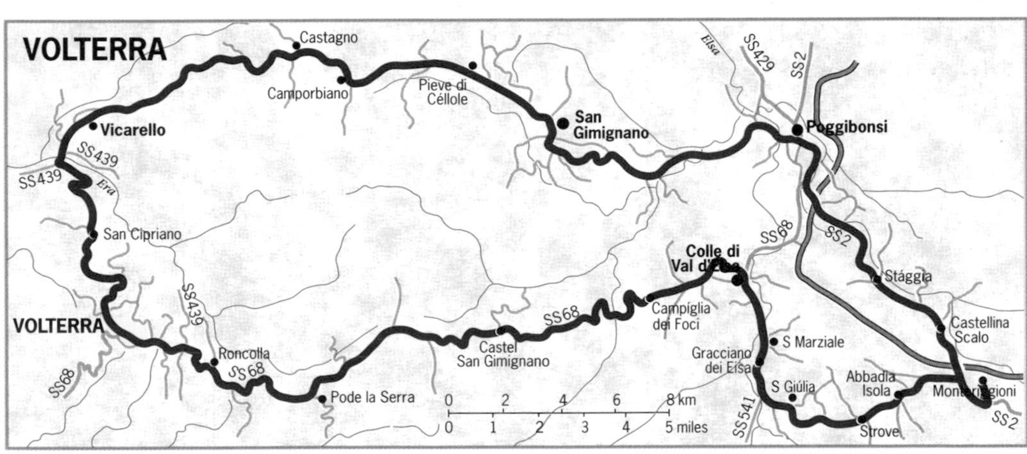

MOTOR TOUR

The theme of this 80km tour is quintessential Tuscany in a day; the highlights, San Gimignano and Monteriggioni, are two of the best-preserved hilltop towns in central Italy and plenty of time should be allowed for thorough exploration.

Leave Volterra on the road signposted to Pontadera and Pisa. On leaving the town, just past the Church of San Giusto, there is a view of the Balze to the left. This is a deserted area of bald yellow hills and steep precipices, created by landslips that have engulfed the remains of extensive Etruscan necropoli. After 8km turn right, then left, then right again, following the signs to San Gimignano; this is reached after 22km of scenic road which passes through the green Volterran foothills.

San Gimignano
Myriad towers thrusting into the sky announce this enthralling city where excellent restaurants and shopping are combined with outstanding art and architecture.'A tipsy miniature New York' is how Sheila Hale aptly described the city which E M Forster used as the setting for his novel, *Where Angels Fear to Tread*. The best of the medieval city's buildings are concentrated in the Piazza del Duomo.

Follow the signs for Poggibonsi then, skirting the town, follow the signs for Siena, which leads on to the SS2. Monteriggioni appears on the left some 10km south of Poggibonsi on the SS2, just beyond the junction with the autostrada.

Monteriggioni
This unusually well-preserved Sienese fortress town was in the front line of Florentine aggression from the 13th century onwards. The walls and 14 towers are as impressive and complete today as they were in Dante's time.

Head back on the N2 towards Poggibonsi then take the first left to Abbadia Isola, a Romanesque monastery with animal carvings round the gables and a pretty cloister. Continue following the signs to Colle di Val d'Elsa; on arrival, ignore the lower town and take the Volterra road to reach the old upper town.

Colle di Val d'Elsa
The mellow, palace-lined streets of the town offer the chance to browse in shops selling antiques and locally made glass and enjoy some very fine architecture spanning the 13th to 16th centuries.

Follow the scenic SS68 to return to Volterra, which is reached after 25km.

THE ETRUSCAN COAST

Some parts of Tuscany have the appearance of being locked in the past; venerable, ancient and immune from change. The coastal plain of the Maremma, stretching from Tuscany's border with Lazio up to Grosseto, is not one of these. In recent years it has undergone a transformation and is no longer the little-visited backwater of 15 years ago.

The long sandy beaches are now packed in summer and the area has so many holiday villages, caravan sites and marinas that solitude is a rare commodity. The changes are due in part to the initiative of the mayor of Porto Santo Stefano, Susanna Agnelli, sister of the Fiat tycoon. She has helped to turn Monte Argentario into a resort favoured by prosperous Italians, attracted by its wild and still unspoilt Mediterranean beauty. In the wake of the rich have come ordinary Italian families, refugees from the cities in camper vans and caravans.

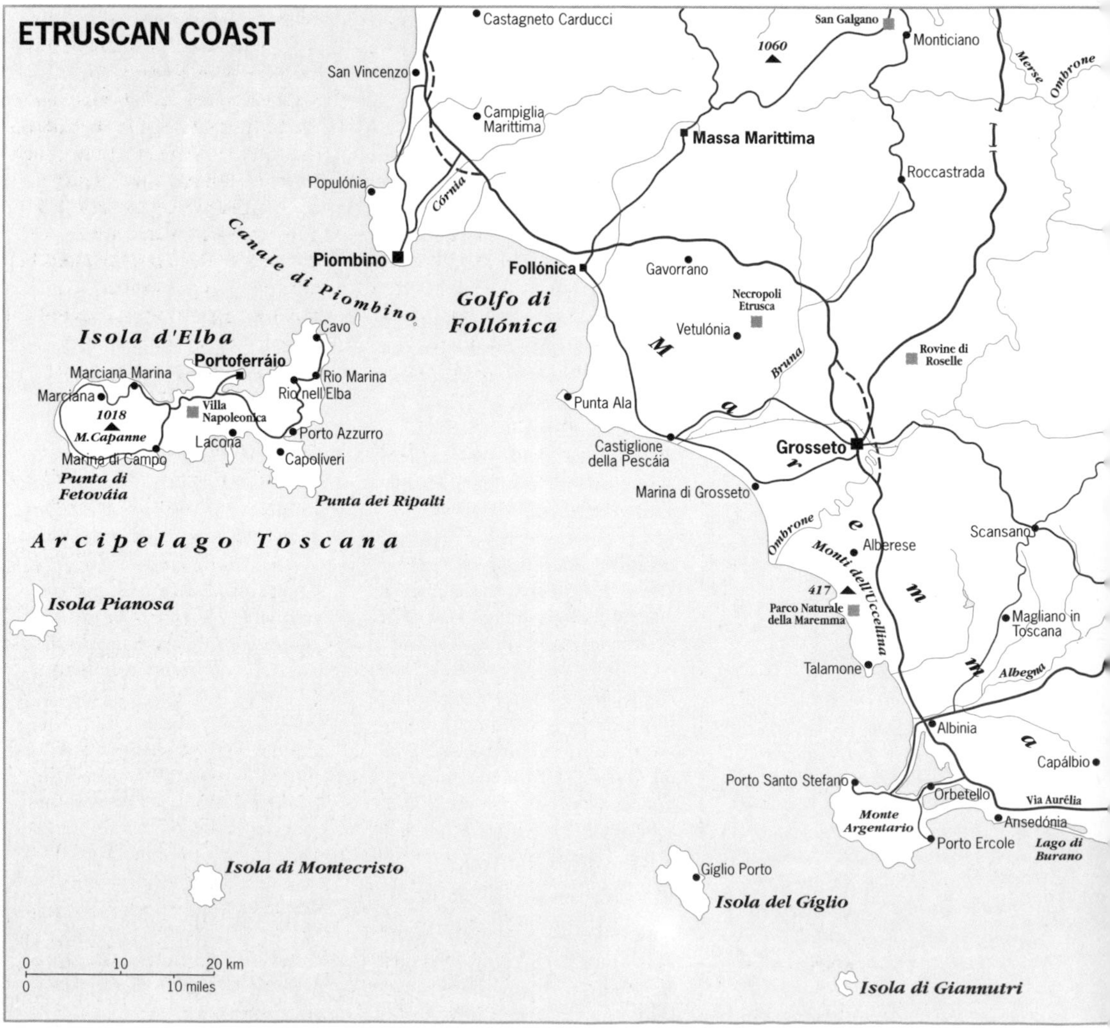

The speed of this change is in direct contrast to its past history. The Maremma slumbered for centuries and travellers were warned away from an inhospitable area of insalubrious swamps and stagnant water. The area was plagued by malaria-carrying mosquitoes although, as the name malaria (bad air) denotes, it was not realised until this century that mosquitoes were the cause. The marshes had been drained by the ancient Etruscans and the land was put to good use after the Romans conquered the region. They built a port at Ansedónia, whose rock-cut canal can still be seen, and farmed the fertile plain from huge imperial estates. With the collapse of the Roman Empire, the drainage courses silted up and the area reverted to wilderness, inhabited by a handful of fishermen and cattle breeders. The complete absence of farmhouses built before this century indicates that the region was, literally, 'avoided like the plague'. One consequence is that, with nobody to steal the masonry, several ancient buildings have survived. An early Christian church, perhaps dating from the 5th century, stands opposite Ansedonia's railway halt, roofless and overgrown with brambles, but intact. On the opposite side of the busy N1, the Via Aurélia, a country road leads past the boundary walls of the 1st-century BC Villa delle Colonne, still standing to their full height. A short way beyond, a track leads uphill to Settefenestre (Seven Windows), so called because the undercroft of this Roman villa is pierced by seven great arches. The modern farm, built to one side of the 1st-century villa, still uses the original Roman well and the undercroft is used for storage, as in Roman times. Students from the universities of Rome, Pisa and London excavated the villa in the 1970s and found the remains of several more substantial villas in the area, enabling the agrarian economy of the Roman landscape to be reconstructed.

The impetus to reclaim the Maremma began under the 19th-century Grand Dukes of Tuscany and gained momentum under Mussolini in the 1920s and 1930s. The swamps were redrained, new houses built and farmers given incentives to move there. The railings of the public park in Orbetello still bear fascist symbols; slogans of the era, such as 'houses for all the people' could still be seen on the walls of public buildings until painted over as recently as 1975, by then regarded as offensive to a carefree generation anxious to put the past behind them.

Widespread use of DDT, before it was banned, eradicated the mosquito problem and today the Maremma is prosperous. The fertile red soil of the plain – *terra rossa* – is used for growing tomatoes, peppers, aubergines and courgettes in great quantity; the Mediterranean atmosphere and excellent fish restaurants have proved a magnet to visitors. The region has benefited economically without losing too much in the process. Out of season, Talamone, on the southern edge of the Parco Naturale della Maremma, is a delightful spot to watch the local fishermen land their catch and mend their boats. The park itself preserves an unspoiled stretch of *macchia*, thick scrub made up of broom, cistus, lavender, rosemary and other fragrant herbs. Within the park, rather [illegible], the *butteri*, still raise white Maremmana cattle, huge and docile beasts despite ferocious-looking horns. The *butteri* are serious farmers but they do find time to give demonstrations of their riding and lasso skills to visitors in summer and compete with their transatlantic counterparts in rodeos.

Many visitors come here just to lie on the beach, go walking, bird-watching, canoeing or horse-riding, or to take day trips to Elba and other islands in the Tuscan archipelago. The region also offers beautiful hilltowns inland and extensive Etruscan remains at Roselle, Vetúlonia and Sovana. It is worth remembering, too, that the Etruscan and Roman ruins of Vulci, literally just over the border in Lazio, are some of the most complete and impressive in Italy; and that Tarquinia, further south, has the best painted tombs in Italy and one of the finest museums of Etruscan art.

There are several ways to approach the Maremma but one of the most scenic roads is the one from Volterra, through Pomarance and Larderello to Massa Marittima. This passes through the ore-rich Colline Metallifere. Around Larderello itself there is one of the strangest sights Tuscany has to offer: huge polished steel pipes, zigzagging across the wild landscape, belching out jets of sulphurous steam from leaky joints and valves. In this volcanic region the hot underground rocks are used to heat water for electricity generation. Larderello proclaims itself the 'world centre for geothermal energy'. A museum in the town is devoted to the subject and to other local industries, such as borax mining. Visitors may choose not to stop in what is a grim town of cooling towers and featureless industrial buildings but the web of pipes in the surrounding landscape, resembling the creation of some megalomaniac post-modernist sculptor, is irresistibly fascinating.

Since the war, Elba has become a top holiday resort, where small bays give way to a wealth of beaches

CAPÁLBIO

MAP REF: 110 C2

Capálbio's quiet charm has made it a favourite resort for affluent Italians. The most interesting buildings are the 12th-century church and the Aldobrandeschi fortress at the centre of the village but for most visitors the main attractions are the well-kept beauty of the narrow streets and the views from the restaurant terraces over Monte Argentario to the Tyrrhenian Sea. In the winter months Capálbio is filled with huntsmen dressed in camouflage green; the Maremma Hunting Reserve lies to the north, the source of the wild boar and venison served in many a local restaurant.

Nearby Lake Burano (Lago di Burano), south of Capálbio, is a nature reserve maintained by the Worldwide Fund for Nature. The shallow freshwater lagoon is a feeding ground for birds migrating between eastern Europe and Africa and a nesting area for some of the few cranes left in Italy. The most spectacular displays are at sunset when flocks return to the lake from their various daytime haunts. To the east of Capálbio, the French sculptor Nikki de Sant Phalle is creating the Giardino dei Tarocchi, a sculpture park inspired by the mystical characters of the Tarot. The huge flamboyant sculptures of concrete, glass and ceramic can be viewed at weekends.

ELBA

MAP REF: 110 B3

Elba is the largest of the islands in the Tuscan archipelago and it can be reached by regular ferries connecting Piombino on the mainland with Portoferráio, Elba's port and main town. Thousands of visitors make the day trip in summer, concentrating on the lively Galeazze market in Piazza Cavour and the fish restaurants of the old town of Portoferráio. The port is guarded by two fortreses built in 1548 – the Forte del Falcone and the Forte delle Stelle. Above the latter is the Palazzina Napoleonica dei Mulini, a small palace built around two ancient windmills which was Napoleon's home for nine months. Under the terms of the 1814 Vienna Congress, Napoleon was given Elba as his personal principality on condition that he remain there. Instead he escaped, in February 1815, only to suffer a final humiliating defeat at Waterloo later the same year. His former home is furnished with books and silver from the Palace of Fontainebleau and period furniture from the house of his sister, Elisa, who lived in Piombino. Six kilometres west of Portoferráio, on the Marciana road, is Napoleon's country villa, San Martino, set amidst attractive gardens. The nearby church of the Misericordia displays a bronze death mask of the great imperialist.

Elba's 150km coastline is indented with sandy coves, perfect for bathing, diving, fishing and water sports. Many of the best beaches, however, are privately owned and accessible only to guests at the island's many resort hotels and holiday villages, while the public beaches can be uncomfortably crowded. The west of the island is far less developed and there are hiking trails around and up Monte Capanne, the island's highest peak (1,018m). There is also a cable car link to the summit from Marciana Alta, Elba's best-preserved medieval town, where the local archaeological museum displays Roman and Etruscan finds from ships wrecked off the island's coast.

Open-cast mining is still practised in the eastern part of the island, around Rio Marina and Rio nell'Elba. The ancient Etruscans were the first to exploit the island's deposits of ferrous oxide, shipping the iron ore to the mainland via Portoferráio (hence its name, Iron Port). Workshops in Rio Marina sell jewellery made from local quartz, onyx and beryl and Elba's complex geology is illustrated in the town's Museo Mineralogica. The rocky coves between Rio Marina and Cavo are popular with beachcombers searching for brightly coloured pebbles and other mineralogical treasures.

Elba: Napoleon's country home at San Martino

Ancient mosaic remains near Grosseto

GROSSETO

MAP REF: 110 C3

Grossetto is a large and frenetic city with few charms to detain the visitor. Heavy bombing during World War II took its toll, though the high brick walls surrounding the old town have survived; they were built between 1574 and 1593 by the Medici Dukes and the bastions have been landscaped to form shady public parks. The main reason for visiting is the Museo Archeologico e d'Arte della Maremma, essential for an understanding of the nearby Etruscan ruins at Vetúlonia and Roselle. The well-presented museum explains the ancient topography of the Maremma region and the finds include a black bowl scratched with the 22 letters of the Etruscan alphabet, providing a key to the lost language of these enigmatic people. The museum also houses a good collection of Sienese School paintings.

Nearby The ruins of two great Etruscan cities lie close to Grosseto. Vetúlonia, to the northwest, is a sleepy rural village surrounded by the overgrown ruins of the acropolis and 6th-century BC walls. Considerable imagination is needed to make sense of the jumbled foundations, aided by the displays in the small Museo Archeologico. More rewarding are the tombs at the crossroads below the village. Take the right-hand road, signposted to Grosseto, and the tombs lie just beyond on the left. The first, the 6th-century Tomba del Belvedere, stands by the roadside. Two others can be found by following the farm track: the Tomba della Petraia (after 600m) and the Tomba del Diavolino II (after 1.2km). Both are impressive domed structures dating from the 7th century BC.

Vetúlonia went into sudden decline in the 6th century BC; scholars now think that the rise of Roselle, north of Grosseto off the SS223, may have been the reason. Archaeologists are still working at Roselle so the freshly uncovered walls and streets are easier to interpret; much of the 6th-century city has been revealed, including residential and industrial quarters, sacred buildings and chamber tombs. Overlying these are parts of the 1st-century BC Roman city that superseded it.

The town of Porto Azzurro, Elba

Visitors flock to the well-stocked shops of Orbetello like bees to the honey pot

MAREMMA NATIONAL PARK

MAP REF: 11O C2

The Parco Naturale della Maremma is both a playground and a nature reserve. Some visitors come for the unspoiled beach which stretches for 6km either side of the Marina di Alberese, others for the flora and fauna of this important area of untouched Mediterranean vegetation. Access to the park (officially open only at weekends and on Wednesdays) is from Alberese, where there is a ticket office selling entry permits and maps and a small museum devoted to local wildlife. (Entry to the park can only be made on foot or by bus from Alberese; cars are not permitted). In Alberese it is also possible to arrange excursions on horseback or by canoe along the park's drainage canals. Marina di Alberese is accessible by car and has picnic facilities shaded by groves of parasol pines. Other parts of the park are accessible only on foot along paths that are, in theory, waymarked, though this cannot be relied upon. Fortunately Poggio Lecci can be used for orientation; this is the highest peak (417m) in the Uccellina hills that run through the park, parallel to the coast. Several of the adjoining peaks are crowned by 16th-century watchtowers, part of a chain built by the Medici Dukes for coastal defence.

The park's vegetation is extremely varied. Sea lilies and sea holly grow on the shoreline, which is backed by groves of parasol pines juniper and mastic trees. The marshes around the Ombrone river estuary are colonised by large areas of bullrush, reeds, glasswort and saltwort. Mediterranean scrub (*macchia*) covers the hills in a dense mosaic of stunted rowans, arbutus (strawberry tree), asphodels, euphorbias, rosemary, broom, sea lavender, cistus (rock rose) and many varieties of orchid. Clouds of butterflies feed on the scrub, while lizards and snakes bask among the undergrowth. Stone martens, porcupines, weasels and fallow deer inhabit the park but are rarely seen. More visible is the birdlife, especially around the coastal lagoons, or *bozzi*. Look out for marsh herons, pintails, widgeon, shovellers, tufted ducks, stilt plovers, curlews, storks and even the occasional flamingo.

MASSA MARITTIMA

MAP REF: 11O B3

Although Massa Marittima stands on the edge of the ore-rich Colline Metallifere, an important mining region since Etruscan times, there is nothing grimy or industrial about this town, the most rewarding of the Maremma region. A brief burst of prosperity in the 13th century, when substantial copper, silver and lead deposits were found nearby, paid for the town's majestic buildings. Once the mines were exhausted the town slumbered until new methods of extraction led to an industrial revolution in the mid-19th century. Fortunately this had little impact on Massa Marittima's buildings, which form a stately ensemble round Piazza Garibaldi in the lower town.

The fine cathedral, built of travertine, has an arcade of almost classical purity running round its flank and is partnered by a slender campanile with numerous arched bell openings. Though the church was partly rebuilt in Pisan Romanesque style in the 13th century, it incorporates reliefs from its 11th-century predecessor, including the lively scenes above the portal depicting the life of San Cerbone. This early Christian

Local pasta – Massa Marittima

missionary is shown arriving from the Holy Land by boat and being thrown into a pit full of wild bears who, instead of tearing him limb from limb, tamely lick his feet. San Cerbone's marble sarcophagus in the crypt, the work of Goro di Gregorio (1324) is carved with more charming scenes from the saint's life. Massa Marittima was the birthplace of another saint, San Bernardino of Siena, the itinerant preacher who tried so hard to quell the intercommunal strife of 15th-century Tuscany. The font in which he was baptised is carved with scenes from the life of St John the Baptist, the work of Giraldo da Como (1267).

Noble 14th-century buildings surround the cathedral, including the Palazzo del Podestà which houses a small archaeological museum and picture gallery; Ambrogio Lorenzetti's glowing Maestà (1330) is well worth seeing. A maze of alleys leads up to the Fortezza dei Senesi at the centre of the Città Nuovo, the New Town, founded after the Sienese conquered Massa Marittima in 1337. The conquest was to do them little good since the coveted silver mines were exhausted soon after. The story of mining in the vicinity, from the Middle Ages to the present day, is told by two museums; the Museum of the Art and History of Mining in the upper town, and the Mining Museum behind the cathedral in Via Corridoni.

MONTE ARGENTARIO

MAP REF: 110 C2

Monte Argentario was an island until the shallow waters separating it from the mainland silted up in the last 200 years BC. Forgotten and inaccessible for centuries, the island has undergone a complete change since 1980, having been transformed into an up-market holiday resort favoured by Italy's jet set. Expensive yachts fill the harbour towns of Porto Ercole and Santo Stefano, with their exclusive discotheques and excellent fish restaurants. Both have public beaches nearby. The south of the island, reached by an unpaved road, remains relatively inaccesible for the time being and offers good walking country. Ferries from Porto Santo Stefano go to Isola del Giglio, with its sandy beaches, and Isola di Giannutri, whose clean waters are popular with aqualung divers.

ORBETELLO

MAP REF: 110 C2

Orbetello is now a popular holiday resort whose main attractions are well-stocked shops selling everything from antiques to designer fashion, and numerous fish restaurants. Much of the fish comes from farms located in the shallow lagoon whose waters lap the town walls, coming to within feet of the 13th-century cathedral. Part of the northern lagoon is now a bird sanctuary under the care of the Worldwide Fund for Nature. The massive walls ringing the core of the town date from the Spanish occupation of Italy under Charles V when Orbetello was occupied by a major Spanish garrison. The baroque city gates and the Polviera de Guzman arsenal (which houses a small museum) still lend a Spanish air to the town.

Nearby Ansedónia, perched high on a promontory overlooking Orbetello, is an area of luxury holiday villas with immaculate gardens. Less manicured are the overgrown ruins of the Roman town of Cosa, partly revealed by excavations, standing in an olive grove at the highest point of the hill. A museum at the centre of the site explains the history of this prosperous trading colony, founded in 273BC. Another good reason for visiting is the superb view from the crumbling Roman walls, over Monte Argentario. The road through Ansedónia descends to the local railway station; just beyond, a track to the right leads to a long stretch of sandy beach where, until recently, beachcombers could find handfuls of Roman pottery fragments. This was the site of Cosa's port; to the right of the beach car park a long stretch of narrow rock-cut canal survives, formerly linking the Roman port to Lake Burano.

Porte Ercole, Monte Argentario

THE ANCIENT ETRUSCANS

Because a fool kills a nightingale with a stone, is he therefore greater than the nightingale? Because the Roman took the life out of the Etruscan, was he therefore greater than the Etruscan? Not he! Rome fell and the Roman phenomenon with it. Italy today is far more Etruscan in its pulse than Roman: and will always be so. The Etruscan element is like the grass of the field and the sprouting of corn, in Italy: it will always be so.
D H Lawrence, *Etruscan Places*

Etruscan tombs from once-mighty Populonia (below and opposite)

The ancient Etruscans are a byword for obscurity, a people whose language and culture became extinct just as Roman civilisation began to reach its zenith in the 1st century BC. Yet the Etruscans continue to exert a strong hold on the imagination; to D H Lawrence they symbolised men 'at their intensest, most naked pitch', and modern Tuscans will speculate about genetic and cultural continuity between themselves and their ancient ancestors, intensely proud of their Etruscan heritage.

The popular image of the Etruscans as a vital people, 'effervescent as flowers' in the words of D H Lawrence, has been fostered by the remarkable series of tomb paintings in Tarquinia (in Lazio, 29km south of the Tuscan border). These delicately erotic scenes depict dancers and musicians, posed in balletic gestures among trees that seem about to burst into the first fresh leaves of spring, their branches full of exotic birds. Other, less well-preserved frescos in Chiusi's Tomba della Scimmia (Tomb of the Ape) depict naked youths dancing and taking their exercise, paintings that convey a sense of freshness, gaiety and innocence. This image of the Etruscans is further reinforced by the objects displayed in the museums of Volterra, Arezzo, Florence and Grosseto: bronze mirrors engraved with tender lovers bathing together or funerary urns on which plump matrons recline with their equally obese husbands, the epitome of marital contentment. Faced with such evidence, it is easy to see how the Etruscans have come to be idealised. How sad, then, that this seductive portrait is all part of a glamorous myth; there is, in the words of Lisa Gerard-Sharp, a poignant commentator on modern Italian life, a deep gulf between 'poetic' and 'scholarly' Etruria, caused by the projection of modern preoccupations upon the scanty evidence of the past.

Even scholars are at variance on the precise origins of the Etruscans. Some have speculated that they may have migrated to Italy from as far away as India. The poses struck by the dancing figures in Tarquinian tombs, with out-turned palms and delicately extended fingers, call to mind Buddhist art, while the figures on Etruscan funerary urns have distinctly Asiatic features and the priestly caste system of the Etruscans reflects the Brahmanism that evolved in the Indus-Ganges plain around 1,000BC. To others, this idea is too far-fetched. The Etruscan alphabet has affinities with Chaldean Greek, so they may have migrated from Asia Minor, as the Greek historian Herodotus believed.

On the other hand, the Etruscans could have developed their alphabet through contact with Greek traders, along with the other cultural influences that are so evident in the painted vases that fill Tuscany's museums, which depict scenes from Greek mythology and Homeric epic. The Etruscans themselves, according to Dionysius of Helicarnassus, claimed to be the indigenous people of Italy.

Contact with Greece began in the mid-6th century BC when traders came to Etruria, attracted by the mineral wealth of Elba and the Colline Metallifere. The earliest Etruscan bronzework and pottery dates from this period; once again, it is not clear whether this technology was learned from the Greeks or developed independently. We do know, however, that the region prospered from this time on and that the population rose dramatically. The first cities were founded, encircled by walls that have survived remarkably intact in Volterra, for example, or in the Umbrian town of Amélia, which Pliny and Cato regarded as one of the oldest cities in Italy.

A stratified society had already developed by the 7th century, with a princely class that played a fundamental role in controlling trade, land ownership and defence; we know the name of at least one king – Lars Porsena of Kamars (modern Chiusi) – who led an attack on Rome in 508BC. The Etruscans were a slave-owning society, and in between aristocrat and slave there was a wealthy merchant class, an artisan class – whose members showed a genius for crafting metal and clay – and a priestly class that specialised in augury and divination, interpreting the will of the gods through the flight patterns of birds, animal entrails and the weather.

By the 6th century BC, Etruria consisted of numerous autonomous kingdoms, or 'lucomonies'. Twelve of the most powerful came together to form a loose confederation called the Dodecapolis, and member cities included Arezzo, Chiusi, Volterra, Orvieto, Perugia, Cortona and Tarquinia, cities that still flourish, along with Fiésole, subjugated and destroyed by Florence in 1125, and Vulci, Roselle, Vetúlonia and Populónia, which today consist of little more than villages and ruins. The confederation joined forces for defence and to conquer new territory, founding colonial outposts such as Felsina (modern Bologna) in the 5th century and pushing north as far as Ravenna and south as far as Pompeii. Nemesis came when the Etruscans launched an attack on Greece itself, suffering a defeat at Cumae in 474BC. This marked the beginning of a fundamental change in Etruscan society, characterised by the rapid loss of territory to invading Gauls and Samnites, loss of trade contact with the Greeks, the growing power of a priestly oligarchy and increasing preoccupation with death, the painful parting and the journey to the underworld.

The Romans, a rising force in Italy, took advantage of Etruscan vulnerability and began to conquer the territory of their neighbours in the 4th century BC. Veio was one of the first cities to fall, in 396BC, and Perugia one of the last, in 309BC. Etruscan cities were forced into reluctant alliance with Rome and had to pay tribute in the form of wood, grain, arms and metals to supply the expanding republic.

The Romans, in turn, absorbed much from the Etruscans, especially their religion, which had developed from magical, animistic origins into a coherent and comprehensive set of rules for divination, sacrifice and libation. Etruscan priests were summoned to Rome to lead mass ceremonies intended to purge the city or avert some impending disaster.

Etruscan culture flickered, faded and finally died as the Etruscans became absorbed into the fabric of a new society – except that the story does not quite end there. One of the most celebrated examples of Etruscan bronze sculpture, the Wounded Chimera (now in the archaeological museum in Florence), was discovered near Arezzo in 1554. Cast in the 5th century BC, it depicts a strange mythical beast, part lion, part snake, part goat, taut and straining with the agony of its wounds. Its discovery caused a sensation. Cellini, entrusted with repairing the broken left legs, marvelled at the bronze-casting skills of his ancestors, matched only by the achievements of his own time.

The romantic idea of a link between ancient and modern Tuscany was about to be born, and with it a whole new 'poetic' interpretation of this enigmatic people.

MAREMMA TOUR

This 80km tour takes in the best hilltop towns of the region inland from the Maremma, an area that has been dubbed the 'forgotten corner of Tuscany' because most visitors pass it by; in doing so they miss a landscape of gently rolling wooded hills, of olive groves and sheep pasture and of quiet rural villages where life is lived at a gentle pace. Take swimming costumes and towels for a swim in the springs at Satúrnia and a torch for exploring the Etruscan tombs at Sovana.

Pitigliano

The first town on this tour is spectacularly sited on a plateau above sheer cliffs and ravines carved out by the River Lente. The houses of Pitigliano seem to grow organically out of the ochre-coloured tufa and many have deep cellars cut into the soft rock which are used for storing the locally produced olive oil and Bianco di Pitigliano wines. The town itself is a maze of tiny streets; the warren of the former Jewish ghetto survives, and there is still a small Jewish community, descended from those who took refuge here from Catholic persecution in the 17th century. At the centre of the town, in the Palazzo della Repubblica, the fortified Palazzo Orsini has its own water supply provided by the huge arched aqueduct that sails across the Via Cavour.

From Pitigliano, follow the signs to Albinia, which leads, after 20km, to Manciano.

Manciano

The natural caves in this region of Tuscany have provided a home for man from the 10th millenium BC on, and the small Museum of Prehistory in Manciano illustrates the region's earliest settlement.

Follow the signs for Montemerano, along the SS322, noting the good backward view of Manciano while climbing the hill opposite the town.

Montemerano is encircled by 15th-century walls and art lovers may like to stop for the Siena School frescos in the Church of San Giorgio. Otherwise, follow the signs for Scansano and turn right, after 1km, following the signs for Satúrnia. After 3km, as the road descends, a glimpse is caught of the eventual destination, a waterfall in the valley below. To find it, descend to the valley floor and cross over a bridge. The road bends left then right; just before the right-hand bend, turn left down a track. Park and walk down the track to the falls.

Satúrnia Falls

The shallow falls of Satúrnia cascade over rocks stained blue-green with mineral deposits. Bathing is permitted here, in the pools between the rocks, allowing the warm water to flow over stiff muscles. The hot sulphurated waters spring from the ground several miles to the east and are tapped near by at Terme di Satúrnia, a modern spa offering a range of thermal treatments. But here visitors can enjoy the salubrious pleasures of relaxing in the warm waters for free.

A thermal pool at Satúrnia

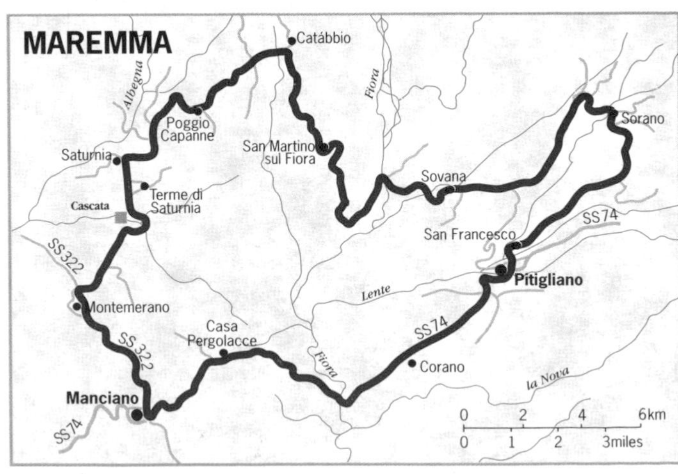

Continue on for another 3km to Satúrnia.

Satúrnia

The Romans named this town after Saturn, the father of the gods, because they believed it to be one of the oldest settlements in Tuscany. Archaeologists have found pre-Etruscan remains and the impressive walls, strengthened under Sienese control in the 15th century, incorporate Etruscan and

Roman masonry. Today the town is being gentrified by second-home owners from Rome who have discovered its sleepy charms and there are an unusual number of good shops and quality restaurants in the town.

Leaving Satúrnia, follow the signs for Arcidosso; carry straight on at the next junction, reached after 1km following signs to Monte Amiata. In Poggio Capanne, after 4km, turn left following signs to Sovana. After another 4km, at the entrance to Catábbio, turn right and continue following signs to Sovana, which is reached after 14km of delightful road which follows deep wooded gorges.

Sovana

This tiny one-street town is a perfectly preserved jewel of medieval architecture in which scarcely any building dates from later than the 14th century. At one end is the 11th-century Rocca Aldobrandesca, an early stronghold of the Aldobrandeschi family which emerged, after several centuries of feuding, as the dominant power in the region. The Teutonic origins of the family are evident in the Lombardic style of the town's two outstanding churches. In the main square, the proto-Romanesque church of Santa Maria has massive octagonal columns and an 8th-century marble canopy sheltering the high altar, carved with interlace and grapevine motifs. From here a cobbled track leads past the Ristorante Scilla up to the 11th-century cathedral of Santi Pietro e Paolo whose portal is carved with a tonsured priest raising his hand in blessing, and a knight on horseback. These have been interpreted as symbols of spiritual and temporal power. Such a theme would be entirely appropriate since Sovana was the birthplace of Hildebrand, the man who became Pope Gregory VII in 1073. Throughout his reign, which lasted until 1085, Gregory was embroiled in conflict with the German Emperor, Henry IV, over the issue of church supremacy, the same issue that was to result in Thomas à Becket's murder in 1170. Gregory himself may have been the patron of this cathedral, a building of considerable grandeur for such a small town. Back in the centre of the town there are several good restaurants and a shop selling fine reproductions of Etruscan jewellery, a reminder that the cliffs below Sovana are riddled with rock-cut Etruscan tombs (see **Sovana walk** on page 108).

Leaving Sovana, turn right and drive for 10km to Sorano.

Sorano

Sorano is another town which seems carved out of the rock. It sits above the dramatic gorge of the roaring river Lente, rising above sheer cliffs of brown tufa. Landslips have placed the future of its cliff-edge buildings in jeopardy, but the characterful narrow streets linking the two immense fortresses at either end of the town are well worth exploring.

Follow the signs to Pitigliano, which is reached after 8km.

MAREMMANA CUISINE

The restaurants in and around Saturnia are regarded as some of the best in Tuscany, renowned for their Maremmana cuisine. Wild boar (*cinghiale*) is a particular speciality, served in the form of translucent slices of *prosciutto* or as a hearty casserole. Wild boar also goes into *scottiglia*, another hunter's dish of various meats cooked with olives. Roasted wild mushrooms often accompany these filling hotpots in autumn. The fertile plains of the Maremma provide the tomatoes and celery that go into *acquacotta*, a thick soup served over garlic-scented bread with a poached egg. Local *pecorino*, sheep's milk cheese, is creamy and mild and for dessert it is usual to be offered sweet chestnut delicacies. Robust wines, such as the local Bianco di Pitigliano and Morellino di Scansano, are the best accompaniment.

The town of Pitigliano

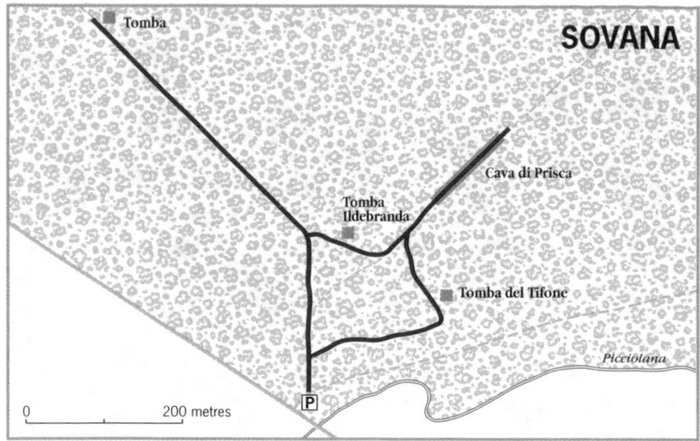

SOVANA WALK

The rock-cut Etruscan tombs below Sovana are some of the best in Tuscany, forming an Etruscan-style Valley of the Kings in miniature. Some tunnel deep into the soft tufa, so it is worth carrying a torch. Children will love this walk, but care needs to be taken because the route is lined with deep shafts and unfenced ravines.

From Sovana, turn left and drive downhill, through a road tunnel, down to the valley floor. After 1.6km, look for a yellow sign on the right pointing to a small car park. Park here and walk up the track, taking the footpath to the left, signposted 'Necropoli di Poggio Prisca'. Take the left fork when the track divides; the path climbs and bends to the right, leading to the first tomb.

1 The so-called Tomba Ildebranda (3rd century BC) is a momentous piece of carving designed to resemble a temple hollowed out of the rock. Archaeologists regard it as the best surviving example of Etruscan architecture from the Hellenistic period, when all things Etruscan were influenced by the art of their Greek trading partners. Six columns survive from the podium along with some eroded fragments of mythological scenes in the pediment. A long corridor below the podium leads to the cross-shaped tomb chamber. Clearly this was the tomb of someone important, but no one knows who, which is why local people have named it after their most prominent citizen, Hildebrand (Pope Gregory VII) who was born in Sovana in the 11th century AD.

With your back to the tomb, there is a good view of Sovana's cathedral on the opposite side of the valley. Facing the tomb, take the track to the left and follow this for 400m through oak woodland rich in wildflowers, lizards and butterflies. This leads to another temple-like tomb with a weathered column and a tomb chamber entered from the bottom of a deep ravine. Retrace your steps to the Tomba Ildebranda and take the track that curves round to the left, leading to the Cava di Prisca.

2 This great rock-cut ravine, 120m long, served as a ceremonial way down to the necropolis, its dark echoing gloominess perhaps representing the entrance to the underworld. At the upper end of the tunnel-like ravine, the marks of chisels and picks can clearly be seen in the face of the bare stone.

Retrace your steps and, just before reaching the Tomba Ildebranda, take the track that leads off to the left. This leads to the Tomba del Tifone.

3 This 2nd-century BC tomb has a pediment decorated with a sphinx-like head, gaunt and enigmatic after 2,000 years of weathering.

Turn your back on the tomb and follow the path downhill which leads back to the car park.

There are many more intriguing tombs in the Sovana area; the Colombaria a Lacunari, with its pigeon-holes for cinerary urns and the Tomba del Sileno, both on the Pitigliano road, are particularly rewarding; a guide to the tombs can be bought in Sovana itself.

Olive groves around Volterra

REGIONAL MAP

Map symbols

A4 Motorway - dual carriageway

A7 Motorway - single carriageway

A1 Toll motorway - dual carriageway

A6 Toll motorway - single carriageway

Motorway junction

Motorway junction restricted access

Motorway service area

Motorway under construction

Primary route

Main road

Secondary road

Other road

D600 E57 N59 Road numbers

Dual carriageway or four lanes

Road in poor condition

Under construction

TOLL Toll Toll road

Scenic route

Road tunnel

68 Distances (km)

10-6 970 Mountain pass (height in metres) with closure period

Gradient 14% and over. Arrow points uphill

Gradient 6% - 13%

Frontier crossing with restricted opening hours

V Vehicle ferry

Airport

International boundary

Viewpoint

Motor racing circuit

2973 DIAVOLEZZA Mountain / spot height in metres

Urban area

River, lake and canal

■ **Jockfall** Place of interest

Mountain railway

Car transporter (rail)

LA SPEZIA
Portovenere
Lerici
Sarzana
Aulla
Fivizzano
Passo di Pradarena 1572
M. CUSNA 2121
Pievepelago
Sestola
M. CIMONE 2165
Abetone
Vergato
Porretta Terme
Ponte Venturina
Castiglione dei Pépoli
Loiano
Passo della Raticosa 968
Firenzuola
Passo della Futa 903
Marradi
Carrara
Massa
Marina di Carrara
Marina di Massa
Seravezza
Forte dei Marmi
Pietrasanta
Marina di Pietrasanta
Lido di Camaiore
Camaiore
Viaréggio
Piazza al Sérchio
Castelnuovo di Garfagnana
Barga
Fornaci di Barga
Borgo a Mozzano
Bagni di Lucca
La Lima
San Marcello Pistoiese
Passo della Collina 932
Pistóia
Prato
San Piero a Sieve
Borgo San Lorenzo
San Benedetto in
Dicomano
Sesto Fiorentino
Colonnata
Fiésole
FIRENZE
Pontassieve
Reggello
Lucca
Collodi
Pescia
Montecatini Terme
Monsummano Terme
Vinci
Lastra a Signa
Empoli
San Giuliano Terme
PISA
Cáscina
Fucécchio
San Miniato
Pontedera
Marina di Pisa
Tirrénia
LIVORNO
Ponsacco
Collesalvetti
Casciana Terme
Castelfiorentino
San Casciano in Val di Pesa
Tavarnelle Val di Pesa
Greve in Chianti
Incisa in Val d' Arno
San Giovanni Valdarno
Montevarchi
Búcine
Certaldo
Poggibonsi
San Gimignano
Colle di Val d' Elsa
Castellina in Chianti
CHIANTI
Monteriggioni
Siena
Volterra
Saline di Volterra
Castiglioncello
Rosignano-Marittimo
Solvay
Cécina
Pomarance
Larderello
COLLINE METALLIFERE
TOSCANA
Asciano
Marina di Castagneto-Donorático
San Vincenzo
Monticiano
Buonconvento
Montalcino
Massa Marittima
Roccastrada
Populónia
Piombino
Follónica
Golfo di Follónica
Canale di Piombino
Í di Gorgona
Capráia
Capo Vita
I Palmaiola
Cavo
Portoferráio
Marciana Marina
Marina di Campo
Lacona
Porto Azzurro
Capolíveri
Ísola d'Elba
Punta di Fetováia
Punta dei Ripalti
Punta Ala
Castiglione della Pescáia
Grosseto
Marina di Grosseto
Roccalbegna
Arcidosso
Scansano
Parco Naturale della Maremma
Magliano in Toscana
Manciano
Punta d Marchese
Isola Pianosa
Punte Libéccio
Punta Brigantini
Orbetello
Porto Santo Stéfano
Monte Argentário
Porto Ércole
Ansedónia
Capálbio
Punta d Fenáio
Gíglo Porto
Í del Giglio
Punta d Capel Rosso
Í di Montecristo
Í di Giannutri
ÓLBIA
CAGLIARI
A
B
C
1
2
3
4
5

E
F
5
Faenza
Forlì
Cesena
Rimini
Riccione
San Marino
Pésaro
Fano
Senigállia
Ancona
Urbino
Fossombrone
Sansepolcro
Arezzo
Città di Castello
Gúbbio
Fabriano
Macerata
Perúgia
Assisi
Foligno
Spoleto
Todi
Orvieto
Terni
Rieti
Viterbo
L'Aquila
Avezzano
Tivoli
Roma
Frascati
Ascoli Piceno
Norcia
Camerino
Jesi
Osimo
Recanati
Tolentino
Cortona
Montepulciano
Chiusi
Città della Pieve
Bolsena
Montefiascone
Narni
Orte
Civita Castellana
Bracciano
Cerveteri
Ladíspoli
Fiumicino
Lido di Ostia
Albano Laziale
Subiaco
M A R C H E
U M B R I A
L A Z I O
MONTI SIBILLINI
MONTI DELLA LAGA
MONTI SIMBRUINI
MONTI ERNICI
MONTI SABINI
MONTI MARTANO
MONTEFELTRO
CAMPO FELICE
Lago Trasimeno
Lago di Bolsena
Lago di Vico
Lago di Bracciano
M. VETTORE 2476
M. TERMINILLO 2213
M. VELINO 2487
M. CATRIA 1701
Passo di Mandrioli 1173
Passo Viamaggio 983
Passo di Capannelle 1283
Vallelunga
LEONARDO DA VINCI
CIAMPINO
A1
A14
A24
A25
A12
E45
E35
E80
D
E
F
4
3
2
1

PRACTICAL GUIDE

Accommodation

Self-catering accommodation is likely to be the most economic choice for those travelling to Tuscany and Umbria as a family or group of four or more. The region is amply supplied with farmhouses, villas and apartments for rent, but it is necessary to book up to six months in advance for the peak holiday season.

Italy has an excellent system for grading hotels and fixing room prices. Hotels are inspected annually and awarded 1 to 5 stars, depending on their facilities. The grading is then used to fix the maximum price the hotel can charge for a single room (*una camera singola*), a twin-bedded room (*una camera doppia*) and a double-bedded room (*una matrimoniale*). One and 2-star hotels are excellent value for the budget traveller, though they only offer basic facilities, such as a shared bathroom and toilet, and may be located on a noisy street. Four and 5-star hotels offer comfort and luxury at a price. As well as large, well-furnished rooms with en-suite bathroom and TV, mini-bar and IDD telephone, they will usually have excellent restaurants, as well as sports facilities such as a swimming pool, tennis courts and riding stables.

Most hotels fall into the 3-star category and are very reasonably priced. Standards do vary, however. Traditional city centre hotels, constrained by the limitations of the building they occupy, may have smaller rooms and fewer facilities than a rural hotel. Even so, clean rooms with an en-suite bathroom are standard.

Rural hotels, often located in converted farmhouses, villas or even monasteries, are very popular with Italians themselves and are most likely to be fully booked during the main holiday season. City centre hotels offer a better base for sightseeing, shopping and nightlife. The main disadvantage is that with traffic restrictions in force in most cities, you may have to leave your car some way from the hotel.

Tourist offices in most major towns offer a room-finding service covering a range of accommodation, including rooms in private houses, cheap *pensione* and *Agriturismo*; the latter is a recently developed system for helping farmers supplement their income by taking guests. The accommodation offered is usually simple but cheap, on working farms or vineyards, and meals are taken with the host family (although some self-catering apartments are available).

Arriving

To enter Italy, visitors from the USA, EC and Commonwealth countries need only a valid passport. Other nationals should apply for a visa in advance from an Italian embassy. If you are driving to Italy you must carry your driving licence, car registration documents and evidence of insurance cover (an international Green Card or insurance certificate) at all times; you may be asked to produce all three at random checks.

Pisa's Galileo Galilei Airport is served by frequent scheduled and charter flights and is less prone to industrial disputes than many Italian airports. A number of travel agents specialising in Italian travel offer attractively priced fly-drive packages to Pisa and these offer the cheapest and most flexible option for touring the region; these services are, however, heavily booked in summer when advance reservations are essential. It is a short drive from Pisa airport to the two main motorways serving Tuscany and Umbria, the A12 coastal *autostrada* and the A11 for Florence, Arezzo and Perugia.

Pisa Aeroporta railway station is located right next to the airport and trains leave at least hourly for Pisa Centrale (journey time 5 minutes) and Florence (1 hour). Tickets can be bought at a special booth inside the airport, which also has a bank, restaurant and small duty-free shop. For airport information, tel: (050) 28088.

Several airlines now offer flights to Florence Peretola airport but these are largely aimed at business travellers and the fares are higher than to Pisa. The airport is located 4km northwest of Florence and there are taxi services to the city.

Travelling to the region by rail can be more expensive than a charter flight, unless you hold a rail pass that qualifies you for reduced fares. One trans-European service calls at the Santa Maria Novella station in Florence: the Italia Express (connections from London to Lille, and from there via Strasbourg, Basel and Milan). The Palatino runs from Paris via Turin and Genoa, and Florence can be reached by a single change at Pisa. There is also a direct train from Brussels but this exists only during the summer.

Camping

Camping is very popular in Italy though to most Italians this does not mean sleeping under canvas, but travelling in mobile camper vans. There are excellent sites all over the region, especially around Lake Trasimeno and along the coast. Sites are graded from 1 to 3. Grade 1 sites offer only simple facilities, such as a communal washblock, whereas grade 3 sites will usually supply electricity and water to each plot, and provide a restaurant, shop, telephones and sports facilities as well as chalets and caravans for rent.

Details of campsites can be obtained from local tourist offices, but the best sites are booked up in the peak season and advance reservation is advisable. For booking forms and a list of sites write to the Centro Internazionale Prenotazioni Federcampeggio, Casella Postale 23, 50042 Calenzano, Firenze.

Chemists

Chemists (*farmacie*) are identified by a sign displaying a green cross on a white background. They are staffed by trained pharmacists who can prescribe drugs, including antibiotics, that are only available by doctor's prescription in other countries. Normal opening hours are from 9am to 1pm and from 4pm to 7pm, Monday to Friday. The address of the nearest chemist on emergency duty will be posted in the window. In rural areas, where there may be no alternative, it is acceptable to ring the doorbell out of hours in an emergency.

Crime

Tuscany and Umbria are relatively crime free, but it always pays to be careful. Do not leave valuables in your car. Report any loss promptly at the nearest police station. The key word is *denuncia*, meaning statement, without which you will not be able to make an insurance claim.

When shopping, beware of forged notes and remember that all the designer-name goods sold at bargain prices by street traders are counterfeit.

Customs

All items intended for your personal use can be imported duty free and there are no limitations on the import of currency. Special rules apply to the import of hunting weapons (information from Italian embassies). EC residents aged 17 years or over can import the following duty free (non-EC residents have the same limits, except that the tobacco allowance is doubled; higher limits apply to goods purchased duty and tax paid within the EC):

Tobacco: 100 cigarettes or cigarillos or 50 cigars or 250 grammes of tobacco.

Alcohol: 1 litre of spirits or 2 litres of still, sparkling or fortified wine.

Toiletries: 50 grammes of perfume or 250 cc of toilet water.

New limits are due to be introduced shortly; look out for notices at airports or ask a travel agent for details.

Disabled Visitors

Wheelchair users will find that the steep and unevenly paved streets of a typical hilltown in Tuscany or Umbria are extremely difficult to negotiate, and you will need a strong and tireless companion. Few concessions to the needs of disabled people are made anywhere in Italy. Churches and museums are often approached by steep flights of stairs and hotel lifts tend to be too small for a chair. One welcome concession is that free parking spaces are reserved for orange badge holders close to major tourist sites. Sources of further information include the offices of the Italian State Tourist Board, whose hotel lists indicate those suitable for disabled visitors, and Radar (25 Mortimer Street, London W1M 8AB, tel: 071-637 5400). A useful publication, *Access to Florence*, can be obtained from Mrs V Saunders, Project Phoenix Trust, 68 Rochfords, Coffee Hall, Milton Keynes, MK6 5DJ.

Driving

Without a car it is virtually impossible to see the best of rural Tuscany and Umbria. On the other hand, if you are going to base your holiday in Florence, forget the car and use public transport: traffic is banned from the city centre and finding space in the peripheral car parks is never easy.

Bringing your own car to Italy will probably cost more than renting on arrival, and there are plenty of travel agents offering fly-drive packages to Pisa, where cars can be collected on arrival at the airport. The price should include unlimited mileage and insurance as well as a 24-hour emergency breakdown service. In either case, drivers must always carry a driving licence, the car registration douments and an insurance certificate, or international Green Card, at all times. Holders of old-style green driving licences, must also carry an official Italian translation (obtainable from motoring organisations such as the AA and RAC). A red warning triangle to display in the event of an accident or breakdown is also a necessity. If you do bring your own car, it is worth buying petrol coupons, either in advance from motoring organisations such as the AA and RAC, or at the Italian frontier, in order to qualify for petrol at discount prices.

Drivers are generally courteous and law-abiding and the bad reputation of Italian motorists is based almost entirely on the behaviour of big city drivers. Most of the region's roads, except for the *autostrade*, are narrow, steep and twisting. Plenty of time should be allowed for every journey, because what looks like a short distance on the map actually takes a long time to drive taking hairpin bends and steep gradients into account. Drivers will rarely get into top gear and should expect not to exceed an average speed of 48kmh.

Signposting in the region is good especially on country roads. Town driving can be more confusing because of the plethora of signs; look for the word *Centro*, or *Centro storico* to navigate towards the city centre, or the words *Tutti Direzione* if you want to by-pass the centre.

Cars drive on the right and the speed limits are 50kmh in built-up areas, 90kmh on ordinary roads and 110kmh on the *autostrada*. Seat belts must be worn in the front of the car and by children travelling in the rear. Using the horn is prohibited in built-up areas except in emergency; flash your lights instead as a warning. Outside towns it is customary to use the horn to warn that you are about to overtake and to warn of your presence on a blind bend.

Vehicles are banned from the centres of most towns in the region from 7.30am to 6.30pm on weekdays. There is never enough parking space around the periphery to fulfil the demand and in some areas parking is totally banned (these are identified by a graphic sign showing a pick-up vehicle towing a car away). As a general principle, when you arrive in a town, look for car park direction signs (a large square sign with the letter P painted in white on a blue background). In some streets, generally those furthest from the centre, parking is free on most days, but always look for signs detailing the one morning a week when parking is banned for street cleaning. In other streets there are meters which take 100, 200 and 500 lire coins, where you can park for up to two hours. In some squares you buy a ticket from an attendant. There are also privately run multi-storey or underground car parks in most cities; you can park here for as long as you wish, but they are expensive. By far the majority of street parking, however, falls into the *zona disco* category. This means that parking is free for one hour – and sometimes two – provided that cars display a disc (purchased from petrol stations) showing the time of arrival. Once the time is up drivers must move on and find another space; frustrating but necessary, because traffic police are very vigilant.

Petrol stations are usually open from 7.30am to 12noon and 4pm to 7pm Monday to Friday. Many are closed on Saturday and all close on Sunday and public holidays, except for *autostrade* service stations. Some display a sign saying *Aperto 24 Ore*; this means that they have an automatic petrol pump which accepts 10,000 lire notes – but if the note is crumpled or creased the machine will either reject it or swallow it but give no petrol in exchange. Very few petrol stations accept credit cards. Two types of petrol are sold: *Super* (4-star) and *Super senza piombo* (unleaded). Diesel is sold as *gasolio*.

If you break down, switch the hazard lights on immediately and place the red warning triangle 50m behind the vehicle. Find a telephone and ring 116, the number for the Automobile Club d'Italia (ACI) which provides a free breakdown service to foreign visitors. It is well worth using this number too if you have an accident; the ACI will help with police formalities and the exchange of insurance details. If necessary they will also help to find a garage for repairs.

Electricity

The supply is 220 volts and the plugs are the standard continental type, with two round pins. An adaptor is needed to use three-pin appliances and a transformer if the appliances normally operate at 100–120 volts (eg US and Canadian standard).

Entertainment

Ask at tourist information centres for details of forthcoming events. For the most part, entertainment in the Tuscany and Umbria means taking to the streets for the evening stroll, the *passeggiata*, followed by a good meal. There are cinemas and theatres in many towns but visitors need to understand Italian to make the most of them. Music lovers are well catered for: many churches host concerts and organ recitals, especially at the weekend. The best chance of enjoying an evening's entertainment is to attend one of the region's numerous festivals (see **Calendar of Events**) although advance booking is necessary for the most popular (eg Spoleto's *Festival dei Due Mondi*).

Health

For minor ailments it is best to seek the help of a pharmacist (*Farmacia* – see **Chemists**). Every public hospital has a casualty department (*Pronto Soccorso*) where treatment is free. Call an ambulance by dialling 113. Otherwise, medical care has to be paid for. In theory, EC nationals can seek reimbursement of the costs; provided, that is, they have had the foresight to complete an official E111 form in advance of their visit. In practice, there is a lot of form-filling and bureaucracy involved, and it is simpler to take out travel insurance providing cover for emergency medical care in one's own country.

There are no special health regulations governing visitors to Italy from most countries. Adequate precautions need to be taken against sunburn, and it is sensible to carry insect bite cream; mosquitoes are a problem, especially in the countryside or when dining out of doors.

Media

In big cities, such as Florence, Perugia and Siena, there is no difficulty in buying the major European newspapers, although perhaps a day late. For readers of Italian, *La Nazione*, published in Florence, is the paper that most Tuscans and Umbrians read and it contains details of local events.

Money

The Italian lira (plural lire) is usually abbreviated to L or £. The lira is a relatively stable currency and the exchange rates have not fluctuated much in recent years (£1 equals 2,150 lire, but it is more convenient to think in terms of £1 equals 2,000; US$1 equals roughly 1,000 lire). Many Italians would like the government to simplify the currency by knocking off three zeros (so that 1,000 lire would become 1 lira), but so far this measure has been defeated every time it comes to a parliamentary vote.

Notes come in denominations of 1,000, 2,000, 5,000, 10,000, 50,000 and 100,000 lire; coins in denominations of 50, 100, 200 and 500 lire. Telephone tokens (*gettoni*) are also accepted as coinage: their current value is 200 lire. The days when coins and small notes were in short supply are now over. Travellers should not normally be met with hostility if they offer a 50,000 lire note in payment – except for small items such as a cup of coffee or a postcard. Museum attendants, for some reason, also seem to resent giving change for big notes. 10,000 lire notes are useful for buying petrol from automatic pumps and for buying telephone cards from vending machines. Coins are also very useful: a supply of 100 and 200 lire coins are needed for parking meters, making local telephone calls and feeding the electricity meters in churches that illuminate frescos.

Banks in Italy normally open from 8.20am to 1.20pm weekdays. Some city centre banks also open in the afternoon from 2.30 to 3.45pm. None open at weekends, and a wise traveller in Italy also keeps an eye on the festive calendar: some banks change their opening hours just before and just after bank holidays and big festivals.

Fortunately there are several other sources of money if you run out over a weekend. Many banks have hole-in-the-wall exchange machines which accept the major European currencies and US dollars and pay out lire in exchange. Instructions are given in several languages and the exchange rate is good; the machines are, though, apt to reject notes that are creased or damaged. Equally useful are cash machines displaying the blue and red EC sign. If your credit card displays the same sign you can use these machines to draw cash, provided you feed in the correct personal identity number (check with your bank or card company before you go if you have forgotten this number). If anything goes wrong, and the machine swallows your card, it can usually be retrieved by presenting your passport to the bank within three days.

The major credit cards (Visa, Mastercard/Access, American Express and Diners' Club) are accepted in many hotels and restaurants and up-market shops (look for a sign saying *Carta Si* – Card Yes – in the window). Despite the high price of petrol, however, very few garages accept cards. You will also have to pay cash for your groceries; small shops only accept cash and the out-of-town hypermarkets issue their own charge cards and only accept these.

Eurocheques are very widely accepted in Italy and are as good as money: each cheque can be cashed at a bank for up to 300,000 lire. Neither will any problem be encountered with cashing Travellers' Cheques, though for all bank transactions it is necessary to present your passport.

When looking for the best possible rates of exchange, it is usually advantageous to use bank or credit cards, because the exchange calculation is done at the inter-bank rate, which is more favourable than the tourist rate. Most banks in Italy also charge a small commission for changing cash or Eurocheques, though visitors should not be charged for cashing a Travellers' Cheque.

Opening times

Shops are usually open Monday to Saturday from 9am to 1pm and from 4pm to 7pm (8pm in summer). In cities, large stores may stay open until 9pm on Thursday or Friday, but are closed on Monday morning. In rural areas shops may close for one afternoon midweek, usually Wednesday. Flower and cake shops open in the morning on Sundays and public holidays, but very little else, although bars remain open all day six days a week. All bars and restaurants must shut at least once a week by law. The day in question will be posted outside, or on the shutters. Many businesses, including restaurants, close for two weeks in August, the traditional holiday month in Italy.

Banks are open Monday to

Friday, 8.20am to 1.20pm. Some reopen from 2.30pm to 3.45pm.

Petrol stations open Monday to Friday from 7.30am to noon and 4pm to 7pm. Many are closed on Saturday and all close on Sunday and public holidays, except for *autostrade* service stations.

Post offices are open Monday to Saturday 8am to 1.30pm, although many bars and tobacconists displaying a 'T' sign sell postage stamps.

Tourist offices follow shop opening hours, though in Florence and some other large cities they may open on Sundays in summer.

Museums are a law unto themselves. As a general guide, expect them to be closed on Mondays; on Tuesday to Saturday they should be open 9am to 1pm and 2pm to 5pm, and on Sundays 2pm to 5pm. These rules apply mainly in the summmer (April to September); in winter expect them to open later and close earlier. There are some exceptions (the Uffizi in Florence opens every day and throughout the lunch hours), but more commonly you will find a museum closed when it should be open because of 'staff shortages', a euphemism that covers all sorts of ills. Hotels in Florence now post weekly or monthly bulletins showing the opening hours, insofar as these can be pinned down, and you can also get reasonably up-to-date information from tourist information centres. In rural areas, you may have to seek out a custodian, whose name should be posted on the museum door, or ring a bell to gain admittance.

Churches are usually open from 8am to 12noon or 1pm and from 2pm to 7pm (or dusk in winter). Tourists are discouraged from wandering round the church when there is a service on. In rural areas, you may have to seek out a keyholder, especially in winter.

Beautiful, wild, Tuscan landscapes, stretching as far as the eye can see

The wonders of modern technology in the ancient city of the Medici

Police

Italy has different police forces for different functions. Visitors are most likely to encounter the *vigili urbani*, traffic police whose main job is to prevent infringement of parking regulations and keep unauthorised vehicles out of city centres during prohibited hours. Their name is apt; they are very vigilant and visitors are not immune from traffic laws. If you commit an offence and fail to pay the fine on the spot, you can expect a letter to arrive on your doormat at home in due course.

Local police matters are handled by the *polizia urbana*. They also carry out random checks on vehicles, so if you are flagged down whilst travelling, do not worry. They will want to see your driving licence, car registration documents and insurance card or certificate and are generally very friendly as long as your papers are in order. If you need their help in an emergency, dial 113. If you need to report a theft, go to the police station (*questura*) and make a statement (*denuncia*) using an official multi-lingual form, keeping one stamped copy for yourself as evidence for making an insurance claim. You will also see armed police – the *carabinieri* – on duty as you travel; they are a national police force, technically a branch of the army, whose role is the handling of serious crime.

Post Office

Many bars and tobacconists sell postage stamps for letters and postcards: look for a sign with the white letter T on a blue background. For other transactions you will need to go to a post office: most are open Monday to Saturday 8am to 1pm though city-centre branches may open as late as 7pm.

Public Holidays

Most businesses are closed on the following national holidays:
1 January
6 January (Epiphany)
Good Friday
Easter Monday
25 April (Liberation Day)
1 May (Labour Day)
15 August (Assumption)
1 November (All Saints)
8 December (Immaculate Conception)
25 and 26 December
In addition, many businesses close for a period during August and individual towns close for big festivals.

Public Transport

The only city in which visitors are likely to need to use public transport is Florence, where the private car is a liability. Everywhere else, even in the larger cities such as Pisa, Perugia or Siena, the historical centre is so compact that all the sites are within comfortable walking distance. The same is true of Florence, but visitors may want to use a bus for out-of-town excursions (eg to Fiesole). Most buses can be caught from the Piazza del Duomo or Santa Maria Novella station. Tickets can be bought from bars and tobacco shops displaying the ATAF sticker; each ticket is valid for 70 minutes' travel and should be fed into the stamping machine at the rear of the bus when you enter.

Travelling around Tuscany and Umbria by train and bus is possible if you have time and energy. The railways are good and inexpensive, but the stations are often located at some distance from the historical centre, and it can be a long, hot, uphill climb in summer, especially if carrying luggage; taxis are available at the station, at a price. The railway network will take the traveller to the major towns, but for exploring rural areas it is necessary to use the excellent, but slow, bus network. Tourist information offices will provide timetable details.

Restaurants

Eating out in Tuscany and Umbria is a great pleasure and will furnish many happy memories, but there are certain points to bear in mind in order to avoid an embarrassing situation. In a *ristorante* or a *trattoria*, customers are usually expected to order at least three courses. If you only want a simple meal, go to a *pizzeria* where it is perfectly acceptable to order just a pizza or a plate of pasta. Vegetarians would be wise to stick to *pizzerie*, because restaurants in Italy are determinedly carnivorous in their emphasis. In general a *ristorante* will be more expensive and more up-market than a *trattoria*, though the distinction has been substantially eroded over the last decade. *Antipasti* are optional; most diners will order a first course (*primo*) of pasta, rice (*risotto*) or soup (*minestra*), followed by a main course (*secondo*) of meat or fish. This is served without accompaniment; if you want salad (*insalata*) or vegetables, you will have to order additional side dishes (*contorni*). The meal finishes with either fruit (*frutta*), cheese (*formaggio*), dessert (*dolci*) or ice cream (*gelato*), followed by a coffee (*caffè* – invariably an espresso, unless requested otherwise).

There is an extra cover charge (*pane e coperto*) in all establishments, even *pizzerie*. Usually service is included in the prices (look for the words *servizio compreso*); if not it will be added to the bill. Even if service is included, it is customary to leave a small tip.

Senior Citizens

Some museums, but by no means the majority, offer reduced priced admission to senior citizens from EC countries on production of a passport as evidence of age. More concessions may follow with EC harmonisation.

Student/Youth Travel

As with senior citizens, Italy makes few concessions to students; school children (under 18) are admitted free or at a reduced price to a few museums, but otherwise the full price is charged. Holders of student railcards can obtain discounts on the already cheap railway system.

Telephones

Old-fashioned public telephones, operated by tokens (*gettoni*) are rapidly becoming part of Italian folklore as they are replaced by modern card and coin-operated phones. Coin-operated phones accept 100, 200 and 500 lire coins and can be found in many streets and squares; you can also phone from a bar if it displays a sign consisting of a dial on a yellow background. Insert the coins before dialling and insert more if you hear a beep while still speaking; unused coins will be refunded after a call by pushing the return button. In many cities telephone booths can be found in or near the post office, the railway station or the main shopping street (look for signs directing you to the *Centro Telefono Pubblico*). Vending machines in the booths dispense phone cards (the machines accept 5,000 and 10,000 lire notes) which can then be used to make long-distance and overseas calls (phone cards can also be bought in many tobacconists). Many hotel rooms also have IDD phones, but the hotel mark-up makes this an expensive way of making a call.

To dial a number in the same province you should omit the area code; otherwise you need to dial the city or district code, then the subscriber number. If the number is engaged you will hear a series of rapid pips; the dialling tone is a series of longer notes. To make an international call, dial 00, then the country code, the area code (minus the initial 0) and the subscriber number. To call Italy from another country, dial the international access code followed by 39, then the area code minus the initial 0 and the subscriber number.

Time

Italy observes Central European Time (one hour ahead of Greenwich Mean Time) from the end of September to the end of March. Daylight Saving Time comes into effect for the summer when the Italian clocks go forward by an hour, in common with most of Europe.

Tipping

In general, tips are not expected and are received with pleasure: a few coins for the barman, 1,000 lire for taxi drivers and porters, a little more for waiters – these will be received with smiles.

Toilets

Railway stations, airports, bus stations, *autostrada* rest areas and service stations and some museums have public toilets but elsewhere they scarcely exist; restaurants provide toilets for their customers but bars do not as a rule, so if you ask to use the toilet (*bagno*, *toiletta* or *gabinetto*) in a crisis, remember that the barman is doing you a special favour if he says yes. In restaurants one toilet may serve for for both sexes; if there are two they are likely to be marked *signore* or *donne* for women and *signori* or *uomini* for men.

Tourist offices

Every town in Tuscany and Umbria has a tourist information centre, usually well signposted and often located in or near the main square. They are generally open from 9am to 1pm and 4pm to 7pm, but the hours will vary according to the season – in popular destinations in summer they may stay open through the lunch period, whereas in winter they may close earlier in the evening.The staff will help you find accommodation locally, and answer questions on transport, opening times and entertainment. The emphasis is on local information; if you want more general information, contact the Italian State Tourist Office in your own country before departure or one of the following regional tourist authorities:

For Tuscany: Assessorato Regionale Turismo, Via di Novoli 26, 50127 Firenze (tel: 055 439 311).

For Umbria: Assessorato Regionale Turismo, Corso Vannucci 30, 06100 Perugia (tel: 075 5041).

Calendar of Events

February: Pre-Lenten Carnival in Viareggio. A huge parade of floats, renowned throughout Italy for their satirical content.

March: Three-week Italian Antiques Fair in Todi. Attended by leading dealers from all over Italy.

Good Friday: dramatic re-enactment of the Passion in Assisi.

Easter Monday: the *Scoppio del Carro*, (Explosion of the Cart) in Florence celebrating the Resurrection.

April: Tulip Festival floral parade in Castiglione del Lago. Food and wine festivals in Panicale, Montefalco and Città della Pieve.

May: Celebrations for the beginning of spring start in the last three days of April and build to a climax in the first week of May. *Cantamaggio* is a parade of festively decorated carts plus street theatre and concerts, in Terni. *Calendimaggio* in Assisi; singing, banner-waving, archery and dance competitions plus dressing up in medieval costume. *Corso dell'Anello* jousting competition in Narni, preceded by a torchlit parade. *Corso dei Ceri* (Candle Race) in Gubbio on 15 May, followed by the *Palio della Balestra*, a medieval archery contest, at the end of the month. *Maggio Musicale* (May Music) festival begins in Florence and lasts into June.

June: Corpus Domini parade in Orvieto and floral carpets for *Corpus Christi* in the streets of Spello. *Estate Fiesolana* arts festival in Fiesole. *Festa di San Ranieri* regatta in Pisa on 16–17 June. *Calcio in Costume* played in Florence on 17 and 24 June, and 1 July. On 24 June there are fireworks for the feast of St John. *Concorso Internazionale Pianistico* piano contest in Terni in even-numbered years. Rockin' Umbria pop festival in Perugia. *Festival dei Due Mondi* begins in Spoleto.

July: *Palio* in Siena on 2 July. Umbria Jazz based on Perugia. Concert and theatre festival in San Gimignano.

August: *Palio* in Siena on 16 August. Opera festival in Torre del Lago Puccini, beefsteak festival in Cortona, regatta in Livorno. International choir contest in Arezzo and international chamber music festival in Città di Castello.

September: *Sagra Musicale Umbra*, an important festival of religious music in Perugia. *Giostra del Saracino* (Joust of the Saracen) in Arezzo.

October: food and wine festivals all over the region.

November: Truffle festival and agricultural show in Città di Castello.

December: Re-enactments of the Nativity in Assisi and many Umbrian churches.

Tourists invade Pisa all year long

·GLOSSARY·

Italian is a rhythmic and euphonious language that is easy to pronounce once a few basic rules are understood.

C or *cc* before *e* or *i* is pronounced *ch* (cinque = chinque, cappuccino = cappuchino). Otherwise *c*, *cc* and *ch* are pronounced *k* (caldo = kaldo, piccante = pikante, Chianti = Kianti).

G or *gg* before *e* or *i* is pronounced *j* (giovedi = jiovedi, formaggio = formajio). Otherwise *g*, *gg* and *gh* are prounced hard as in get. *Gli* is pronounced like the middle part of million (Castiglione = Castillionay). *Gn* is prounounced *ny* (bagno = banyo).

H is not pronounced (hortus = ortus).

S between vowels is pronounced *z* (casa = caza). *Sc* before *e* or *i* is pronounced *sh* (scena = shena); otherwise it is pronounced as *sc* in scampi.

Z is pronounced *ts* (grazie = gratsie).

The stress nearly always falls on the last but one syllable. Where it does not, you will sometimes see a stress mark over the accented syllable (Mèdici, Accadèmia, Nicolò, caffè).

Accentuation can alter the way a vowel is pronounced. *A* when stressed is like *a* in father (*andare*); *e* when stressed is like *a* in fate (*mele*); *i* when stressed is like *i* in machine (*primo*) and like *y* when followed by another vowel (*piove*); *o* when stressed is like *o* in rock (*notte*); *u* is pronounced like *u* in June (*uscita*) but like *w* when followed by another vowel (*uomini*).

Basic words

Even if you speak no other Italian, the following phrases will be indispensible.

Good morning buon giorno
Good afternoon/evening buona sera
Goodbye arrividerci
Goodnight buona notte
Please per favore
Thank you grazie
You are welcome prego
Excuse me mi scusi/permesso
That's fine/OK va bene
Yes si
No no
I don't understand non capisco
I don't speak Italian non parlo Italiano
Do you speak English? parla Inglese?
I am English/American sono Inglese /Americano (feminine Americana)
Toilet bagno
Ladies signore/donne
Gents signori/uomini
Hot caldo
Cold freddo
Open aperto
Closed chiuso
Entrance entrata
Exit uscita

Hotel

Single/twin-bedded/double-bedded room una camera singola/doppia/matrimonale
With bathroom/shower con bagno/doccia
Child's bed/cot letto di bambino/una culla
How much per night? quanto costa al girno?
Too expensive costa troppo
Anything cheaper? meno caro?
Floor piano
Key chiave
Dining room sala di pranzo
What time is breakfast/dinner? a che ora e la colazione/cena?
Laundry service servizio lavanderia
Come in! avanti!

Restaurant

Have you a table for one/two/three/four? avete un tavolo per uno/due/tre/quattro?
A different table? potremmo spostarci?
A quiet table? un tavolo tranquillo
The menu la carta
The bill il conto

Drinks

Black coffee caffè/espresso
White coffee cappuccino/caffè latte
Tea tè
Mineral water (carbonated/still) aqua minerale (gassata/non gassata)
Beer (draught) birra (alla spina)
Fruit juice succo di frutta
Orange/lemon squash aranciata/limonata
Red/white/rose/sparkling wine Vino rosso/bianco/rosato/spumante
Dry/sweet secco/dolce
Another (beer) please un altro (birra) per favore

Menu terms

Aceto **vinegar**
Affettati **cold meats**
Affumicato **smoked**
Al burro **cooked in butter**
Al forno **baked**
Alla brace **charcoal grilled**
Alla griglia **grilled**
Bianco **boiled**
Bruschetta **garlic bread**
Burro **butter**
Carne **meat**
Contorno **vegetable side dish**
Crudo **raw**
Diavola **spicy (often hot)**
Farcito **stuffed**
Fatto in casa **homemade**
Fettina **a slice**
Formaggio **cheese**
Fresco **fresh**
Fritto **deep fried**
Gelato **ice cream**
Pane **bread**
Pesce **fish**
Pezzo **piece (of meat or fish which is ordered by the 100 grammes, such as beefsteak)**
Piatto del giorno **dish of the day**
Piacere **cooked to your taste**
Tramezzino **sandwich**
Uovo **egg**
Zucchero **sugar**

Numbers

1 uno
2 due
3 tre
4 quattro
5 cinque
6 sei
7 sette
8 otto
9 nove
10 dieci
11 undici
12 dodici
13 tredici
14 quattordici
15 quindici
16 sedici
17 diciasette
18 diciotto
19 diciannove
20 venti
30 trenta
40 quaranta
50 cinquanta
60 sessanta
70 settanta
80 ottanta
90 novanta
100 cento
1,000 mille

·INDEX·

A

Abbadia Isola 97
Abbadia San Salvatore 85
Abbazia di Monte Oliveto Maggiore 78
Abbazia di San Eutizio 64
Abbazia di Sassovivo 74
accommodation 112
airports and air services 112
Alberese 102
Alpi Apuane 12, 13, 14
Alviano 61
Amélia 61, 105
Anchiano 29
Angelico, Fra 40
Ansedónia 98, 103
Arezzo 30, 32–3, 73
Arni 17
Arno 12, 30
Asciano 78
Assisi 52–3, 54, 55, 73

B

Badia a Coltibuono 81
Bagni di Lucca 14
Bagno Vignoni 89
banks 114
Barga 14–15
Bevagna 56, 75
Bibbiena 33
Boboli Gardens 21
Boccaccio, Giovanni 79
Bolsena 66
Borghetto 58
Borgo a Mazzano 15
Browning, Elizabeth and Robert 91
Buggiano 22
Buonconvento 78

C

Camáldoli 35
camping 112
Capálbio 100
Capanne di Collegiacone 56
Caprese Michelangelo 34
Carrara 15
car rental 113
Carsulae 74
Cascata delle Mármore 74
Cascia 55, 56
Cáscina 12
Casentino 30, 34
Castellina in Chianti 80
Castello dei Cavalieri di Malta 59
Castello di Brólio 81
Castello di Castagnoli 81
Castellúccio 64, 65
Castellúcio 87
Castelnuovo di Garfagnana 16–17
Castèl Rigone 59
Castel Ritaldi 75
Castiglione del Lago 56, 58
ceramics 58
Cerreto 62
Certaldo 79
chemists 112
Chianciano Terme 79
Chianciano Vecchio 79
Chianti 80
Chiusi 80, 104
Città della Pieve 57, 73
Città di Castello 57
Colle di Val d'Elsa 84, 97
Collodi 16
Colonnata 15
Cortona 35
Cosa 103
credit cards 114
crime 112–13
currency 114
customs regulations 113

D

Dante 42
Deruta 58
disabled visitors 113
Donatello 36, 37, 39, 41
driving 113

E

eating out 116
Elba 100
Elsa Valley 84
Empoli 16
entertainment 114
entry formalities 112
Eremo delle Carceri 53
Eremo di Camáldoli 30, 34–5
Etruscans 104–5
Eugubine Tablets 61

F

Faenza 58
Ferentillo 63
festivals and events 72–3, 117
Fiésole 46–7, 73
Florence (Firenze) 30–1, 36–46, 72, 73, 90–1
Fonti di Clitunno 75
food and wine 67, 82–3, 107

G

Gaiole in Chianti 81
Galileo 46
Galleria del Cipollaio 17
gardens 21
Garfagnana 13, 16
Geppa 62–3
Ghiberti, Lorenzo 38
Giardino dei Tarocchi 100
Giotto 30, 53
Grosseto 101
Grotta del Vento 17
Grotta di Monte Cucco 58
Grotta Giusti 22
Gualdo Tadino 58
Guardea 61
Gúbbio 60–1, 72, 73

H

health matters 114
hotels 112

I

Isola del Giglio 103
Isola di Giannutri 103
Isola Maggiore 59
Isola Polvese 59

L

La Foce 87
Lago di Burano 100
Lago Trasimeno 58
language 118
La Pietra 21
Larderello 99
La Verna 33
Le Crete 76, 79
Leonardo da Vinci 29
Lippi, Filippo 70
Livorno 18
local time 117
Lucca 18–19
Lucignano 48
Lugnano in Teverina 61

M

Machiavelli 43
Magione 59
Manciano 106
Marciana Alta 100
Maremma 98–9
Márlia 21
Marmitte dei Giganti 17
Masaccio 39
Massa Marittima 102–3
media 114
medical treatment 114
Medici family 42–3
Meleto 81
Michelangelo 34, 36, 37, 39, 41
money 114
Monsummano Terme 22
Montalcino 84
Monte Amiata 85
Monte Argentario 98, 103
Montecatini Alto 22
Montecatini Terme 22, 23
Monte Cucco 58
Montefalco 62, 75
Montefegatesi 14
Montefranco 63
Monte Luco 81
Montemerano 106
Monte Pisanino 17
Montepulciano 86, 87
Monterchi 48
Monteriggioni 86, 97
Monte San Savino 48
Monte Vettore 65
Monti del Chianti 76
Monti Sibillini 65

N

Narni 62, 73
Nórcia 55, 64–5

O

Oltrarno 44
opening times 114–15
Orbetello 99, 103
Orrido di Botri 14
Orvieto 66–7, 72–3
Otrícoli 62

P

Palio 73, 95
Panicale 56–7, 73
Parco dell'Orecchiella 13
Parco di Pinocchio 16
Parco Naturale della Maremma 99, 102
Parco Naturale della Viriglia 80
Parco Naturale delle Alpi Apuane 13
passeggiata 8
Passignano sul Trasimeno 59
Perugia 50, 68–9, 73
Perugino 57
Péscia 22
Piancastagnáio 85
Piano Grande 64, 65
Piccolomini, Aeneas Silvius 77, 86
Piediluco 73
Pienza 77, 86–7
Piero della Francesca 32, 48
Pieve di Romena 34
Pisa 12–13, 24–5
Pistóia 26–7
Pitigliano 106
plantlife 9, 65, 102

Póggio a Caiano 21
Poggio Lecci 102
Poggio Pinci 78
police 116
Politian 77, 86
politics 10–11
Ponte Buggianese 22
Ponte del Diavolo 15
Ponte delle Torri 75
Pontedera 12
Poppi 34
Porto Ercole 103
Portoferráio 100
Porto Santo Stefano 103
post offices 116
Prato 27, 73
public holidays 116
public transport 116
Puccini, Giacomo 29

R

Radda in Chianti 80–1
rail services 112, 116
Ranco di Sigillo 58
Renaissance 38–9
Riétine 81
Rio Marina 100
Roccaporena 56
Roselle 101

S

St Benedict 55, 64
St Clare 55
St Francis 54–5
St Rita 55
San Cassiano 14
San Damiano 52–3
San Galgano 93
San Gimignano 88–9, 97
San Gusmé 81
San Miniato 28
San Pellegrino in Alpe 17
San Pietro in Valle 63
San Quírico d'Orcia 89
Sansepolcro 48
Sansovino, Andrea 48
Santa Maria degli Angeli 53
Sant'Antimo 84–5
San Vito 59
Sarteano 79
Satúrnia 106–7
Savonarola 43
Scheggino 63
seasons 7
senior citizens 116
Sérchio Valley 13
Serravalle 22
Settefenestre 99
Shelley, Percy Bysshe 29, 90
Siena 73, 77, 92–5
Sodoma, Il 78
Sorano 107
Sovana 107, 108
Spaltenna 81
spa towns 23, 79
Spello 70, 73, 74
Spoleto 70, 71, 73, 75
Stia 34
student and youth travel 116

T

Talamone 99
Tarquinia 99, 104
telephones 116–17
Tempio di Clitunno 75
Terni 74
tipping 117
Todi 74
toilets 117
Torgiano 58
Torre dei Lombardi 59
Torri 93
tourist offices 117
travelling to Italy 112
Trevi 74–5
Tuoro sul Trasimeno 58–9

U

Umbertide 73

V

Vagli di Sopra 17
Valdichiana 76–7
Valdinievole 22
Vallo di Nera 63
Vallombrosa 30, 49
Valnerina 62
Vasari, Giorgio 30–1
Vertine 81
Vetúlonia 101
Viareggio 29, 73
Villa Adriana 20
Villa della Petraia 21, 47
Villa delle Colonne 99
Villa dell'Ombrellino 21
Villa di Careggi 20–1, 47
Villa di Castello 21, 47
Villa di Póggio a Caiano 16
Villa Garzoni 16, 21
Villa La Fernandina 16
Villa Mansi 21
Villa Reale 21
villas 20–1
Villa Stibbert 47
Villa Torrigiani 21
Vinci 29
Volpaia 81
voltage 114
Volterra 96–7
Vulci 99

writers in Tuscany 90-1

Z

Zoo Fauna Europa 35

ACKNOWLEDGEMENTS

The Automobile Association would like to thank the following photographers and libraries for their assistance in the preparation of this book.

KEN PATERSON was commissioned to take the photographs for this book and his photgraphs appear on the following pages:

1, 3, 4/5, 6a, 6b, 7, 8a, 9, 10a, 10b, 12, 13, 14a, 14b, 15, 16a, 16b, 17, 18, 19a, 19b, 20a, 20b, 21, 22, 23a, 23b, 24a, 24b, 26, 27a, 27b, 28a, 28b, 29a, 29b, 30, 31, 32, 33, 34, 35, 36a, 36b, 38a, 39, 40a, 40b, 41, 44, 45a, 45b, 47, 49, 50, 52a, 52b, 54a, 55a, 58a, 58b, 59, 60, 61, 62, 63, 64, 65a, 65b, 66a, 66b, 67, 68b, 69, 70b, 74, 76a, 76b, 78a, 78b, 79, 80, 81a, 81b, 82b, 83a, 83b, 84, 85a, 85b, 86, 87a, 87b, 88, 89, 92a, 92b, 93, 94, 95a, 95b, 96a, 96b, 96c, 98, 99, 100, 101a, 101b, 102, 103b, 104a, 104b, 105, 106, 107, 108, 115

The remaining photographs are from the following libraries:

AA PHOTO LIBRARY
Eric Meacher 82a
Barrie Smith 38a, 42a, 42b, 43, 46, 116, 118
Anthony Souter 8b, 68a, 70a

J ALLAN CASH PHOTOLIBRARY 57 Cascia

C CATLING 56a Bevagna San Michele, 56b Bevagna Piazza Silvestri

INTERNATIONAL PHOTOBANK Cover, Siena Rooftops

MARY EVANS PICTURE LIBRARY 54b St Rita, 55b St Francis, 90a, 90b Dante, 90c Shelley, 91b Robert Browning

SPECTRUM COLOUR LIBRARY 11, 72a, 72b, 73 Il Palio (Siena)

THE BRIDGEMAN ART LIBRARY 48 Della Francesca *The Annunciation*